Controversies in American Politics and Society

David McKay, David Houghton and
Andrew Wroe

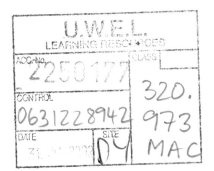

BLACKWELL *Publishers*

First published 2002

2 4 6 8 10 9 7 5 3 1

Blackwell Publishers Ltd
108 Cowley Road
Oxford OX4 1JF
UK

Blackwell Publishers Inc.
350 Main Street
Malden, MA 02148
USA

British Library Cataloguing in Publication Data

A CIP catalogue record for this book is available from the British Library.

Library of Congress Cataloging-in-Publication Data

McKay, David H.
    Controversies in American politics and society / David McKay, David
  Houghton, and Andrew Wroe.
        p.   cm.
    Includes bibliographical references and index.
    ISBN 0–631–22894–2 (hbk : alk. paper) — ISBN 0–631–22895–0 (pbk. :
  alk. paper)
      1. United States—Politics and government.   2. Political
  planning—United States.   I. Houghton, David Patrick.   II. Wroe, Andrew.
  III. Title.

JK275 .M34 2002
320.973′09′051—dc21
                                                                2001004194

Typeset in 10.5 on 12 pt Sabon by Ace Filmsetting Ltd, Frome, Somerset
Printed in Great Britain by Antony Rowe Ltd, Chippenham, Wiltshire

This book is printed on acid-free paper.

Contents

List of tables and figures   viii

Introduction: Conflict and Controversy in American Society   1

Part I Institutions and Processes   7

1 **Divided Government: Does it Matter?** *David McKay*   9
   The causes of divided government   11
   The consequences of divided government   14
   But do the voters approve of divided government?   17

2 **Trust in Government: a Crisis of Democracy?** *Andrew Wroe*   20
   Performance   21
   Political explanations   24
   Socio-cultural explanations   27
   Conclusion   29

3 **Voting and Non-voting: America's Flawed Democracy?**
   David Houghton   31
   Theories of voting behaviour   34
   Theories of non-voting   37
   A symptom of sickness or of health?   41

4 **Campaign Finance Reform: Creating a Level Playing Field**
   David Houghton   44
   The case against campaign finance reform   47
   The case for campaign finance reform   48
   Money and politics   50
   Conclusion   52

5 **Containing Presidential Power** *David Houghton*   55
   The 'imperial presidency' thesis   56
   The 'post-imperial presidency' and the 'imperial Congress'   57
   The War Powers Resolution   59
   The Iran-Contra scandal   61
   Conclusion   64

6   **The Supreme Court: the Politics of Judicial Activism**   *David McKay*   67
Activism, passivity and interpreting the constitution: the enduring
debate   68
The Burger Court: confusion in the face of rapid social and
political change?   69
The Rehnquist Court: conservatism revived?   72
Conclusion: should the Court continue its activist role?   75

7   **Direct Democracy: Power to the People?**   *Andrew Wroe*   78
The theoretical and historical debate in brief   82
The contemporary debate   82
Responsive or responsible laws, or both?   88
Conclusion   90

Part II   Policies   **93**

8   **Gun Control: the Right to Bear Arms**   *Andrew Wroe*   95
Arguments for guns and against control   96
Arguments against guns and for control   99
Conclusion   104

9   **Immigration: a Nation State or a State of Nations?**   *Andrew Wroe*   106
The immigration debate: environmental arguments   108
The immigration debate: economic arguments   109
The immigration debate: cultural arguments   112
Conclusion   116

10   **Affirmative Action: the Continuing Dilemma**   *Andrew Wroe*   118
The history of affirmative action   118
The case for affirmative action   122
The case against affirmative action   123
Class-based affirmative action?   125
Conclusion   126

11   **The Politics of Health Care: Anxiety amid Plenty**   *David McKay*   128
Self-reliance, health care and public expectations   128
The failure of the Clinton Health Care Plan   132
The health care controversy: an unending story?   134
The New Federalism, George W. Bush and the future of health
care reform   137

12   **Capital Punishment: the Politics of Retribution**   *David McKay*   139
The death penalty in historical perspective   139
The courts and capital punishment   142
Capital punishment in the twenty-first century: the debate
continues   144
The future of capital punishment   148

13 **Welfare Reform: Providing for the Old but not for the Poor?**
David McKay   150
The early days: 'protecting soldiers and mothers'   151
Three failed reform attempts   151
The 1990s reforms: the end of welfare as we know it?   155
Welfare reform: has it worked?   157
Conclusion: Protecting the old but not the poor: the new American
philosophy?   159

14 **Abortion: the Right to Life Debate** *Andrew Wroe*   161
A brief history of abortion and the abortion issue   162
Roe v. *Wade*   163
The constitutional argument   164
Philosophy and science   166
The difficult cases: rape, incest and the death of the mother   169
Conclusion   170

15 **Manifest Destiny and *Realpolitik*: Realism versus Idealism in
Foreign Policy** *David Houghton*   172
The realist–idealist debate   172
The case for realism   176
The case for idealism   179
Conclusion   181

16 **America as a Global Economic Player: Free Trade versus
Protectionism** *David Houghton*   183
The Battle over NAFTA   185
The WTO and the 'battle of Seattle'   188
The contemporary case for free trade and globalization   188
The case against free trade and globalization   189
A case of 'doublethink'?   190

Further Reading   193
Index   200

Tables and figures

TABLES

1.1	Composition of Congress, by political party, 1961–2001	10
1.2	Presidential vetoes and divided government, 1932–2001	16
3.1	Average voter turnout at national elections, selected countries, 1991–2000	32
3.2	National voter turnout in presidential election years, 1960–2000	32
7.1	Initiative use, by the number on the ballot, 1898–1998	80
7.2	Success of California initiatives, by nature of inter-group conflict, 1986–96	86
9.1	Immigration to the United States, 1800–1998	107
11.1	National expenditure on health, selected countries, 1960–97	129
11.2	US health expenditure, actual and projected, 1970–2007	135
12.1	Executions, by method, 1976	147
13.1	Average Aid for Dependent Family payments per family in selected regions and AFDC population as a percentage of regional population, 1990	152
13.2	Temporary Assistance for Needy Families, percentage of total US population, 1990–2000	157

FIGURES

2.1	Trust in government	21
7.1	The geographical distribution of states using the initiative	79
11.1	Health insurance coverage, by poverty level, 1998	136
12.1	Executions, by year, 1608–2000	141
12.2	Public opinion on the death penalty, 1953–2001	144
12.3	Race of defendants executed	145
12.4	Race of Death Row inmates	146
12.5	Race of victims	146
12.6	Total executions, 1976–2000	147
13.1	Percentage of the population on welfare since 1960	153

Introduction: Conflict and Controversy in American Society

Perhaps the most enduring feature of American society and its political system is the juxtaposition of apparently deep conflicts and divisions with a remarkable capacity not only for survival but also for regeneration and renewal. More than once foreign commentators have written the United States off as a system in danger of failure or even disintegration. Such sentiments were common at the time of the Civil War and its aftermath, during the Great Depression of the 1930s and during the riots and assassinations of the 1960s.

Even in the calmer environment of the last thirty years controversy and conflict have never been far from the surface. Of course, it could be argued that all societies are to a greater or lesser extent characterized by division and disputes. In most cases, however, these either relate to ethnic, religious or linguistic divisions that have existed for centuries or they involve problems that are common to most societies. In modern Europe, for example, some of the deepest conflicts are ethnic or religious in nature, as Northern Irish and Basque nationalism and the trials and tribulations of the Balkans show. But for most countries, including mainland Britain, France, the Scandinavian states and Germany, the problems tend to be broadly similar in nature. In all four, such things as economic performance – and in particular questions relating to employment – the provision of pensions and other benefits, education and health care systems tend to dominate political discourse. As far as politics is concerned, debate tends to focus on the role of political parties and how their programmes can be turned into public policy. More rarely does debate turn to more fundamental questions such as the level of trust in political institutions or the political role of the courts.

While these same issues are obviously important in the United States, the nature of what may be called the 'controversy agenda' is different, and at two levels. First, it tends to be substantively different in content. In the United States passions are aroused by a range of issues that either do not apply or are of little import in Europe. This applies both to policy areas such as abortion, capital punishment, affirmative action and gun control, and to political questions such as non-voting, divided government and the role of direct democracy. Second, the nature of public debate on these and other issues is qualitatively different in the United States. Debate is often more passionate and reaches deep into society.

This is particularly true of those policy questions that involve moral absolutes (abortion, capital punishment) or which raise questions of justice and fairness (direct democracy, campaign finance and affirmative action). In contrast to the situation in many European countries, these issues are hotly debated not just by educated elites but by large numbers of ordinary Americans. Often the debates take place in isolation from each other. Activists in the abortion debate, for example, may devote all their political energies to that question and play little part in other areas of public policy. While not unique to the United States, 'single-issue politics' is much more pervasive in America than in Europe. As a result, the two main political parties are often not the main vehicles for the articulation of interests in such areas as abortion and affirmative action. For either party fully to embrace one side or another in these disputes would be to invite electoral re-criminations. Instead, advocacy groups and individual politicians – with or without the approval of state and national parties – play the lead role. This will become apparent in the chapter-by-chapter discussions that follow.

This is not to say that more traditional 'distributional' issues such as health care, welfare and education are also not the subjects of passionate debate. They are, as subsequent chapters will show. But even in these areas the nature of the debate is different from that in Europe. Possibly because they are less cynical than Europeans or have been inculcated with a spirit of optimism and opportunity, Americans expect fast and effective solutions to societal problems. Perhaps this is why they argue the pros and cons of an issue with such vehemence and passion. Hence the debate on welfare reform includes those who actually believe that through job training and the provision of child care virtually *all* government-provided welfare can be eliminated. Similarly, many affirmative action programmes have been premised on the belief that positive discrimination can purge educational disadvantage from society. And even when these expectations are dashed, the beliefs remain, the agenda is modified and the battle is joined anew.

For this reason some commentators have identified an almost religious dimension to the values underpinning many of these debates. Samuel Huntington has called it a 'creedal passion' that raises expectations beyond what can realistically be achieved.[1] But his conclusion that dashed expectations will bring disharmony has proved to be over-pessimistic. In the twenty years since the publication of *The Promise of Disharmony* the 'politics of passion' have been as persuasive and influential as ever, but measured by most objective indicators – riots, protests, the rise of alternative political parties – there has been remarkably little disharmony. Certainly there has been intellectual and political conflict over practice, policies and programmes. But open and violent conflict has been much rarer and largely confined to an extremist fringe. This brings us back to the fact that, in spite of apparently deep divisions and conflicts, the American system seems remarkably resilient. It *can* adapt in the face of great social and economic change – if sometimes with difficulty.

The purpose of this book is not, however, to explain this resilience – although some of the reasons can be inferred from the discussion in the individual chapters. It is, rather, to familiarize readers with the nature of the current debate in a wide range of issue areas. Sixteen areas are covered, and for the most part they coincide with the more important debates raging in politics and society. That said, we do not pretend to be comprehensive in our coverage. The actual choice of issues sometimes reflects the interests of the authors rather than their relative importance. Certainly a number of vital questions, including the debate on environmental protection and the role of gender in society, have been excluded on these grounds. We intend to correct such biases in a later edition.

The controversies are broadly divided between those that concern political processes and institutions and those that involve substantive public policy questions. The choice of the former was certainly easier than the choice of the latter. At the turn of the century all the process controversies are at the very heart of political debate, and in almost every case they have assumed that status only in the last few decades. Hence the debate on divided government (the presidency controlled by one party and Congress by another, chapter 1) has naturally been a matter of concern only since divided government became the norm rather than the exception after 1968. The issue here is clear: can a government divided into partisan camps by an institutional division of power be an effective government? Declining trust in government (chapter 2) also originates in the 1960s, as does the decline in voter turnout (chapter 3). In both cases, commentators worry that the antipathy shown towards government on the part of many Americans and the apparent indifference to democratic participation reflect a deeper malaise in society. The debate on campaign finance reform (chapter 4) goes back much further, but it is only in recent years with the growth of 'soft money' campaign contributions that the issue has assumed a place at the centre of the reform agenda. Why, the critics ask, should a privileged few apparently be able to 'buy' election outcomes?

Chapter 5 is of a slightly different order. The debate on containing presidential power originates with Vietnam and Watergate and, it could be argued, is now moot, given that modern American presidents seem much less powerful than before, given the constraints imposed on them by divided government, public opinion and the media. While this is true, the presidency remains the main focus of political attention, both at home and abroad. Presidents retain great power, not least in foreign affairs. Even a president such as George W. Bush, who was elected by a minority of the voters, and has to live with *de facto* divided government,[2] has shown this.

Judicial power (the subject of chapter 6) has become a matter of great importance, given that the majority on the Supreme Court is at present both conservative and highly activist. The Court was, of course, the effective final arbiter of the 2000 presidential election, and we can expect further forays into the political thicket over the next few years. We can be sure that all will be highly controversial. The final area covered in this part of the book is the use of direct democratic devices in many of the states. Does the use of initiatives and referendums improve the quality of public policy or are these devices a cover, either for discrimination against minorities or for the exercise of power by the financially advantaged?

All the subjects covered in Part II have a uniquely American tinge. Chapter 8 concerns the debate on gun control and shows how the assumption that the public have the right to own guns is deeply embedded both in the American consciousness and in American politics. The United States has, of course, always been a nation of immigrants, and the debate on immigration and immigration control is as passionate now as at any time in recent history. Chapter 9 provides an account of this debate by focusing on the economic, social and cultural advantages and disadvantages of mass immigration. Controversy on affirmative action (chapter 10) is also at a high level, with some proposing an end to all such programmes while others remain convinced that affirmative action will remedy all the wrongs visited upon America's racial minorities and especially African Americans.

The great paradox of American health care is that almost nobody is happy with the system, yet it has become the most expensive in the world. Chapter 11 tries to explain why this is so by outlining the many attempts to reform health care delivery over the last twenty years. Foreign observers are constantly amazed that the American states continue to execute large numbers of their own people. Chapter 12 provides a background to the capital punishment debate and assesses the prospects of reform. Another area where the United States seems to have departed from the norm is in the provision of welfare for the poor. Chapter 13 asks why Americans are so reluctant to provide for the needy and assesses the prospects of the radical welfare reform measures introduced in 1996. Equally fierce passions are aroused by the abortion issue that is the subject of chapter 14. Why is it that so many Americans ascribe such an important status to the human foetus while others argue passionately that women should always have the right to choose?

The final chapters (15–16) deal with the role of the United States in the broader world. Both issues (realism versus idealism in foreign policy and the free trade versus protectionism debate) have a renewed poignancy in the context of the post-Cold War world and of the economic consequences of globalization. Can the United States carve out a constructive role in this new world, or will it revert to an unthinking and potentially dangerous isolationism?

Each of the chapters follows the character of the ongoing debate in each of the issue areas. In some cases this involves placing most of the emphasis on academic debate. With direct democracy and divided government, for example, much of the substantive evidence on both sides of the debate has been provided by academic political scientists. This is not to say that the broader society is not also engaged with the pros and cons. It is merely to state that the claims of both sides can be confirmed or disconfirmed primarily through the use of scientific evidence. In other issue areas, while scientific evidence may indeed be invoked, it is less important because the subject matter involves moral absolutes. Hence, with abortion, capital punishment and gun control, both sides of the debate start from diametrically opposed value positions that are unlikely ever to be reconciled. In these chapters, therefore, some attempt is made to explain why it is that such views are held.

With these and a number of other issues the debate is fairly clear cut and lends itself to an account of the argument used by each side. In these chapters, therefore, we have listed the arguments for and against each perspective in a fairly systematic way. In other cases, while the issues involved remain highly salient and controversial, it is not sensible to list the pros and cons in this way. No one is *against* the principle of health care reform, for example. The debate is about how to choose between competing reforms. Similarly, both liberals and conservatives see advantages in an activist Supreme Court and both groups have in the past seen advantages in a passive Court. This chapter is, therefore, more concerned with explaining these nuances than with providing a simple list of the arguments for and against activism. Few argue that declining trust in government is a good thing. Some may claim that it is indicative of a mature democracy, but no one seeks to *encourage* a decline in trust. Accordingly, chapter 2 provides competing explanations for falling trust.

All the chapters have one thing in common, however. All are designed to provide an up-to-date and dispassionate account of the nature of debate on those issues that at the beginning of the twenty-first century dominate political discourse. They are also intended as an introduction to these debates. Hopefully readers will be sufficiently stimulated to study some or all of these subjects in greater depth. Few countries are intrinsically as interesting as the United States, whether in terms of its extraordinary political arrangements, its social make-up or its historical development. This was true 100 years ago when the United States was widely regarded as a beacon of democracy in a predominantly autocratic world and it remains true to this day, even when the country and its people are often regarded with envy and suspicion. We are confident that, having read the chapters that follow, readers will agree that the debates and arguments that dominate American public life are likely to remain a subject of international importance and interest for many years to come.

NOTES

1 Samuel P. Huntington, *American Politics: The Promise of Disharmony* (Cambridge MA, Harvard University Press, 1981).
2 Although the vice-president's casting vote in the Senate originally gave the Republicans a nominal majority, this lasted just four months until the defection of Jim Jeffords to become an Independent. In the House this majority is just seven.

Part I

Institutions and Processes

- DIVIDED GOVERNMENT: DOES IT MATTER?   *David McKay*
- TRUST IN GOVERNMENT: A CRISIS OF DEMOCRACY?   *Andrew Wroe*
- VOTING AND NON-VOTING: AMERICA'S FLAWED DEMOCRACY?
  David Houghton
- CAMPAIGN FINANCE REFORM: CREATING A LEVEL PLAYING FIELD
  David Houghton
- CONTAINING PRESIDENTIAL POWER   *David Houghton*
- THE SUPREME COURT: THE POLITICS OF JUDICIAL ACTIVISM   *David McKay*
- DIRECT DEMOCRACY: POWER TO THE PEOPLE?   *Andrew Wroe*

1 Divided Government: Does it Matter?

- ■ THE CAUSES OF DIVIDED GOVERNMENT
- ■ THE CONSEQUENCES OF DIVIDED GOVERNMENT
- ■ BUT DO THE VOTERS APPROVE OF DIVIDED GOVERNMENT?

No one disputes that the most important feature of the American political system is the separation of the legislative power vested in Congress from the executive power vested in the president. For much of the nineteenth century – although not notably during the Civil War and its aftermath – Congress made the laws and the president duly executed them. During the twentieth century the relationship between the two branches changed dramatically. With the rise of federal responsibilities at home and abroad, the presidency became the dominant branch. By mid-century a pattern was established. Presidents were expected to produce comprehensive programmes that became the basis of congressional action. Congress may have sometimes blocked presidential initiative and the legislature often delayed or modified the president's programmes. Rarely, however, did it offer an alternative strategy, and in the foreign policy arena it effectively ceded the initiative to the president.

This process was greatly aided by the fact that until the late 1960s it was rare for the White House and Capitol Hill to be controlled by different political parties. In the 1900–68 period unified government prevailed 79.4 per cent of the period, and when divided government did occur it was viewed as a temporary aberration and always in response to the perceived failure of an administration at mid-term. This was the case in 1911, 1919, 1931, 1947 and 1955, and only in 1955 did it last for more than two years. Indeed, by the 1960s observers were able to claim that, following the great political realignment during the Great Depression, the Democrats were likely to find themselves dominant not only in Congress and the presidency but also in state and local government. The Republicans may occasionally have gained a foothold at one level, but never at all levels and always for a relatively short period.[1] Prior to the Depression, the Republicans occupied an analogous position. As a result, administrations were often able to overcome the constitutional obstacles to effective government inherent in the American system. By providing 'connective tissue' between the branches, political parties helped produce such achievements as the reforms of the Progressive era (under the Republicans) and the New Deal and Great Society (under the Democrats).

After 1968 this apparently fortuitous coincidence of events changed dramatically. Divided government became the norm rather than the exception. Between

Table 1.1 Composition of Congress, by political party, 1961–2001

			House			Senate		
	Party and president	Congress	Majority party	Minority party	Other	Majority party	Minority party	Other
1961	D (Kennedy)	87th	D-263	R-174	–	D-65	R-35	–
1963	D (Kennedy)	88th	D-258	R-174	–	D-67	R-33	–
1965	D (Johnson)	89th	D-295	R-140	–	D-68	R-32	–
1967	D (Johnson)	90th	D-247	R-187	–	D-64	R-36	–
1969	R (Nixon)	91st	D-243	R-192	–	D-57	R-43	–
1971[a]	R (Nixon)	92nd	D-254	R-180	–	D-54	R-44	2
1973[a, b]	R (Nixon)	93rd	D-239	R-192	1	D-56	R-42	2
1975[c]	R (Ford)	94th	D-291	R-144	–	D-60	R-37	2
1977[d]	D (Carter)	95th	D-292	R-143	–	D-61	R-38	1
1979[d]	D (Carter)	96th	D-276	R-157	–	D-58	R-41	1
1981[d]	R (Reagan)	97th	D-243	R-192	–	R-53	D-46	1
1983	R (Reagan)	98th	D-269	R-165	–	R-54	D-46	–
1985	R (Reagan)	99th	D-252	R-182	–	R-53	D-47	–
1987	R (Reagan)	100th	D-258	R-177	–	D-55	R-45	–
1989[e]	R (Bush)	101st	D-259	R-174	–	D-55	R-45	–
1991[e]	R (Bush)	102nd	D-267	R-167	1	D-56	R-43	–
1993[e]	D (Clinton)	103rd	D-259	R-175	1	D-57	R-43	–
1995[e]	D (Clinton)	104th	R-235	D-197	1	R-53	D-47	–
1997[e]	D (Clinton)	105th	R-227	D-207	1	R-55	D-45	–
1999[e]	D (Clinton)	106th	R-223	D-211	1	R-55	D-45	–
2001	R (Bush)	107th	R-221	D-212	2	D[f]-50	R-49	1

D Democratic, R Republican. Data for beginning of first session of each Congress. Excludes vacancies at beginning of sessions. – represents zero
a   Senate had one independent and one conservative Republican.
b   House had one independent Democrat.
c   Senate had one independent, one conservative Republican and one undecided (New Hampshire).
d   Senate had one independent.
e   House had one independent.
f   Democratic majority from May 2001.
Source: US Congress, Joint Committee on Printing, Congressional Directory annual; beginning 1977, biennial.

1968 and 2000 the two branches of the federal government were under divided control 81.25 per cent of the time. The Democrats no longer looked like the 'majority' party – although more voters continued to identify with the Democrats than with the Republicans.[2] Instead, elections to the presidency, the House and the Senate became increasingly competitive. In the 2000 elections the contests for all three institutions ended in what was very close to a dead heat. The loser in the presidential race, Al Gore, won the popular vote and lost the electoral college by just one vote. The Senate was divided fifty–fifty and the Republicans' working majority in the House was reduced to seven. (See table 1.1.) In May 2001 the defection of James W. Jeffords of Vermont from the Republicans to an Independent gave the Democrats control of the chamber.

The initial reaction to this new era of divided government was generally negative. Democrats, in particular, disliked the development. Having grown accustomed to controlling both branches of government, and having used this advantage greatly to expand the role of the federal government in society, they viewed Republican presidents Nixon and Reagan as threats to their economic and social agenda.[3] Democrats continued to see themselves as the majority party – a claim bolstered by the fact that they continued to dominate the Congress all the way through to 1994 (apart from Republican control of the Senate between 1981 and 1987). Predictably, Republicans were increasingly frustrated with their inability to capture both Houses of Congress, and officials in the Reagan and Bush (senior) administrations were quick to blame the Democratic Congress for the ballooning budget deficit in the 1980s and early 1990s.

Journalists and other commentators were also negative in their judgement. How, they argued, could public policy and the affairs of state be properly conducted when Congress and the president were constantly bickering and often pursuing quite separate agendas? A new vocabulary on the ineffectiveness of government emerged, with such labels as political 'gridlock' and 'ungovernability' being employed as descriptions of Washington politics.

Political scientists were generally more dispassionate in their analyses and divided their efforts between trying to explain the *causes* of divided government and assessing the *consequences* of the phenomenon. Let us look at each of these in turn.

THE CAUSES OF DIVIDED GOVERNMENT

Not surprisingly, most of the explanations of the causes of divided government originally dwelt on the Democratic domination of the House of Representatives. For during the twenty years of Republican presidents from 1968 to 1992 (with a break of just four years for the Carter presidency) the Democratic grip on the House remained firm. Generally, scholars were of one of two schools – those who believed that Democratic control of the House was *purposeful*, or resulted from a clear preference among voters for such an outcome, and those who believed that it was *structural*, or derived from the ways in which House elections were organized and financed. As far as structural factors are concerned, much attention was paid to the incumbency advantage, or the fact that, once in office, Representatives were able to build up good campaign organizations and establish name recognition among voters. Eventually they not only had more money than those challenging their seats, they were also better at knowing how to campaign and win elections.[4] While this seemed to be true of the earlier period (the

1960s and 1970s) it became increasingly obvious during the 1980s that incumbency was not the key to Democratic success. Indeed, in open seats, where incumbency was by definition irrelevant, the Democrats still consistently outperformed Republicans. This led many observers to conclude that the voters were actually *choosing* a Democratic House because Democrats provided a range of specific benefits, from better social security to more traditional pork-barrel items such as federal projects in home constituencies.[5]

This view seemed to be nicely complemented by the apparent dominance of the Republicans at the presidential level. What seemed to be happening was that voters were opting for congressional Democrats who provided federal largesse and presidential Republicans who championed strength abroad while at the same time acting as a check on the often profligate Democrats in Congress.[6]

However, while this neat and appealing analysis seemed applicable during the Reagan years, it suffered from a number of weaknesses. There was, first, the fact that both Reagan and George Bush senior were increasingly perceived not as guardians of the public purse but as fiscally irresponsible. The federal budget deficit increased rapidly during the early 1980s and again during the early 1990s. Second, applying the purposeful voter model to the Senate never seemed quite to work. The Senate was, after all, controlled by the Republicans between 1981 and 1987, and competition for most Senate seats was always keen. Whether or not the Democrats or the Republicans controlled the chamber seemed to be as much a matter of chance (or of the electoral appeal of particular candidates) as the deliberate party choice of the electorate. Third, in 1992 the Democrat Bill Clinton was elected president, and for two years at least the United States reverted to unified government. The Clinton victory was, of course, greatly facilitated by a perception that George Bush was responsible for the economic recession of 1991–2. Admittedly, victory in the Gulf War boosted his popularity. But that proved to be a temporary phenomenon. What mattered to most voters was the state of the economy. The association of 'strength abroad' with Republican presidents became less and less relevant, as did the general importance of foreign affairs.

All these developments, of course, pale into insignificance compared with the events of November 1994, when, against all expectations, the Republicans recaptured the Senate and the House. In the case of the House it was a truly startling event. After forty years of uninterrupted Democratic control the Republicans took over. Moreover they retained control in 1996 when Clinton's margin of victory over the Republican Bob Dole was substantial. Since then the Republicans' grip on both houses has been weakened to the point that by 2001 party control was very evenly divided.

Rather than undermine the purposeful voting model, the events of 1994 seemed, in a rather perverse fashion, to confirm its validity. The reasoning went like this. During the Bush and, in particular, the Reagan years a Democratic Congress had failed to stem federal spending and rising taxation. The preferences of the typical voter had shifted from the liberal welfare statism of the 1960s and 1970s to the fiscal rectitude and moral conservatism of the 1990s. When, as was the case in 1994, the voters were presented with a coherent conservative agenda they would opt for it. Just this happened with the *Contract with America*, the manifesto produced for the 1994 mid-term elections by House minority leader Newt Gingrich and other conservative Republicans.[7] With a resounding victory, they were quick to claim that the voters had, in fact, specifically chosen the conservative agenda. They also fully expected that this agenda would be consolidated with a Republican presidential victory two years later. In the event it was not to be. Instead the Democrats won the 1996 presidential election, and the Republican majority in both the House and the Senate was gradually eroded in 1996, 1998 and 2000.

By far the most convincing explanation of the origins of divided government is the effect of a 'broad pattern of electoral disintegration' that has been in progress since the late 1960s.[8] In other words, over the last forty years traditional party political cues have been in decline. Voters show less devotion to the parties and are much more likely to split their tickets between presidential and congressional candidates – and indeed between House and Senate candidates and national and state candidates.[9] The appeal of individual candidates irrespective of their party label has thus become significantly more important. In addition, at any one election particular issues may dominate, as was the case with Vietnam in 1968 and the economy in 1992. In such a context the electorate behave in a much more volatile manner, making electoral prediction difficult. Split ticket voting often results. The new breed of fickle voter is also less inclined to vote. Should neither candidate be appealing, or should the salience of the issues be low, voters may simply decide to stay at home. This applies even to better educated and informed voters.[10] Searching for a consistent pattern in such an environment is extremely difficult. In 1996, for example, were the voters approving Bill Clinton's handling of the economy or was the result a negative comment on the suitability of the ageing and uncharismatic Republican candidate Bob Dole?

Claims of a Republican realignment, which were common following the 1980 Reagan victory and the 1994 mid-term elections, have proved premature. Perhaps the ultimate example of this pattern of electoral disintegration was the result in 2000. The country appears to have been evenly divided, but not because the electorate is made up of 50 per cent of solid Republicans and 50 per cent solid Democrats. On the contrary, all the evidence is that most voters' electoral allegiance is weakening and that the 2000 outcome was partly chance – certainly so with regard to the presidential contest, where the electoral college rules just happened to work in a way that produced a near dead heat.

Even the congressional result was dictated by the happenstance of which candidates were up for election in the Senate, and in both House and Senate contests were decided as much by local factors, including the particular appeal of candidates, as by national trends. As there is little sign of the trend towards electoral disintegration abating, we can expect that the era of divided government is here to stay. This is not to say that in any one electoral cycle we may not witness a period of unified government. Indeed, the 2000 election theoretically produced unified government. It was a very strange and almost certainly transient variety of unified government, however. Indeed, it lasted only a few months. In May 2001 Vermont Senator Jim Jeffords left the Republicans to become an Independent.

THE CONSEQUENCES OF DIVIDED GOVERNMENT

As earlier suggested, in the opinion of most commentators divided government was a thoroughly bad development. Traditionally, the political parties have provided the organizational and ideological 'connective tissue' between the branches. In its absence, the electorate are deprived of a clear platform on which they can make a considered choice. One of the most vehement critics of divided government was James L. Sundquist, who argued that effective government actually depends on common party control of the two branches. Without it not only is the efficiency of government affected but also democratic accountability is reduced. Sundquist calls this an American form of coalition government. As he puts it:

> In the American form of coalition government, if the president sends a proposal to Capitol Hill or takes a foreign policy stand, the opposition controlled house or houses of Congress – unless they are overwhelmed by the president's popularity and standing in the country – simply *must* reject it.[11]

Much of this critique is predicated on the assumption that the president is bound to lead and the Congress bound to follow. Austin Ranney has summarized this point in the following terms:

> The ideas underlying all of them [presidential leadership theories] are that America, like every other country, must somehow take swift, coherent and purposeful action . . . that Congress . . . cannot by itself initiate such action; the president is the only official who can take the lead; and that the basic problem of American government is finding and perfecting institutions that will enable the president to lead Congress with maximum effectiveness.[12]

The message is, therefore, clear: divided government will (and indeed already has) led to indecisive and incoherent government. Balancing the budget will be difficult, initiating new and innovative programmes will be problematical. The United States will be unable to execute foreign policy efficiently. In the worst case, the national defence could be threatened because presidents would be unable to act with speed and certainty, constrained as they would be by an obstructionist Congress.

As of the early 1990s, much of the empirical evidence appeared to support this contention. The United States had acquired a chronic budget deficit problem, with Congress and the president constantly blaming each other for the impasse. In addition, the 'Reagan revolution' in economic and welfare reform came to a grinding halt in 1982 when the Democratic Congress refused to accept further reductions in federal expenditure.[13]

What is interesting about this analysis is that, while it seems eminently feasible, it is grounded more in supposition than in careful empirical analysis. Among the questions that have to be asked are the following:

1   Did the divided government of the 1970s and 1980s (and indeed of the late
    1940s) produce a more difficult environment for policy making than the 1945–
    68 period?
2   How does the experience of the 1990s fit into the pattern? Was Clinton more
    successful during his two years of unified government (1993–5) than during
    the subsequent six years of divided government?

In his *Divided we Govern*, published in 1991, the Yale scholar David Mayhew
directly addressed the first question.[14] Mayhew took two plausible indicators of
government effectiveness – the volume of laws passed and the volume of high-
publicity congressional investigations into the executive branch – and attempted
to find a pattern for the 1946–90 period. What he found was that there was
virtually no difference at all between the periods of divided control and those of
unified control. While Mayhew looked only at those laws that at the time or later
were judged to be *significant* he did not ask whether they were *effective* or *desirable* laws. It could be argued, for example, that during the Great Society period a
number of laws were passed that were of great historical significance – for example, the 1964 and 1965 Civil Rights Acts[15] and the creation of medical care for
the old (Medicare) and for the poor (Medicaid). In these and other cases Congress passed the legislation because of the unusually high degree of ideological
unity within the Democratic Party during that period. The Democrats also had a
very large majority in both the House and the Senate at the time. In historical
perspective it would be difficult to identify *any* law passed in the 1950s that was
as significant as these Acts.

   On the other hand, those who believe in purposeful voting would argue that
the American voters were *choosing* such an agenda. Therefore at particular times
in history the electorate may prefer an activist federal government led by a pros-
elytizing president. At such times laws of great significance are passed. At other
times, the electorate may prefer Congress to check the activism of presidents.
Hence, during the Reagan years, the electorate may have split their votes between president and Congress because they were more ambivalent about the need
for such radical reductions in the role of the federal government.[16] Mayhew's
analysis misses these nuances because he chose a simple measure of the supply
of legislation rather than one that concentrates on the demand for government
action.

   Sundquist's claims about the relationship between divided control and effective government may also fail to match the experience of the 1995–2001 period.
This was, of course, the era of divided control when the Democrats controlled
the White House and the Republicans the Congress. This period is interesting in
a number of ways. The House Republicans under (initially) the leadership of
Newt Gingrich were unusually ideological, united as they were behind the right-
wing manifesto in the *Contract with America*. In spite of this, they managed to
legislate some of the *Contract* even if the Senate and the president contrived to
water down some of the measures. Perhaps the most notable achievement of the
Republican Congress was the passage of a comprehensive welfare reform package in 1996. Reforming the welfare system had been on the national agenda for

decades, and successive presidents including the (unified) Johnson presidency, the (divided) Nixon incumbency, the (unified) Carter years and the (divided) Reagan administration had all failed, often in spite of Herculean efforts.[17] Second, during the period of *unified* control (1993–5) Bill Clinton suffered a number of major defeats at the hands of the Democratic Congress. The most notable was, of course, the failure to enact a major health care reform package which had been the centrepiece of his 1992 campaign. (See chapter 11, below.) He also experienced very serious problems negotiating the 1993 budget with the Democratic Congress – more serious, in fact, than equivalent budget negotiations brokered with opposition Congresses by Eisenhower in 1957/8, Nixon in 1971 and Reagan in 1981.[18] Even more striking is the fact that the budget was eventually balanced and a surplus accumulated not during this unified period but during the subsequent period of divided government. Admittedly, this achievement was greatly aided by a booming economy and a growing consensus in both parties that a burgeoning deficit was economically and politically unsustainable. None the less, the achievement is notable – especially given all the dire warnings during the 1980s and early 1990s that the deficit was largely the product of divided government.[19]

To be fair, some of these warnings were based not on divided government *per se* but on the fact that for much of the 1980s Congress itself was divided. Each House could, therefore, blame the other for failing to control the deficit but merrily carry on spending so as to please constituents.[20] There may indeed be

Table 1.2 Presidential vetoes and divided government, 1932–2001

President	Total	Major Bills vetoed per year in office	No. over-ridden	Divided or unified government
Roosevelt	2	16	2	Unified
Truman	6	8	5	Divided (1947–8)
Eisenhower	2	25	1	Divided (1955–60)
Kennedy	0	0	0	Unified
Johnson	0	0	0	Unified
Nixon	13	24	4	Divided
Ford	11	44	7	Divided
Carter	5	13	1	Unified
Reagan	15	19	5	Divided
Bush	15	37	1	Divided
Clinton	20	25	2	Divided (1995–2001)

Source: author. For a definition of major Bills see David McKay, 'Presidential strategy and the veto power: a reappraisal', *Political Science Quarterly*, 104 (1989), table 5.

something to this, given that, apart from a blip during the 1991–2 recession and its aftermath, the deficit generally declined after 1987 at a time when both Houses were under the control of either the Republicans or the Democrats.

A final dimension of divided government is its effect on the veto power. There was a time when the presidential veto was wielded only as a last resort or in order to control the tendency of Congressmen to grant individual constituents special favours. This is no longer the case, however. Today, presidents often find themselves obliged to veto measures championed by the opposition in Congress. Sometimes this means exercising the veto over major items of legislation, including money Bills and foreign policy measures. As can be seen from table 1.2, the relationship between the veto and divided government is strong. All Truman's vetoes were exercised during divided government, as were all of Clinton's. However, once the Republicans controlled Congress after 1994, Bill Clinton refused to sign a number of important Bills, including a Republican plan to use the budget surplus for tax cuts rather than social spending. This pattern of vetoes would suggest that divided government really *does* make a difference and leads to a markedly more adversarial relationship between the branches.

But do the Voters Approve of Divided Government?

Understanding exactly what voters intend when they vote is always problematical. In the American case it is particularly so because Americans vote for national offices at two levels (presidential and congressional) and for three institutions (House, Senate and President). Further complexity is added because the electoral cycles of the three institutions are not completely synchronized. At mid-term all the House seats are up for grabs but only one-third of the Senate seats. Again, during presidential elections only one-third of the Senators are elected. Add to this the decline of party cues and the rise of candidate voting and it is all too easy to see why simple explanations of voter motivations are hard to come by. The puzzle is further compounded by the decline of trust in government. As is catalogued in chapter 2, this has been a growing and disturbing phenomenon over the last forty years, and the secular trend of declining trust seems to parallel the rise of divided government. So, irrespective of whether divided government is the voters' conscious choice, they certainly do not appear to like the results. Also, even if by most measures the policy consequences are not always negative, there is little doubt that division has led to a more confrontational and adversarial style of government.[21] It is very likely that a link exists between confrontational politics and the public's regard for institutions and politicians.

Of course, at the heart of this problem is the constitutional separation of powers. Given that very distinct constituencies are in place for the election of members of Congress and the presidency, and given that the constitution assigns to both branches very extensive powers, the potential for conflict has always been there. Add to this the veto power and the other checks and balances, and the potential for conflict is clear. It may be that the mid-century period (1932–68) was exceptional because party identification and party loyalties were so strong at the time. With the decline of party has come an element of electoral disintegration, with its attendant split ticket voting and divided government. While it is not possible to measure the impact this development will likely have on American politics, two things are clear. First, there is no prospect of the sort of constitutional reform that some commentators have called for in order to eliminate what they claim are the deleterious effects of divided government.[22] British-style parliamentary arrangements may indeed encourage more efficient policy making, but there is no prospect of the United States abandoning the separation of powers. Indeed, it is hardly even a subject of serious discussion. Second, the most recent periods of completely divided government when both Houses were dominated by the opposition party (1987–93, 1995–2001) have been marked by a remarkably favourable political and economic climate. Except for two years in the early 1990s, the economy boomed. For the two branches to be haggling over how the budget surplus should be spent hardly smacks of crisis politics. But renewed recession would transform the budget arithmetic in just a few short years and return inter-branch budget negotiations to crisis and confrontation. Abroad, the end of the Cold War has lowered the stakes of international politics. President and Congress may disagree over foreign issues, but the costs of such disagreement are relatively low. Should this benign international environment change for the worse – and history tells us that at some time it surely will – then the perils inherent in divided government will become apparent. Such was the case in 1947–9, when pundits warned of the dire consequences for world peace that might result from divided government.

For these reasons, students of American politics should always be sensitive to just how important the separation of powers is for the functioning of the political system. The causes and consequences of divided government are likely to continue to dominate political discourse, therefore, for the first few decades of the twenty-first century.

NOTES

1   See William Nisbit Chambers and Walter Dean Burnham (eds), *The American Party Systems: Stages of Political Development* (New York and Oxford, Oxford University Press, 1975), chapter 7.
2   For comprehensive data see Harold W. Stanley and Richard G. Niemi, *Vital Statistics on American Politics, 1999–2000* (Washington DC, CQ Press, 2000), figure 3.1.
3   For a critique of the Nixon agenda see Alan Gartner *et al., What Nixon is Doing to Us* (New York, Harper & Row, 1973), and of the Reagan agenda Gary Wills, *Reagan's America* (New York, Penguin, 1987).
4   For a summary of this research see Charles O. Jones, 'New directions in US congressional research', *Legislative Studies Quarterly*, 6 (1981), pp. 455–68.
5   See, in particular, the discussion in Gary C. Jacobson, *The Electoral Origins of Divided Government: Competition in the US House Elections, 1946–1988* (Boulder CO, Westview Press, 1990).
6   See Byron Shafer, *Bifurcated Politics* (Cambridge MA, Harvard University Press, 1988).
7   Newt Gingrich, Dick Armey and the House Republicans, *Contract with America*

(Washington DC, Republican National Committee, 1994).

8   Jacobson, *Electoral Origins*, p. 39.

9   On split ticket voting see Martin Wattenberg, *The Rise of Candidate Centred Politics in the USA* (Cambridge MA, Harvard University Press, 1991).

10 See the references at chapter 3, below.

11 James L. Sundquist, 'Needed: a political theory for the new era of coalition government in the United States', *Political Science Quarterly*, 103 (1988), p. 630.

12 Cited in Sundquist, 'Needed: a political theory', p. 622.

13 For a review of the politics of this period see John E. Chubb and Paul E. Peterson (eds), *The New Direction in American Politics* (Washington DC, Brookings Institution, 1985).

14 David R. Mayhew, *Divided we Govern: Party Control, Lawmaking and Investigations* (New Haven CT, Yale University Press, 1991).

15 The 1964 Civil Rights Act banned discrimination in education, employment and public facilities. The 1965 Voting Rights Act outlawed discrimination in voting.

16 On this point see Morris Fiorina, *Divided Government* (New York, Macmillan, 1992), pp. 88–92.

17 See David McKay, *Domestic Policy and Ideology: Presidents and the American State, 1964–1987* (Cambridge, Cambridge University Press, 1989), also the discussion in chapter 13 below.

18 For a summary of the Eisenhower, Nixon and Reagan experience see Herbert Stein, *Presidential Economics: The Making of Economic Policy from Roosevelt to Reagan and Beyond* (New York, Simon & Schuster, 1984).

19 See, for example, Matthew D. McCubbins, 'Government on layaway: federal spending and deficits under divided party control', in Gary W. Cox and Samuel Kernell (eds), *The Politics of Divided Government* (Boulder CO, Westview Press, 1991), pp. 113–54.

20 Ibid.

21 On this theme see Eric Uslaner, *The Decline of Comity in Congress* (Baltimore MD, University of Maryland Press, 1995).

22 Including James Sundquist; see his *Constitutional Reform and Effective Government* (Washington DC, Brookings Institution, 1987).

2 Trust in Government: a Crisis of Democracy?

- ■ PERFORMANCE
- ■ POLITICAL EXPLANATIONS
- ■ SOCIO-CULTURAL EXPLANATIONS
- ■ CONCLUSION

Americans are deeply dissatisfied with government. While they feel very proud to be American and express high support for American ideals such as democracy, liberty and equality of opportunity, in the 1990s never more than 40 per cent said they trusted government most of the time or just about always. Indeed, in 1994 only 21 per cent trusted government, while fully 77 per cent trusted it only some of the time or never. Furthermore, clear majorities think public officials don't care about people, think that government is run for and by big interests, and believe government wastes money. While Americans have always been suspicious of authority – their country was after all born of a revolution against the autocratic rule of George III – figure 2.1 shows that trust has declined precipitously since the 1960s. Three-quarters trusted government in 1964, but by 1980 less than a third did. Since then trust has increased, fallen and increased again, but the trend is unclear and the fluctuations are minor compared with the overall downward shift in the post-1960s period. And trust has fallen across socio-demographic groups fairly evenly. It is down among male and female, white and black, south and non-south; across education, income and occupation level; across generation, age group, religion and party identification. Moreover, Americans increasingly display hostility towards a host of professional people and societal institutions such as academics and universities, doctors and hospitals, journalists and the media, business leaders and big corporations.[1]

Does all this really matter, however? While one answer is that it is healthy to be suspicious of government (we will return to this later), the more usual response is that of course it matters. First, on a psychological level, it matters greatly that people are distrustful, angry, murderous even. The former two emotions make people feel unhappy, and the last is deadly. For example, when Timothy McVeigh committed the most deadly peacetime act of domestic terrorism in US history in April 1995 – his fertilizer-based truck bomb devastated the Alfred P. Murrah federal building in Oklahoma City, killing 168, nineteen of whom were children – his target or 'enemy' was the federal government and its 'agents'. Second, on a political level, it matters because it cannot be healthy for people to be so suspicious and cynical about politicians and the political system. One

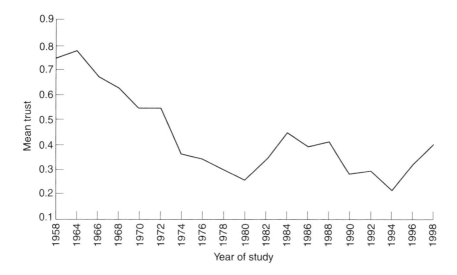

Figure 2.1 Trust in government. The curve represents the proportion trusting government 'just about always' or 'most of the time'.
Source: authors' own calculations, from National Election Studies (Ann Arbor MA,University of Michigan, 1948–98)

consequence is that people will disengage from the political system and democracy will no longer prove an effective way of representing Americans' interests. In fact, in the longer run, how long will Americans continue to express support for the principle of democracy when the reality (or, more accurately, as we shall see, their perception of reality) continually fails to meet expectations? And what would be the consequences of a loss of faith in a principle that the American people hold dear? The end of democracy, perhaps, and its replacement with a less benign system?

The illness, then, looks serious. But the United States is not unique. Many other industrial democracies are experiencing a decline in trust, although nowhere is it as serious as in the United States. Still, while the aim of this chapter is to review and critique the potential causes of the illness in America, the experience of others may help our diagnosis. The potential causes can usefully be divided into three types: performance, political and socio-cultural.[2] Let us examine each of them to discover whether any, some or all are responsible for the contemporary dissatisfaction Americans feel towards their government.

PERFORMANCE

Perhaps the reason why Americans distrust government is that government is too big and too inefficient. It attempts to do too much and does it poorly, and this in a nation with a historic antipathy towards government. Before the Great Depression hit the United States in 1929 the federal government played little role in the life and economy of the nation. Federal government spending as a percentage of GDP was about 5 per cent, while today it stands at about 25 per cent. On one level, then, the size of government, together with the perception that it is inefficient and ineffective and, at the same time, overly meddlesome and regulatory, could be responsible for the fall in trust. Ronald Reagan captured this mood when he famously said that 'government is the problem, not the solution'. Yet, on another level, Americans are very supportive of many government programmes such as social security (pensions) and Medicare (medical care for the elderly) – so much so that they are electorally sacrosanct. This suggests an ambivalent attitude towards government. Americans distrust it because it is too big and too inefficient, yet they want it, for example, to provide and enforce environmental and consumer regulations and to protect them from foreign and domestic threats. Is this ambivalence irrational? Not necessarily, if we distinguish between scope and performance. Americans may not mind big government so long as it does its job properly, but size may become an issue when it does not. Distrusting government and wanting to reduce its scope are thus perfectly rational responses to government failure.

If the evidence shows that government has failed, then negative perceptions of it would seem to be entirely understandable. But has it? While this is a very difficult question to answer, one scholar has made an ambitious attempt. Employing seventy or so indices on which he thinks most Americans have shared goals (e.g. *per capita* income, dwellings with serious defects, the infant mortality rate, the cost of health care, personal freedom) across a range of policy fields (prosperity, quality of life, opportunity, personal security and values), Derek Bok suggests that between the 1960s and 1990s the United States has 'made definite progress . . . in the majority of cases'.[3] For example, racial and gender discrimination and child poverty are down, the economy is doing well, and social security and Medicare are providing greater comfort in older age. But are the improvements large enough to satisfy most people?

Bok's second measure thus examines the changing rate of progress over time on the same indices employed in the first measure. He acknowledges that the rate of progress on some indices between 1975 and 1990 is not as rapid as that made between 1960 and 1975. Some, such as income and productivity, show that things are still getting better today but they are not getting better as quickly as they were. On balance, though, Bok suggests that the evidence is 'mixed . . . and it would therefore be difficult to assert categorically that America or its government has performed less well in the past fifteen to twenty years than during the preceding two decades'.[4]

Bok's final measure compares the United States' performance with six other industrial democracies (Britain, Canada, France, Germany, Japan and Sweden). He finds that:

> in roughly two-thirds of these cases, the United States has performed less well than most of the other nations since 1960. In roughly half of the cases, our record is

actually at or near the bottom of the list. America continues to have the most pro-ductive economy, the highest standard of living, and the best scientific research in the world. But poverty rates are higher, health care costs are greater, and programs for children more restricted than in other countries surveyed. The United States also provides its citizens less personal security; more of its people lack health insurance, the risk of violent crime is higher, the workplace tends to be less safe, and the safeguards from layoffs and arbitrary firing are less effective. Finally, efforts to regulate the economy often seem to produce fewer results and lead to more litiga-tion, delay, and expense than in other leading democracies . . . Close analysis sug-gests that government practices and programs have played an important part in our performance in almost all of the[se] cases.[5]

This evidence suggests that Americans are perhaps right to be concerned about the performance of their government when compared with people living in simi-lar industrial democracies. Yet most indices also suggest that things have im-proved for Americans since the 1960s, the time when dissatisfaction began to grow. This indicates that Americans' judgement of government is harsher than the mixed evidence suggests it should be.

While Bok takes some account of economic performance, he does not give it primacy. Yet political scientists have long believed that the state of the economy and people's perceptions of their own financial performance are important deter-minants of election outcomes. If they can influence the selection of government, could they not also determine the perception of government? Economic factors are perhaps worth a second, closer look.

The evidence suggests that the personal economic performance of the ordinary working American – Joe Six-pack, as Americans sometimes call him – has dete-riorated since the mid-1970s. Sure, Joe has watched the post-1973 economy grow at 2.5 per cent per annum on average, and, while this is not as impressive as the pre-1973 3.5 per cent, it is an increase none the less. However, Joe's wages have not grown at anything like 2.5 per cent. Median real hourly wages in America have fallen on some estimates by a staggering 25 per cent.[6] To compensate for this decline many people are working longer hours, and many families now have two or more breadwinners, not the traditional one. Yet, even with these changes, breaking down average family income by quintiles (creating five income groups, from low to high, with equal numbers in each) shows that between 1979 and 1983 income fell for the first, second and third quintiles while increasing for the fourth and fifth.[7] This change has been driven both by an increase in permanent inequality (the rich get richer while the poor get poorer) and an increase in risk and uncertainty (the difference in income between bad times and good times has increased). In both cases Joe would feel hard done by.

Joe's lower wages and increased job insecurity have a number of interrelated causes. One is the increase in global competition, especially from developing coun-tries and the newly industrialized countries, and the associated freer movement of labour and capital, which have all put downward pressure on wages and up-ward pressure on unemployment (especially of the unskilled). While not neces-sarily the government's fault, regional free-trade pacts such as NAFTA and WTO-negotiated tariff reductions certainly are the responsibility of the US government.

Another is the IT revolution, which has led to the loss of many well paid, secure, unionized blue-collar jobs in manufacturing and the growth in non-unionized white-collar jobs in the service sector. Yet another is the move towards more 'macho', authoritarian management styles, decreasing unionization of the workplace, lean business philosophies ('restructuring', 'downsizing', 'outsourcing' and so on), and corporate mergers and take-overs, which have all reduced the demand for both blue-collar workers and white-collar staff. The US government is not responsible for all these changes. However, if governments become in-creasingly active in the management of the economy and try to take credit for economic good times, they should not be surprised when the public react to nega-tive developments.

It is plausible that these changes could have influenced the downturn in trust. But the timing does not always fit. While the late 1990s improvement in trust co-incided with an increase in median real wages and a narrowing of income in-equality, the steep decline of trust in the 1960s antedates most personal economic difficulties. Indeed, the average family income of all quintiles increased in real terms between 1966 and 1979. Moreover, mistrust of government applies equally across income groups and job types.[8] It is not, however, equal across personal *perceptions* of economic performance. Individuals who think they will be better off next year are more trusting of government than their pessimistic peers. And in 1964 the number of people who thought they would be better off next year began to fall. What this means is that increasing economic pessimism (rather than economic performance) 'fits' well with the onset of mistrust in the 1960s; declining pessimism also fits with the improvement in trust in the late 1990s. It looks, then, very much like a plausible case.

POLITICAL EXPLANATIONS

There are several political factors that might explain the decline in trust. Let us first deal with the less plausible ones in order to remove them from considera-tion. The first is called the Cold War thesis, and it goes something like this. During a crisis Americans will pull together, support their leaders and present a united front against the enemy. Some scholars think this 'rally round the flag' effect happened during the Cold War. But when the war ended and the enemy disappeared in the late 1980s Americans had no real enemy to rally against. The uncertainties and disorder in what President Bush called the New World Order replaced the certainties and order of the old order. And, as Gavin Esler put it, the fed scare replaced the red scare.[9] At first glance, this appears to be an intuitively attractive hypothesis. However, the end of the Cold War in the late 1980s does not coincide with the beginning of the decline of trust in the 1960s. Of course, there is no reason why the war's end could not have contributed to the decline, but the absence of any major change in the already downward trajectory of trust suggests that the Cold War thesis is not the main explanation.

Another possible war-related thesis stems from the United States' victory in the Second World War and perhaps the 'battle' against the Great Depression a decade earlier, which were widely regarded as triumphs of central planning and the federal government. In the post-war reconstruction period, the federal government retained its high-profile role at home and abroad, economic growth was high, and there appeared to be opportunities and well-paid jobs for everyone. In short, very specific and unusual events and the government's reaction to them created a perception that government 'works'.[10] This in turn produced inflated and overoptimistic expectations about what government could achieve during 'normal' or non-crisis times. When the government failed to meet such unrealistic expectations from the late 1960s onwards, the public's trust in it inevitably declined. A problem with this argument is that we do not have good pre-war data on trust and other measures. Another problem is that older people who witnessed the government success during the Depression and the war are as likely today as younger people to view government suspiciously.[11] A final problem is that trust has fallen in most industrial democracies, including those that cannot be said to have succeeded in the war (Germany and Japan especially), which suggests that there is something more to today's malaise. It is, however, worth noting that trust in government is consistently lower in Germany and Japan than elsewhere, suggesting that, while the decline in trust may have little to do with post-war euphoria, high levels of trust elsewhere may have had a lot to do with wartime success.

A more likely reason for increasing distrust may be that today's voters do not feel that their opinions are represented and articulated by the two main political parties. David King has shown that the Republican and Democratic Parties have become more ideologically polarized since the 1960s while the general electorate have not.[12] Under such conditions, it would hardly be surprising for voters to feel alienated from, and thus distrustful of, political parties and government. If such well founded alienation persists, the consequences for Americans' support for the principle of democracy could be serious. Ironically politicians have never dedicated so much time and so many resources to 'listening' to the folks back home. Now focus groups have joined opinion polls in the politicians' armoury of eavesdropping devices. They may help politicians in their re-election battles, but they can also encourage further scepticism about politics. The professionalization of the campaign 'industry' has encouraged the 'commodi-fication' of politicians and their 'message'. Professional listening, of course, requires money, which in turn requires fund raising, which further alienates voters already suspicious of the influence money buys, which means more time and effort must be spent listening to voters – and so the circle begins again. This is a cynical view of politics, but it is one many Americans find convincing. It may be an exaggeration, but it is founded in truth.

Less worrying for democracy's long-term prospects, but perhaps the most obvious and compelling political explanation, is that confidence in government may have declined owing to a series of incompetent, dishonest and unsavoury leaders. The decline in trust that began in the mid-1960s coincides with America's descent into the Vietnam mire abroad and social conflict at home. Ultimately, Johnson chose not to seek re-election in 1968, leaving office a broken man. Nixon soon followed. Ford and Carter did little to regain people's confidence. During

Reagan's tenure some confidence did return, but it proved temporary. Bush left office with very low poll ratings and Clinton's personal peccadilloes were legion. While all this is true, it is also the case that knowledge of the personal shortcomings of political leaders is now widespread, whereas in earlier eras it was not. Television and the sound bite now prevail. Before the 1960s politicians often gave 'off the record' briefings that remained just that. After Watergate the whole slant of reporting changed. Journalists realized that the way to get ahead professionally was to dig for dirt, and report it. Sensationalist, scandalous, 'gotcha' stories make the best copy, but they also project and engender a jaundiced view of the political world.

These changes in tone and content influenced the public's knowledge and perception of their leaders. For example, in stark contrast to the media's treatment of Gary Hart and Clinton, Kennedy's numerous infidelities, though well known among the Washington elite, were never reported. Some presidential candidates today release their private medical records and others go to great lengths to demonstrate their physical and mental health, yet few Americans knew their longest serving president, Franklin D. Roosevelt, wore leg braces and spent much of his time in a wheelchair (a result of polio in early adulthood). The press simply refused to tell the American people.

Of course, most Americans get their news from television. But the time allocated to news programming by mainstream television channels is limited, and the time devoted to political stories on news programmes is even more limited – and declining. Accompanying (or perhaps because of) this diminution is a decline in party identification and a rise in candidate-centred commercial political advertising. Come election time, television stations are saturated with political advertisements. Many are attack ads, in which opposition candidates are ruthlessly savaged. If the candidates themselves spend most of their time and money attacking opponents rather than reporting their own triumphs or qualifications, it is easy to see why Americans have become disheartened with their leaders and the political process. There is also little role for the political party in these ads. Politicians' direct appeal to the electorate helps destroy the connective tissue or glue that the parties form between citizens and government. Negative sentiments are also encouraged by polemical radio talk shows and Internet politics sites. Many of these sites and, especially, shows exhibit an extreme level of anti-government propaganda and paranoia. Furthermore, little distinction is made between editorial comment and hard news.

What all this adds up to is a nation that knows very little about the substance of politics but is essentially hostile to the federal government. That the federal government is despised by many and mistrusted by more seems hardly surprising, given its portrayal in the contemporary media. Indeed, so entrenched is anti-government sentiment that politicians often run for government by running against government. Politicians do everything they can to portray themselves as 'outsiders' taking a 'new broom' to 'clean up Washington'.

Socio-cultural Explanations

Three socio-cultural explanations – post-materialism, social capital and the decline of civic republicanism – have been offered as potential explanations for citizens' increasing mistrust of their government. Post-materialism argues that this is no bad thing. In a democracy it is healthy for citizens to mistrust authority, so long as they do not become politically disengaged. Indeed, in a post-material society, citizens do not disengage but move outside the traditional political process to engage in alternative forms of politics, such as direct action, political discussion, boycotts and petition signing.

The concept of post-materialism, first developed by Ronald Inglehart, holds that citizens of economically developed countries are likely to experience 'relatively high levels of existential security, . . . [which] reduces the tendency for mass publics to defer to authority'.[13] Freedom from the need to chase the material basics of life frees up time and energy to concentrate on non-material concerns, such as the environment, education, health, crime and the efficacy and honesty of leaders, as well as on more esoteric values such as liberty, happiness and self-fulfilment. Such concerns are likely to raise individuals' consciousness of government and its actions, and at the same time raise expectations of it on a wide range of non-material values. 'Conversely, conditions of economic insecurity give rise to the Authoritarian Reflex – the tendency for mass publics to seek and idealise strong, authoritarian leaders.'[14]

Post-materialism is an intuitively attractive hypothesis. On the one hand, it offers a credible explanation of why Americans increasingly mistrust the police force, army and government as well as universities and bureaucracies. All are authorities and all have seen their stock fall with the public. On the other, it offers a credible explanation of why trust has fallen across all industrial democracies with mature economies. Moreover, America's economic dominance and high standard of living may explain why distrust of government is higher in the United States than in other industrial democracies.

However, while post-materialism is theoretically appealing, some scholars argue that there is little evidence to support it. Inglehart uses World Values Surveys to show the percentage of people agreeing that 'more respect for authority would be a good thing' declining between 1981 and 1990. However, the decline was small. Moreover, over 70 per cent were 'very proud' to be American.[15] Also, we saw earlier that we should be wary of headline economic data; the real story is that people feel concerned about their personal finances, and this does not fit neatly with Inglehart's story of material contentment. Linked with this is another problem: distrust does not differ significantly across income groups or occupations, suggesting that the materialist/post-materialist dichotomy may actually be a proxy for something else. Finally, Inglehart believes rising levels of interpersonal trust should accompany the new, non-traditional political activity. Yet, as Inglehart himself acknowledges, Americans' trust in their fellow citizens declined between 1964 and 1994 – precisely the time when declining trust in government was most apparent.[16]

For this reason, the social capital argument may provide better explanatory leverage. Social capital theorists, of whom Robert Putnam is the leading proponent, are very interested in interpersonal trust and its decline. They argue that social capital is the invisible commodity that binds communities together. It is like a reservoir of interpersonal or intra-community trust that builds up as a result of shared, group-based, face-to-face experience. This may be going ten-pin bowling together on a social level or attending a PTA meeting on a political level. It is, in other words, the glue that links individuals together in the form of communities. And communities are coming unstuck because people do not work and play together as they used to – in large part because they spend too much time watching television. And this decline in social capital has resulted in a decline of trust at all levels. People trust each other less, and they trust the government less.

Like post-materialism, it is an appealing hypothesis. However, Putnam has been severely criticized. His critics claim that it is not clear why social capital has declined, or what the consequences of such decline are. They also argue that the social capital theory is fuzzily conceptualized. And, finally, they argue that the evidence shows that Americans are not less involved in communities but are, rather, involved in different ways. In other words, Putnam's use of evidence is flawed.

The final socio-cultural explanation, the decline of civic republicanism, is most associated with Michael Sandel. He argues that the dominant political philosophy in the United States today is 'procedural liberalism'. This means that the government plays the role of neutral arbiter between competing interests, ensuring only that each does not encroach on others' individual rights; it makes no attempt to impose on or encourage in its citizens some sense of a higher public good. In this moral void, citizens compete with each other for a slice of the national pie, but are otherwise disengaged from the governing process. Such a lifeless polity, Sandel believes, breeds disenchantment with government and the democratic process. The answer is a style and system of government that involve and engage citizens through self-rule, as was the case in the young American republic. It is the move away from it and towards procedural liberalism that has bred 'democracy's discontent'.

A less theoretical form of Sandel's argument sometimes finds expression in what are often labelled communitarian critiques of modern society. These critiques say Americans are becoming increasingly narcissistic. The focus on rights and the individual rather than on responsibilities and the community places increasing demands on the government. The 'me' generation gives nothing back to society; it only demands and takes. Because it cannot meet such demands, government is accused of 'failing' – so trust in it declines. A more conservative version of this argument promotes the idea that the 'counter-culture' of the 1960s destabilized American life. Women went out to work, families broke up, children lived in poverty without moral guidance, crime and drug use increased, respect for order and authority was lost. An even more conservative version blames the government for encouraging these changes by providing welfare support for those 'choosing' to break societal norms, which in turn creates dependence on government.

CONCLUSION

While Sandel's thesis (and its more conservative variants) is certainly interesting, it is difficult, and probably impossible, to measure its impact on declining trust. No scholar has yet tried, and none is likely to. While this does not mean that we should reject it out of hand, it remains simply an interesting hypothesis. Similarly, while scholars have tried to test scientifically Putnam's social capital thesis, as yet we are unsure of its significance.

We know that the end of the Cold War is unlikely to have had a great impact on Americans' trust of government, and that government performance alone cannot explain all the decline, although it probably explains some. More likely candidates include workers' sense of job insecurity and lower real hourly wages. Because these are partly a result of globalization, increasing economic interdependence and lean business philosophies, we should probably ascribe at least some – and possibly a significant amount – of explanatory power to the nature of modern capitalism.

Other likely candidates include Vietnam and Watergate. They fit well with the decline of trust, and link neatly with increasingly negative perceptions of America's political leaders. It would, however, probably be wrong to put too much emphasis on the incompetence and dishonesty of various presidents and members of Congress. These are probably constants, while media reportage of them is not. The media's negative portrayal of politics and politicians is very likely to be responsible for at least some of the downturn in trust. But we must not forget that media negativism is a result at least in part of Vietnam and Watergate.

Ultimately, it is impossible to judge which is most important. It is also very difficult to rule some theses in or out. Political scientists still have much work to do to. While it would be encouraging to conclude this chapter on a high note by claiming that the late 1990s improvement in trust should bode well for the future, a more sober conclusion is in order. The other chapters in this book demonstrate that the American political system faces some serious institutional, procedural and policy-oriented problems. Ultimately, declining trust must relate to these problems. We can conclude, then, that failures in the political system – real or imagined – have undermined trust and that an improving polity relates closely to an improving society.

NOTES

1   A comprehensive set of distrust data can be found on the National Election Study website at http://www.umich.edu/~nes/nesguide/gd-index.htm#5. Alternatively see Harold W. Stanley and Richard G. Niemi, *Vital Statistics on American Politics, 1999–2000* (Washington DC, CQ Press, 2000), figure 3.7.

2   See Joseph S. Nye junior, 'Introduction: the decline of confidence in government', in Joseph S. Nye junior, Philip D. Zelikow and David C. King (eds), *Why People don't trust Government* (Cambridge MA, Harvard University Press, 1997), pp. 6–17, and Pippa Norris, 'Introduction: the growth of critical citizens', in Pippa Norris (ed.),

Critical Citizens: Global Support for Democratic Governance (Oxford, Oxford University Press, 1999), pp. 21–5.

3   Derek Bok, 'Measuring the performance of government', in Nye *et al.*, *Why People don't trust Government*, p. 61.

4   Bok, 'Measuring the performance of government', pp. 61–2. It is not clear, however, why Bok compares 1960–75 to 1975–90, given that trust started to decline in the mid-1960s.

5   Bok, 'Measuring the performance of government', pp. 63–4, emphasis in original. It is worth noting that trust has also fallen in most of the countries that Bok uses as comparators, which suggests that performance is not everything.

6   A. Gosling and T. Lemieux, 'Labour market reforms and changes in wage inequality in the United Kingdom and the United States', in Richard Blundell, David Card and Richard Freeman (eds), *Seeking a Premier League Economy* (Chicago, University of Chicago Press, forthcoming).

7   Robert Z. Lawrence, 'Is it really the economy, stupid?', in Nye *et al.*, *Why People don't trust Government*, especially figure 4.1.

8   See Gary Orren, 'Fall from grace: the public's loss of faith in government', in Nye *et al.*, *Why People don't trust Government*, table 3.1, and Lawrence, 'Is it really the economy, stupid?', especially table 4.3.

9   Gavin Esler, *The United States of Anger* (London, Penguin, 1997), especially chapters 3 and 14.

10   Nye, 'Introduction', in Nye *et al.*, *Why People don't trust Government*, p. 16.

11   Orren, 'Fall from grace', table 3.1 in Nye et al., *Why People don't trust Government*.

12   David C. King, 'The polarization of American parties and mistrust of government', in Nye *et al.*, *Why People don't trust Government*.

13   Ronald Inglehart, 'Postmaterialist values and the erosion of institutional authority', in Nye *et al.*, *Why People don't trust Government*, p. 218.

14   Ibid., p. 218.

15   Ibid., figure 9.4.

16   Various National Election Studies and General Social Surveys. A *Washington Post/Henry J. Kaiser Foundation/Harvard University* poll in 1995 suggested that one-third of Americans trust other people – down from over half in the 1960s.

3 Voting and Non-voting: America's Flawed Democracy?

- ■ THEORIES OF VOTING BEHAVIOUR
- ■ THEORIES OF NON-VOTING
- ■ A SYMPTOM OF SICKNESS OR OF HEALTH?

In November 2000 the United States went through one of its most controversial and divisive presidential elections in living memory. America uses a 'first-past-the-post' or 'winner-takes-all' system of electing the president, and although the Democratic candidate Al Gore received a wafer-thin majority of the popular vote, Republican George W. Bush received a similarly slim majority in the electoral college. Florida's twenty-five electoral college votes proved crucial in deciding the outcome, and after various court challenges in that state and ultimately in the Supreme Court of the United States, Gore finally conceded defeat on 13 December. George W. Bush took office as the forty-third President of the United States on 20 January 2001.

While this kind of result is mathematically possible in all first-past-the-post systems – it happened in Britain, for example, as recently as 1974 – it was the first time that an American president had taken office without winning a majority of those who voted since 1888, when the Democrat Grover Cleveland captured more popular votes than his rival, the Republican Benjamin Harrison, but Harrison became president by virtue of garnering more electoral college votes. Perhaps surprisingly, however, this outcome produced no great uproar among the majority of the American public. In a parliamentary system like Britain's, losing the election after winning the popular vote is probably easier for the defeated party to take, because its 'consolation prize' (in all likelihood) will be a number of seats in the legislature comparable to that of the winning party. There is no such consolation in the American system, however, since the loser genuinely 'loses it all'.

Although there were some minor protests on the day of George W. Bush's inauguration, no strong movement to reform the electoral college has yet emerged. What, if anything, does this tell us about America's system of elections? One interpretation would stress the strength and continuity of America's political institutions and its commitment to constitutionalism. While the eventual result was in doubt for some weeks, the Democrats eventually conceded defeat and the system reverted to working in the way it usually operates. Another explanation

Table 3.1 Average voter turnout at national elections, selected countries, 1991–2000 (% of the voting age population)

Country	%
Argentina	81
Australia	83
Austria	78
Canada	60
Denmark	83
Finland	71
France	61
Germany	72
Iceland	89
Ireland	71
Italy	90
Mexico	58
Norway	76
Spain	79
Sweden	84
Switzerland	38
United Kingdom	72
United States	45

Source: International Institute for Democracy and Electoral Assistance.

Table 3.2 National voter turnout in presidential election years, 1960–2000 (% of the voting age population)

Year	%
2000	51.20
1996	49.08
1992	55.09
1988	50.11
1984	53.11
1980	52.56
1976	53.55
1972	55.21
1968	60.84
1964	61.92
1960	63.06

Source: US Federal Election Commission.

(less flattering to US democracy) is possible, however. Perhaps the majority of Americans were simply too apathetic and disengaged to care what the outcome was. Gore and Bush were both centrist candidates, one running as a 'New Democrat', the other as a 'Compassionate Conservative'. While there were some significant policy differences between them, these were often not especially visible in the campaign itself. Perhaps it made little difference to most voters who won.

Only 51 per cent of those eligible to vote actually bothered to do so at the 2000 elections. There was nothing unusual about this; only 49 per cent voted in 1996, and the figures for other recent presidential elections show that not much more than 50 per cent of those eligible to vote ever do vote nowadays. Americans traditionally vote in lower numbers than Europeans do; in Austria, for example, turnout is often above 80 per cent, while traditionally Great Britain enjoys turnout rates in the high 70s (although in 2001 turnout slumped to around 60 per cent) and Sweden in the mid-80s. Only Switzerland has a turnout rate comparable to that of the United States. (Table 3.1.)

There has, moreover, been a notable decline in US electoral turnout since 1960; turnout that year was 63 per cent, but it now consistently hovers around the 50 per cent mark. There was a drop of six percentage points in turnout between 1992 and 1996, although this rose very slightly (by 2 per cent) between 1996 and 2000. The year 1996 saw the lowest level of voter turnout since 1924, despite the fact that in 1993 Congress had passed the National Voter Registration Act (commonly known as 'Motor Voter'), which allows US citizens to register to vote at the same time as they renew a driving licence.[1] (Table 3.2.) Why is turnout so low in the United States? Is declining turnout a sign of voter apathy and disillusionment, an indication that the legitimacy of the American system is being called into question? Can a country where half the voting-age population stay at home, even in closely fought presidential elections like that of 2000, truly call itself a 'representative democracy'? These, as we shall see, are formidable puzzles, and political scientists offer different answers to the questions they pose.

We focus in this chapter on two of the most important and central controversies that scholars of American electoral politics have debated, confining our discussion for reasons of space to presidential elections. First of all, why do people vote the way they do? Political scientists have proposed a range of competing theories in order to try to answer this question. The central debate in the literature – between the party identification school and the issue voting school – is outlined and a case made for each. Second, why – in a nation that supposedly values democracy above many (or all) other values – do so many Americans fail to exercise their democratic right to cast a ballot at presidential elections? Just as there are competing theories of voting, so there are different explanations for why people do *not* vote. Political scientists have also, as we shall see, offered different interpretations of whether low electoral turnout actually matters.

THEORIES OF VOTING BEHAVIOUR

Why do people vote the way they do? The political scientist's response to this question is admittedly not a very satisfying one; after more than forty years of systematic research into the determinants of electoral choice there is no real consensus as to what the most important determinant of voting is. There are, however, two major theories about why people vote the way they do: the 'party identification' model and the 'issue voting' model. The case for each is briefly examined below.

THE CASE FOR THE PARTY IDENTIFICATION MODEL

In their classic work *The American Voter* Angus Campbell and his colleagues at the University of Michigan argue that most voters develop a 'party identification' or 'party ID' during their formative or teenage years.[2] This is a long-term *psychological attachment* to a particular political party. As we grow up we develop an affiliation to one party – often as a result of listening to our parents or neighbours when they talk about politics – and that attachment tends to determine the way we vote for the rest of our lives (unless something very dramatic happens which makes us change our mind). The result is that the American electorate resembles two enormous blocs, one composed of Republican Party identifiers, the other of Democratic Party identifiers.

One important thing to notice about party identifications is that they tend to be highly stable and resistant to change. Your party may lose a few elections, it may perform badly in government, or it may even adopt policy positions on some issues you disagree with, but you will still support the party, because it's *your* party. One consequence is that, for many people, the issues being discussed at the election do not matter nearly as much as party does. Strong party identifiers, for instance, will tend to 'screen out' or ignore altogether information about their party which is unfavourable, even when they disagree with their party's representative on major policy issues. For example, many Republican voters and party members reportedly wanted to drop Dan Quayle as their party's vice-presidential candidate in 1992. Behind the scenes, some party influentials apparently wanted Quayle replaced with someone more popular, like Jack Kemp or Colin Powell. However, there was very little possibility that strong Republican Party identifiers would vote against their party in 1992 because of Quayle. This is because strong identifiers tend to screen out political information they dislike and engage in 'selective perception'.

According to this model of voting behaviour, for most people it does not usually matter who the candidates are or what positions they take on the issues of the day. People who identify with the Democratic Party will usually always vote for the Democratic Party's candidate, and Republican Party identifiers will normally always vote for the Republican candidate. A number of individuals sought the Republican Party's presidential nomination in 2000, for instance, including

John McCain, George W. Bush and Steve Forbes. However, party identification theorists suggest that, no matter which one of these got the nomination, Republican Party identifiers would have voted for him. Equally, no matter whether the Democratic Party had chosen Al Gore or Bill Bradley in 2000, Democratic Party identifiers would have voted for their party's candidate. For the majority of citizens, the act of voting is thus 'habitual' or 'instinctive'. The average citizen is not well informed about politics and does not spend his or her time dutifully scrutinizing the campaign proposals of the main political parties in deciding how to vote. Rather, voters simply 'short-circuit' the complex process of deciding who to vote for by simply selecting that party towards which they have developed a long-term affinity since early adulthood.

It is immediately obvious that party identification cannot explain all electoral behaviour. Since the Democratic Party has for many years had the most identifiers within the American electorate, the Democrats would *always* win if party was all that mattered. Advocates of this approach, however, say that something like two-thirds of the electorate have stable party loyalties and always vote for their party at every election. However, one-third of the electorate is composed of people who are only weakly attached to a political party or who are out-and-out independents. This one-third is made up of 'switchers', individuals who (for one reason or another) lack any stable party loyalty and hence are likely to change their mind as to who they support from one election to another. According to the party identification approach, this one-third *does* make up its mind on the basis of the issues and/or on the personal characteristics of the candidates, and it is this one-third which in practice decides the result of the election.

THE CASE FOR THE ISSUE VOTING MODEL

To some extent the party identification model has gone out of fashion in recent years, in part because it has become progressively clear in the years since Campbell and his associates wrote that fewer voters nowadays actually *have* a strong and stable party affiliation. In the 1992 presidential election, for example, only about 29 per cent strongly identified with the Republicans or the Democrats, whereas 38 per cent did in 1964, a drop of 9 per cent. Voters also seem to have become more ideologically and politically sophisticated since the 1960s. By the 1970s these trends gave rise to an approach to explaining electoral choice that challenged the prevailing party identification orthodoxy: the issue voting model.

In their book *The Changing American Voter* Nie et al. argued that American voters are now a good deal more sophisticated than the party identification model gave them credit for.[3] The authors shared the same underlying approach or starting point as Campbell *et al.*, in the sense that they conceded that the party identification model accurately described the behaviour of voters up to the late 1960s. But, they argue, trends in electoral data necessitate a reassessment of the average voter's capabilities and behaviour. The political environment surrounding the American voter changed dramatically during the 1960s, they argue. The ideological emphasis of Republican presidential candidate Barry Goldwater and the emergence of a range of 'new issues' like civil rights, Vietnam and Watergate, the growth of the mass media and shifts in the nature of the electorate itself all produced major change. With regard to this last factor, a new generation of voters have entered the electorate who were and are disinclined to identify habitually with a particular political party.

Issue voting theorists argue that party is declining greatly as an influence on the vote. They argue that in recent years we have seen a process of *dealignment* going on, a process by which voters are gradually losing their attachment to parties in general and becoming independents instead. Between 1960 and 1993 the number of voters calling themselves 'independents' rose from about 23 per cent to 33 per cent, and by some measures to almost 40 per cent. As the influence of party has gone down, issue voting supporters say, so the importance of issues and candidate characteristics has increased. While previously most people simply voted for their party's candidate because it was 'their party', nowadays they are a good deal more selective and sophisticated. The proportion of voters who do this, moreover, is much greater than the one-third described by Campbell *et al.*, issue voting theorists contend, and may well be 50 per cent or even more.

There are essentially two ways of voting on issues: *prospective* and *retrospective* issue voting. Voting prospectively is the more demanding of the two in terms of the knowledge and information it requires of the voter. In order to vote in this way, a voter must: (1) look at the policies of the two parties and at the positions they take on the issues, (2) compare these two sets of policies and (3) select that party which has the policy positions which look most like their own. So, for example, if I am conservative on social issues, liberal on economic issues and conservative on foreign policy, I will want to choose the party that looks most like me on these things. In all likelihood no party platform will be a perfect match with my own preferences, but prospective voting simply requires me to select that party which comes closest to my own position on the issues.

Retrospective issue voting is rather less demanding of the average citizen. Voters, V. O. Key argued in *The Responsible Electorate*, are not fools; they are rational in the sense that they reward incumbents for concrete achievements and punish them for their failures.[4] Voters are perfectly capable of looking back at the last few years and asking themselves how well the incumbent administration has performed. Economic performance is particularly salient for voters; generally speaking, if things are going well economically the government will be re-elected, and if things are going badly the administration will be removed from office. This kind of issue voting is relatively straightforward and easy to do. It does not require the voter to be highly informed about politics and policy, or even to know a single policy of either party. All that is necessary is for the voter to be aware of how well the president's party (for example) is performing. It may also be more 'rational' to vote retrospectively on the issues than prospectively, since the informational costs are much lower. Weighing up party positions on the issues may also be actively inadvisable, since we know that politicians may break their promises. Given this fact, it makes little sense to pay much attention to what leaders say they will do during the electoral campaign. It makes a lot more sense to look at what they have actually done in the recent past.

How is it that both schools are able to claim that their model explains empirical reality best? Surely data from recent presidential elections can tell us who is right one way or another? Unfortunately this is far from being the case, for statistical data do not speak for themselves. The two rival approaches interpret the same data differently. The reason they are both simultaneously able to make a case for their own model is that both claim the weak party identifiers as their own. The party identification school argues that weak party identifiers nevertheless maintain a party affiliation, and that they ought to be classed as falling under the party identification category. Issue voting supporters, on the other hand, treat those who say they have only a weak identification with party as independents prepared to vote on the basis of the issues and candidates. The party identification school argues that the so-called 'decline' in party identification has been greatly exaggerated; between 1960 and 1988 the percentage of voters identifying with a party declined from 75 per cent to 63 per cent, but this is not an especially marked drop. Some of the most recent work on voting behaviour, it is worth noting, has restated the party identification position and attempted to refute the arguments of Nie *et al.*[5]

When compared with the study of voting, the analysis of non-voting has been somewhat neglected.[6] As already noted, however, only about half those eligible to vote regularly turn out to do so, even at presidential elections. This means that a given member of the electorate is just as likely to be a non-voter as he or she is to be a voter. It is important, therefore, to seek some explanation of why so many voters stay at home on polling day.

THEORIES OF NON-VOTING

Some analysts are puzzled as to why voters bother to turn out at all. Most notably, rational choice theory has had some difficulty explaining why people vote. To understand why, we need to understand what the advocates of this approach mean by 'rationality'. One is assumed to be rational when, having weighed up the costs and benefits of the various choices or courses of action open to us, we select that option which yields the greatest benefits relative to costs. In the terms that economists use, we pick the 'utility-maximizing' option, whose likely benefits exceed the likely costs (the 'best' option, in conventional parlance). Rational choice theory suggests that pretty much everyone is 'rational' in this sense.

Why is this a problem in explaining voter turnout? In essence, it is a problem because by most estimates the costs of voting *vastly outweigh* the likely benefits. While American voters may care very much who wins the election, they also know that their own vote is unlikely to make much difference to the outcome. Even in a presidential race as close as that between George W. Bush and Al Gore in 2000, the odds that one's vote will decide the outcome are infinitesimally small. So the instrumental benefits of voting are quite low. However, the costs of voting in the United States are quite high.

There are fairly high informational costs involved in voting. In order to inform yourself fully about the election you are proposing to vote in, you would need to read about the candidates, learn about the issue positions they have adopted and the differences between them, weigh up how those positions compare with your own preferences, and so on. But in the United States an even greater cost – which also helps to depress voter turnout relative to Europe – is getting registered to vote in the first place. As Wilson and DeIulio note, 'the entire burden of register-ing to vote falls on the individual voters. They must learn how and when and where to register; they must take the time and trouble to go someplace and fill out a registration form; and they must reregister in a new county or state if they happen to move'.[7] Contrast this situation with that which exists in the United Kingdom, where registration is mostly done for the voter by the government. A form is delivered by mail every year which by law you have to fill in, stating who in the household is eligible to vote. Then, just before the election a card is deliv-ered with your details already printed on it. You simply take it to the polling booth and vote. But in the United States you have to take the time and trouble to do all this yourself. It is hardly surprising that turnout is lower.

Hence some versions of rational choice theory seem to suggest that no one will vote! The fact that so many do, on the other hand, is seen by critics of the ap-proach as evidence that rational choice theory is inherently flawed or outright wrong.[8] Most analysts of American elections pose the question the other way around, however. Rather than asking why anyone votes, they ask why so many do not vote. Various theoretical factors have been proposed to explain this. Broadly speaking, they can be divided into institutional explanations and socio-political accounts.

INSTITUTIONAL EXPLANATIONS

First of all, it is possible that America's political system – the separation of pow-ers and federalism – is the source of the problem. Samuel Huntington once fa-mously argued that America's major problem is 'too much democracy'. While this may be an overstatement, it is certainly true that US citizens are asked to vote for candidates at a bewildering array of levels. The vertical and horizontal divi-sions of power inherent in the design of the American republic make this inevita-ble. At the same time, these features also work to frustrate leadership and restrain the democratic will of the majority, not to give it free rein. It is also difficult to achieve proper electoral accountability in such a system. Arguably, all this cre-ates powerful disincentives to voting. For one thing, it decreases the likely ben-efits of voting: even if one's vote contributes to the election of the next President of the United States, there are so many 'safeguards' in the system that the incum-bent may not be able to achieve anything of real substance. Indeed, the need for constant bargaining and compromise across political institutions may mean that the actions of government fail to correspond to *anyone's* preferences.

It is difficult to attribute low voter turnout to this factor alone, however. While it may perhaps be true that the sheer number of elections depresses turnout by 'devaluing the currency' of elections, this certainly cannot explain why turnout has progressively fallen since 1960. One of the basic rules of social science is that we cannot use a constant (in this case, the political system, which has changed little since 1960 in its basic features) to explain variation (in this case, the fall in turnout). If we focus simply on presidential elections, this account also fails to explain why an election held every four years would be 'too much' for the average voter. David McKay rejects this variation of the institutional argument for this reason, noting that 'turnout at presidential elections remains low in spite of their relative infrequency and the disproportionate amount of publicity and attention paid to them by political parties and the media'.[9] Britain also elects its chief executive every four or five years but enjoys much higher turnout levels. Logically, since the US turnout rate is almost unique among Western industrial democracies, in explaining this phenomenon we should look for those political characteristics which the United States does not share in common with Britain.

One such difference, as we mentioned in the previous section, is the relative difficulty of voter registration procedures. This provides another (arguably more convincing) institutional explanation for low turnout in the United States. There is certainly much to recommend this argument. If we look, for instance, at the proportion of *registered* voters who turn out to cast their ballots, we see that the turnout is actually a good bit higher in the United States than it is in Britain. About 86 per cent of those registered to vote in the United States turn out to do so, compared with about 76 per cent of those registered to vote in Britain.[10] This suggests rather strongly that the voter turnout problem in general is an offshoot of the fact that it is harder to register (that is, it takes more time and effort) in the United States than elsewhere. It follows that the whole problem could be effectively resolved if government would only take a more proactive approach to voter registration.

This makes for a compelling argument. However, while it must certainly be a good part of the explanation for lower turnout rates in general (most studies estimate that compulsory registration would increase turnout by about 10 per cent), it is not really plausible as an explanation of why turnout has been *falling* since 1960. Indeed, turnout has fallen at the same time as many states have made it relatively easier to register. ('Motor voter' laws are one example of this but they have done little to arrest the decline.)

SOCIO-POLITICAL EXPLANATIONS

As in other Western democracies, you are more likely to vote in the United States if you are a member of an upper socio-economic group. In particular, the more education you have the more likely you are to vote. This is presumably because education tends to boost one's level of political education, and that in turn makes us more interested in getting involved in politics. It is especially puzzling, then, that turnout should have declined so markedly in recent years, given the increased levels of educational attainment which have occurred over the same period. As Robert Putnam notes, 'over the last generation, when increasing levels of education should have prompted large increases in voting, turnout in developed nations has slumped by up to 20 per cent'.[11] Turnout should also have increased owing to the relaxation of registration laws over this period. Falling turnout in the United States, then, as Richard Brody has suggested, 'confounds our expectations'.[12]

Perhaps the answer to the question lies not in the character of America's laws and institutions but in its broader social and political character. One such argument for declining turnout has been offered by Walter Dean Burnham. He argues that 'a critical dimension of the problem lies in the structure – or degeneration – of political parties as vehicles for the representation of broad mass interests in an electoral market'.[13] He traces the beginnings of the current turnout decline to 1900 and to the 'decay of political parties in the United States during the twentieth century'.[14] The growth of non-voting, as he sees it, reflects the growth of an alienated economic underclass, and the weakening of the parties which might otherwise have integrated that underclass into the democratic system.[15]

There are some notable problems with Burnham's analysis, as Ruy Teixeira has shown. The typical non-voter today is no longer as likely to be drawn from lower socio-economic groups as he or she was in 1960, as the decline of turnout has affected all social groupings. Teixeira finds that 'non-voters are spread across demographic and partisan categories'. Nevertheless, the fact that political parties in Europe 'play a much stronger role in commanding voter loyalty and mobilising citizens to go to the polls' than in the United States – together with the existence of proactive state registration procedures in Europe but not America – helps explain the differences in turnout generally.[16] His explanation for turnout, however, is also socio-political; there has been a decline in many voters' sense of political efficacy (their faith in their ability to influence government), a decline in their political information about campaigns (as measured by newspaper reading) and a decline in party identification. These three trends have collectively led to a 'process of political disconnection or "peripheralization" that has reduced the meaningfulness of electoral participation to Americans', Teixeira argues.[17]

Another socio-political explanation of a slightly different sort is provided by Miller and Shanks.[18] Their explanation for declining turnout is generational: they explain the trend by reference to the voting (or non-voting) habits of different generations of Americans and the effects these have had on turnout as one generation has gradually replaced another. Miller and Shanks argue that the pre-New Deal generation of voters – those who came of age prior to the election of 1932 – had all but disappeared by the late 1980s:

> By 1988, the pre-New Deal generation had been more than replaced by the post-New Deal generation that came into being in the midst of the turmoil following the Kennedy–Johnson era and the 1964 elections . . . the post-1964 generations provided substantial growth in the sheer size of the eligible electorate in the 1970s and 1980s, but they were dramatically less engaged by, and less likely to participate in, national politics than were their predecessors at the same stage of their adult lives. Their turnover rates were dramatically lower than those of the generation made up of the New Deal cohorts whose first votes were cast between 1932 and 1964.

In short, what produced the national decline in voter turnout was 'the gradual replacement of the habitual voters of the pre-New Deal generations with the non-voting post-New Deal cohorts'.[19]

Miller and Shanks explain the decline in American turnout exclusively by reference to internal American factors and the behaviour of different generations. Robert Putnam agrees with this assessment, arguing that 'virtually all the long-run decline in turnout is due to the gradual replacement of voters who came of age before or during the New Deal and World War II by the generations who came of age later'.[20]

There is, however, a cross-national dimension to this question. Putnam has also suggested that, in order to understand fully why turnout has been falling in the United States over the past few decades, we need first to appreciate that this is a trend which has been present right across the Western world. 'Turnout is down in almost all established democracies,' he notes. Logically, it follows that the causes of this decline cannot be wholly peculiar to the United States. Putnam locates this cross-national factor in a decline of what he calls 'social capital' or 'civic engagement'; a decline, that is, in our willingness to join in community activities and a corresponding increase in solitary individualism. 'Compared to our parents' generation, we are less likely to know our neighbours, to invite friends home, to go on picnics or hang out in bars, to belong to trade unions and professional associations or simply to spend time chatting with acquaintances.' To the extent that voting is an expression of civic-mindedness and civic duty, we should expect a decline in voter turnout as the former decreases.[21]

A SYMPTOM OF SICKNESS OR OF HEALTH?

Theories of American voting behaviour are well developed and have been studied in great depth since the 1940s. There is general agreement on the list of factors – principally issues, candidates and party identification – which must be studied, but different theories combine these factors in different ways. There is also no real consensus in the literature as to what really causes non-voting. As a general observation, however, institutional factors seem most useful in explaining why US turnout levels are low *in general* compared with other industrial democracies, while socio-political factors seem to explain better why turnout is currently declining.

Should Americans be concerned that there are so many non-voters, though? In other words, is it a sign that American democracy is in trouble in some way? The honest answer is that no one really knows. On the one hand, low turnout may be a sign of democratic ill health, an ominous portent that people are 'turned off' from the political process and disillusioned with their political institutions and those who occupy them. Many citizens may now be so apathetic about politics following Vietnam, Watergate, Iran-Contra, Whitewater, the Lewinsky scandal and various other blemishes on the body politic that they consider voting a waste of time. According to Walter Dean Burnham, one of the leading advocates of the position that falling turnout does represent such an ominous portent, 'the continued growth of the "party of non-voters" in the United States in current elections can only be evaluated as a critical and major limit on democracy itself'.[22]

It is worth noting that low turnout may be a sign of just the *opposite* state of affairs; in other words, it may be an indication that people are generally happy with the system and for that reason are not motivated to go out and vote. While voter turnout is quite low in comparison with turnout in Europe, this may not mean that American voters are more apathetic than citizens overseas, for voting is far from being the only form of participation in politics (although it is certainly the most obvious and important). To some extent, Americans compensate for non-voting by engaging in other forms of political activity instead. In the early 1970s Nie and Verba gathered evidence which suggests that US citizens as opposed to Europeans are more inclined to work for (rather than join) political parties, that they are more active in community organizations, that they work more with local groups to solve local problems, and that they contact government officials more often by phone or mail.[23] These findings were reinforced by the findings of a 1995 study by Verba *et al.*[24]

There is a downside to this rather comforting conclusion, however: it has to be weighed against newer evidence which shows that participation in these 'alternative' political activities has also declined markedly at the same time as voter turnout. While it is still true to say that Americans do these things more than Europeans, they do not do them as much as they used to.[25] As Robert Putnam notes, the 1970s were the heyday of civic involvement and political engagement, but the present era is a low point in such activity (and likely to get worse, owing to trends in generational replacement). Fewer and fewer Americans nowadays identify with a political party, work for a party, attend political meetings or help with campaigns. 'We are playing virtually every aspect of the civic game less frequently today than we did two decades ago,' Putnam notes. While such trends probably do not represent an indication that the political system is on the verge of collapse, it is becoming increasingly difficult for political scientists to defend trends like these as indications of 'contentment'.

NOTES

1   Stephen Knack, 'Drivers wanted: motor voter and the election of 1996', *PS: Political Science and Politics*, June 1999.
2   Angus Campbell, Philip Converse, Warren Miller and Donald Stokes, *The American Voter* (New York, Wiley, 1960).
3   Norman Nie, Sidney Verba and John Petrocik, *The Changing American Voter* (Cambridge MA, Harvard University Press, 1976). See also Morris Fiorina, *Retrospective Voting in American National Elections* (London, Yale University Press, 1981).
4   V. O. Key, *The Responsible Electorate* (Cambridge MA, Belknap Press, 1966).
5   See, for instance, Eric Smith, *The Unchanging American Voter* (Berkeley CA, University of California Press, 1989); Warren Miller and Merrill Shanks, *The New American Voter* (London, Harvard University Press, 1996).
6   Miller and Shanks, *The New American Voter*, p. 39.
7   James Wilson and John DeIulio, *American Government: Institutions and Policies*, sixth edition (Lexington MA, Heath, 1995), p. 132.
8   See especially Donald Green and Ian Shapiro, *Pathologies of Rational Choice Theory:*

Critique of Applications in Political Science (London, Yale University Press, 1994).

9   David McKay, *Essentials of American Government* (Boulder CO, Westview Press, 2000), p. 127.

10   Ibid., p. 129.

11   Robert Putnam, 'Let's play together', *Observer*, 25 March 2001. See also his *Bowling Alone: The Collapse and Revival of American Community* (New York, Simon & Schuster, 2000).

12   Richard Brody, 'The puzzle of political participation in America', in Anthony King (ed.), *The New American Political System* (Washington DC, American Enterprise Institute, 1978).

13   Walter Dean Burnham, *The Current Crisis in American Politics* (Oxford, Oxford University Press, 1982), p. 12. For a related though not identical argument see Frances Fox Piven and Richard Cloward, *Why Americans Don't Vote* (New York, Pantheon, 1988).

14   Ibid., p. 123.

15   Ibid.

16   Ruy Teixeira, *Why Americans Don't Vote: Turnout Decline in the United States, 1960–1984* (London, Greenwood Press, 1987), p. 112.

17   Ibid., pp. 107–8.

18   Miller and Shanks, *The New American Voter*, pp. 39–114.

19   Ibid., p. 41.

20   Putnam, *Bowling Alone*, p. 33.

21   Putnam, 'Let's play together'.

22   Burnham, *The Current Crisis in American Politics*, p. 12.

23   See Norman Nie and Sidney Verba, 'Political participation', in Fred Greenstein and Nelson Polsby (eds), *Handbook of Political Science* (Reading MA, Addison-Wesley, 1975).

24   Sidney Verba, Kay Lehman Schlozman and Henry E. Brady, *Voice and Equality: Civic Voluntarism in American Politics* (Cambridge MA, Harvard University Press, 1995).

25   Putnam, *Bowling Alone*, p. 31.

26   Ibid., p. 41.

4 Campaign Finance Reform: Creating a Level Playing Field

- **THE CASE AGAINST CAMPAIGN FINANCE REFORM**
- **THE CASE FOR CAMPAIGN FINANCE REFORM**
- **MONEY AND POLITICS**
- **CONCLUSION**

Like the notion of term limitations for members of Congress, campaign finance reform is not a particularly new idea; it has been around at least since the turn of the twentieth century, and has become one of the hardy perennials of American political debate. In 1907, at the prompting of President Theodore Roosevelt, Congress passed the Tillman Act banning donations by banks and business corporations at federal elections, and in 1947 the Taft–Hartley Act imposed a similar ban on trade unions. Thus for many years both businesses and labour unions have been prohibited by law from making direct contributions to the campaign coffers of candidates for federal office. Various smaller reforms and safeguards were put in place during the course of the last century, but there were for many years no limits on what individual citizens could donate to federal campaigns.

This was to change in the 1970s. The most important piece of campaign finance legislation in recent history has been the Federal Election Campaign Act (FECA), passed in 1971. The original law was mostly about disclosure; it required political funding to be made public rather than remaining hidden from view. The Watergate scandals during Richard Nixon's administration, however, soon revealed what were then astonishingly large contributions by individuals to Nixon's re-election committee, some of whom were 'rewarded' with ambassadorships. This created a new resolve to limit what individuals could contribute to campaigns. Largely as a result of Watergate, Congress beefed up FECA in 1974 by adding several amendments. A Federal Election Commission was created to enforce campaign finance laws and to provide public funding for presidential elections. Most importantly, the 1974 law also placed limits or ceilings on how much contributors can donate to a candidate running for office. Individuals, for instance, are limited to $1,000 per candidate per election, and Political Action Committees are limited to $5,000 per candidate per election.

The 1974 law may sound quite stringent, and it no doubt originally appeared that way to its advocates. Unfortunately for supporters of campaign finance reform, however, it proved too stringent for the Supreme Court. In a landmark ruling in 1976 in the case of *Buckley* v. *Valeo*, the Court struck down some provisions of the 1974 legislation. As Elizabeth Drew notes, the decision upheld the constitutionality of limits on contributions made *directly* to candidates but maintained that 'expenditures made independently of campaigns are a highly protected form of speech'. Limits could be placed on the former but not on the latter. The Court also ruled that there could be no limitations on what wealthy candidates might contribute to their own campaigns, on the grounds that one cannot corrupt oneself.[1]

It is also true to say that the legislation has not had the effects intended by its sponsors. First of all, while Political Action Committees (PACs) had existed before the 1974 legislation, the new laws gave them legal sanction by authorizing PACs to raise funds on behalf of candidates. As Elizabeth Drew points out, the birth of PACs had occurred as long ago as the 1940s, when labour unions started to circumvent the ban on direct funding by creating more indirect fund-raising bodies.[2] But the 1974 Act explicitly allowed corporations and unions to set up their own PACs. This has unwittingly led, or at least contributed, to an explosion in the number and activities of such committees. According to Federal Election Commission figures, in 1974 there were 608 PACs in Washington DC, but by 1994 their number had grown dramatically to almost 4,000. Their total contributions at congressional elections over this period rose from about $12.5 million to about $179 million. Over the same period the percentage of total contributions to candidates for the House coming from PACs (as opposed to those from individual contributors or the political parties) rose from 14 per cent to 37 per cent.[3]

While the 1974 law was intended to limit the ability of wealthy contributors to exert a disproportionate impact on election outcomes and policy making, it has operated much like a corset, for what was squeezed in one place has merely 'popped out' at another. Candidates for office have increasingly found inventive ways of getting around it. One way of doing so is through the use of what is commonly termed 'soft money'. There is an important distinction to be made in contemporary American electoral politics between soft and hard money. Hard money refers to financial donations that are *given directly to a particular candidate's official campaign organization* for fighting an election. Soft money, on the other hand, is money that – rather than being donated directly to a candidate – is given instead to a political party for 'general purposes' (such as 'party building', voter registration and political education). In addition, soft money may be used to sponsor negative or positive advertising that supports or criticizes one of the candidates. While the 1974 Act instituted the direct, hard money limits already referred to ($1,000 for individuals per candidate, $5,000 for PACs), there are no limits whatever on what an individual or PAC can donate in the form of soft money. This turned out to be a significant loophole in the 1974 legislation, for individuals wishing to donate unlimited amounts have been able to channel their contributions through the soft money category.

Why is this a problem, as advocates of campaign finance reform see it? In essence it is problematic because in practice soft money has often been used to benefit particular candidates in particular elections; in other words, it has been used to achieve almost the same purposes that hard money was meant to serve.

The main use to which soft money has increasingly been put is the development of 'issue advertisements'. For instance, if you know your opponent is pro-gun control, you can use soft money to attack the gun control position in general, and this in turn becomes a thinly veiled attack on your opponent. Soft money has increasingly been used against particular candidates by both major political parties even more directly and explicitly than that, however. The ruling in *Buckley* v *Valeo* provided a list of words which could not be used in a political advertisement paid for with soft money. They were all words which if used would constitute 'express advocacy' for or against a particular candidate in a particular election. They include the words 'Vote for X', 'Elect X', 'Support X', 'Vote against X' and so on. Although the Court may have intended the list as illustrative only, it has usually been interpreted by the two main political parties as full and comprehensive, so that anything not included is permissible. Many issue advertisements on television across America in the run-up to the 1996 and 2000 elections, for instance, contained explicit attacks on particular candidates but used phrases such as 'Are you really happy with X?', 'X isn't working for us', 'Do we really want someone in Congress who thinks what X does?' to convey the intended message. The use of this indirect language makes soft money issue advertisements easy to spot, as does the fact that they usually carry a caption bearing a message such as 'Paid for by the Democratic/Republican Party of State Y' or 'Paid for by the Republican/Democratic National Committee'.

Numerous examples could be given of such advertisements, but a couple of instances – both broadcast in Pennsylvania during the 2000 congressional campaign – will convey the flavour of their typical character. The first advertisement was run against Democratic Congressman Ron Klink, who was challenging the Republican incumbent Rick Santorum for his Senate seat in Pennsylvania. The caption at the top of the ad read 'Paid for by the Republican State Committee of Pennsylvania' and the text was as follows:

> It's a Pennsylvania ethic – a hard day's work for an honest day's pay. Not for Ron Klink. He has the worst attendance record of any Pennsylvania Congressman. He says he 'never missed a vote on anything important'. Missing votes for a prescription drug benefit, social security, ending the death tax, improving railroad pensions, *aren't important*? Klink *didn't* miss the chance to vote himself a pay raise. A pay raise for missing work? Tell Ron Klink these issues may not be important *to him*, but they are to you.

Note that Klink's rival Santorum is not mentioned by the announcer, and that at no point is the viewer urged to 'vote against' Klink. But Santorum is the intended beneficiary. Santorum defeated Klink in the November 2000 Senate race.

A second example, from Pittsburgh, is the following advertisement, one of several run against the Republican Melissa Hart, who was competing for a House seat against the Democrat Terry Van Horne. The ad contained the caption 'Paid for by the Pennsylvania Democratic Party' and the text was as follows:

> Melissa Hart needs to go back to school. With classrooms overflowing, Melissa Hart voted *against* reducing class sizes in grades K through 3. As parents worry

about school safety, Melissa Hart voted *against* funding for programs aimed at preventing school violence. And while education is the key to opportunity, Melissa Hart even supports *eliminating* the Department of Education. Tell Melissa Hart to stop failing our kids.

Again, the text is clearly designed to benefit a rival candidate who is not mentioned – in this case Van Horne – and the language avoids the items listed in *Buckley* v. *Valeo*. In this instance the advertisement was unsuccessful, since Hart won.

Soft money is now often used to finance issue campaigns in this way, but it is not regulated by the Federal Election Commission and there are, as we mentioned, no limits on what can be spent. According to Anthony Corrado, 'in 1980, when soft money was born, the Republicans and Democrats combined raised an estimated $19 million, with the GOP collecting the largest share, $15 million'.[4] In 1992 a total of $86 million was raised by the two main parties. In 1996 the figure rose dramatically: the Democrats spent about $122 million in soft money, and the Republicans spent about $150 million. By 2000 the combined figure reached about $487 million, with each party gathering a roughly equal share of the total. Soft money now accounts for almost half the contributions received by the Democratic Party and more than a third of those received by the Republican Party.

The blurring of the distinction between soft and hard money greatly worries advocates of campaign finance reform, and it has led to campaign finance proposals receiving renewed attention on the floor of Congress and among the wider public. The most notable example at present is the McCain–Feingold Bill, so called because in the Senate it is co-sponsored by Senator John McCain, a Republican, and Senator Russ Feingold, a Democrat. The Bill would ban the use of soft money in campaigns and ban the kind of issue advocacy commercials mentioned above where they clearly benefit one candidate or another. A version of the Bill actually passed in the House in 1999, but it was filibustered to death by the Senate the same year. As of March 2001 the latest version of McCain–Feingold was being debated.

As with the issue of term limits, though, there are strong and passionately held arguments on both sides of the debate. These are examined below.

The Case against Campaign Finance Reform

1   Many opponents of reform argue that giving a candidate cash is an exercise in free speech which is protected by the First Amendment to the Constitution. They cite the Supreme Court case of *Buckley* v. *Valeo*, the ruling in which is often summarized as the argument that 'money equals speech'. As one section of the decision states:

> The First Amendment denies government the power to determine that spending to promote one's political views is wasteful, excessive, or unwise. In the free society ordained by our Constitution it is not the government, but the people –

collectively as associations and political committees – who must retain control over the quality and range of debate on public issues in a political campaign.

Senator Mitch McConnell of Kentucky, a strong opponent of campaign finance reform, argues that since contributing to a political candidate is a constitutionally protected form of speech, legislation to limit campaign contributions violates the First Amendment rights of all Americans. In themselves large contributions to political parties are not evidence of corruption; rather they are an indication of the donor's democratic right to support his preferred candidates and policies. According to McConnell (speaking in a March 2001 debate on campaign finance reform) 'the real problem is not that there's too much money in politics; there's too little money in politics, particularly hard money . . . . And yet nobody on the so-called reform side is trying to deal with the single biggest problem that we have.' Hence many opponents of a ban on soft money urge an increase in the limits on the donation of hard money.

2   The existing campaign finance system works well; all that is wrong is that specific individuals are breaking the law. The solution is to enforce existing laws, not to create new ones. There is an old saying in America: 'If it ain't broke don't fix it.'

3   A ban on soft money donations to political parties – such as that proposed in the McCain–Feingold Bill – would probably weaken the parties, and might well lead wealthy contributors to switch their contributions to other interested groups. Again, Senator Mitch McConnell is a leading advocate of this position. At a hearing on campaign finance in 2000 he suggested that this scenario would be the chief result of a soft money ban. 'Is this the world you want?' he asked. 'Do you really want a system where challengers and citizens who make up political parties lose? Do we really want a world where the undeniable winners are guaranteed to be so-called special interest groups and PACs, wealthy and celebrity candidates, incumbents, the news media and political consultants?'[5]

4   Other opponents of reform argue that campaign contributions and spending have skyrocketed simply because the objective costs of running a campaign have greatly increased. To be elected to a major federal office today, you need to buy television time and radio time, newspaper space, computers, and so on. While a great deal of money is spent at election time, it is but a drop in the ocean compared to what government spends on its own programmes or what Americans spend on basic household goods. One may also note that campaign spending tends to increase the more competitive elections are; so, paradoxically, increased campaign spending may just be an offshoot of the fact that elections are getting more competitive. (And surely that is a good thing, the critics of reform say.)

THE CASE FOR CAMPAIGN FINANCE REFORM

1   The most often cited argument for reform is that the involvement of 'fat cat' financial contributors skews the political process in favour of the wealthy

and diminishes the practical value of 'one person, one vote'. It is inconceivable that millions of dollars are donated each election cycle out of mere philanthropy, so campaign contributions must be buying something. Critics of the current system, like Elizabeth Drew, argue that arguments against campaign finance reform are mostly concocted justifications of plain self-interest. As Fred Wertheimer notes, allowing individuals to use their own financial resources in campaigns also 'undermines the concept of one-person, one-vote, in that it gives much greater influence to people who have money in the process once the politician is elected than it does to the average voter'.[6]

2   Proponents of reform argue that the 1974 legislation has wholly failed in its objectives, owing in large part to the increasing imaginativeness of politicians, consultants and lawyers specializing in electoral law. The loopholes left by the law and by the way in which it was interpreted by the Supreme Court in *Buckley* v. *Valeo* have increasingly been exploited in creative ways. According to Thomas Mann, in recent years we have seen 'the utter collapse of the federal regulatory system governing campaign finance . . . money from corporate and union treasuries and unlimited contributions from individuals once again is flowing to candidates and parties and is being spent directly to influence the outcome of federal elections'.[7] There is therefore an urgent need for new campaign finance laws to stop the abuse of soft money and issue advertisements. Mann argues that:

> in 1996, sham issue ads exploded on the scene as politicians, consultants, parties, groups and individuals discovered that running campaign ads that avoided the use of 'magic words' such as 'vote for' or 'defeat' provided them a wonderful loophole to advance their electoral interests without being constrained by any legal requirements governing disclosure, restrictions on sources of funding, or spending limits on publicly financed presidential candidates.[8]

3   The Republican Senator John McCain of Arizona argues that campaign finance reform is necessary in order to restore public confidence in America's system of government. Trust in government has declined markedly since the 1970s. Corruption, or the appearance of corruption, lowers voter turnout and turns young people away from the political process. As McCain put it on the CNN programme *All Politics* on 30 June 1999:

> We have squandered the public trust. We have placed our personal and partisan interest before the national interest, earning the public's contempt for our poll-driven policies, our phony posturing, the lies we call spin and the damage control we substitute for progress. And we defend a campaign finance system that is nothing less than an elaborate influence-peddling scheme in which both parties conspire to stay in office by selling the country to the highest bidder.

Genuine campaign finance reform, however – including a ban on soft money – would restore public confidence in the political system.

4   Public opinion is on the side of reform. As McCain noted in the March 2001 Senate debate, 'public opinion polls show that the vast majorities of our

constituents want reform and believe our current system of campaign financing is terribly harmful to the public good'. The necessity for reform is 'self-evident' to the American people, McCain argued. Recent opinion polls bear this claim out. When asked in a March 2001 Gallup poll whether they favoured or opposed new federal laws limiting the amount of money that an individual or group can contribute to the national political parties, 76 per cent said they favoured such a reform, while only 19 per cent were opposed; in the same poll, 54 per cent said they believed that campaign finance reform should be a priority for Bush and the Congress, while 41 per cent thought it should not be. Similarly, in an October 2000 Gallup poll, 61 per cent thought that protecting government from excessive influence by campaign contributors is more important than protecting the freedom of individuals to contribute, compared with 34 per cent who thought the opposite. 72 per cent of the respondents in that poll favoured legislation limiting the amount of soft money that an individual or group can donate, while 24 per cent opposed such limits.

5   Advocates of campaign finance reform dispute the notion that 'money equals speech'. Thomas Mann, for instance, argues that campaign finance proposals such as the McCain–Feingold Bill in no way inhibit the right to free speech, and Drew maintains that the Supreme Court did not actually say that 'money equals speech' in its 1976 *Buckley* v. *Valeo* ruling. In upholding parts of the 1974 FECA and striking out the part which would have prevented candidates for federal office using their own cash in political campaigns, the Court discussed two *competing* values: free speech versus the importance of a system free of corruption. However, it did not say that all campaign finance reforms violate the First Amendment. She suspects that those who mention 'free speech' as an argument against reform do not genuinely believe in this position, but are using it to justify the *status quo* and their own vested interest in the continuation of the present system.[9] The First Amendment is simply a convenient device to beat campaign finance reform with, rather than a genuine argument.

MONEY AND POLITICS

What effects does money have on the political process in America? Does money purchase congressional votes and influence? Individuals and PACs dole out millions in direct and indirect contributions to federal campaigns, so what exactly is all that money buying? Political scientists have long been interested in these questions, but they have tended to answer them in ways that are mostly reassuring for the democratic process. While respected Washington journalists with inside access to administration members and members of Congress have concluded that money plays an increasingly distorting role in the legislative process itself,[10] most 'systematic' political science research has concluded that it does not. Almost all the available research has concluded that money does not buy votes in Congress. Janet Grenzke, for instance, finds in a broad-ranging study that PAC contributions do not change members' voting behaviour.[11] There are one or two exceptions to this consensus, of course. The political scientist Lance Bennett, for instance, argues that campaign contributions do effectively buy the loyalty, and ultimately the votes, of members of Congress. He quotes one unnamed member of Congress as saying, 'I fear that we could become a coin-operated Congress. Instead of two bits, you put in $2,500 and pull out a vote.'[12] However, Bennett's condemnation of the way the system works is rather rare among mainstream US political scientists.

The conventional research on vote buying creates an unresolved puzzle: if PACs are unable to buy the votes of members of Congress, why do they continue to contribute millions of dollars to the campaign coffers of these members? At first sight, there would appear to be only two main answers: (1) PACs are irrational in their behaviour or (2) political scientists are simply wrong, since it is implausible to claim that PACs receive nothing in return for their contributions. But there are other ways in which campaign contributions may affect legislative behaviour. Richard Hall and Frank Wayman, in an innovative analysis, shift the focus of research away from the 'Does money buy votes?' question and ask whether we should be looking at other forms of political influence PAC contributions may have. In short, they conclude that we should. The principal effect of PAC contributions, they find, is to 'buy the time' of members of Congress. Although PACs tend to give cash to those who already support them on the issues, money is used to 'mobilize bias' in congressional committees in favour of the PACs' interests and to 'demobilize' the opposition. Political Action Committees realize that members are constrained by their ideology and past voting record, and that it is difficult to 'buy votes' for that reason. As a result, PACs try to make sure that members of Congress who see things the same way as they do focus their attention on the issues that concern the PAC rather than on other matters which compete for their attention. Whether one is ultimately convinced by this argument or not, Hall and Wayman approach the question of money and politics from an interesting new angle, which at least partially reconciles the positions of the journalists and the political scientists.[13]

This is not to say that political scientists claim that money has no effect on the political process whatsoever. The consensus is that it does have an effect, but the effect is at the *electoral* rather than the policy-making level. Political Action Committees and wealthy contributors tend to channel their donations mainly towards incumbents. This is a rational strategy in many ways; after all, incumbents have a concrete voting record (from which 'liberal' or 'conservative' scores can be computed, for instance) and hence one can 'bet' more safely and reliably upon their future behaviour. Challengers have no established track record as such – at least, not in the institution they are attempting to join – and hence their likely future voting behaviour is slightly murky and unknown. This practice, however, helps to create the well known 'incumbency factor' at congressional elections, where incumbents tend to become electorally entrenched in Congress and seemingly invulnerable to defeat once they get there.

CONCLUSION

Campaign finance reform has become a major issue at various points in American history, usually in response to specific scandals or abuses. The United States is at one such point now. Fuelled by the campaign excesses of the 1996 election – including allegations about Chinese government influence over the result, the controversy over the Clinton administration's 'selling' of the Lincoln bedroom and White House 'coffees' at which campaign donations appear to have been solicited – it is natural that so much attention should have been focused on campaign finance issues in the past few years.

Supporters of campaign finance reform can find some solace in a Supreme Court decision handed down in the case of *Nixon* v. *Shrink Missouri Government PAC* (2000), in which the Court upheld a Missouri law that limits what an individual can contribute to state campaigns. At issue was the question of whether a state had the right to do this, and by a six–three majority the justices ruled that it did. In essence, the Supreme Court ruled in its majority opinion that considerations of corruption outweigh concern about the First Amendment in this case. Justice John Paul Stevens was especially forceful on the point in his concurring opinion:

> Money is property; it is not speech. Speech has the power to inspire volunteers to perform a multitude of tasks on a campaign trail, on a battleground, or even on a football field. Money, meanwhile, has the power to pay hired labourers to perform the same tasks. It does not follow, however, that the First Amendment provides the same measure of protection to the use of money to accomplish such goals as it provides to the use of ideas to achieve the same results.

And yet major change on this issue probably cannot be achieved by the judicial branch acting alone; an Act of Congress will be needed. It is fair to say, though, that the prospects for the passage of a major overhaul of the system are rather dim. Although a majority of Americans say in opinion polls that they want campaign finance reformed in some way, it is probably a 'passive' majority rather than an 'intense' one.[14] In other words, while most Americans are critical of the role of money in politics, it does not appear to be one of the issues that most concern them. It has often been suggested that the American political system is 'crisis-activated', and it may well take the appearance of a scandal of major proportions – similar in scope to Watergate, perhaps – before Congress is willing and able to enact a major overhaul of the campaign finance process.

Even if McCain–Feingold or some similar Bill is passed, it is perhaps questionable whether in the long term it will be successful in restraining the flow of campaign contributions at federal elections in any case. To return to the corset analogy, the history of attempts at reform in this area suggests that, when laws have squeezed in one place, cash contributions merely pop out in another. When corporations were banned from making donations to federal election campaigns by the Tillman Act of 1907 they immediately came up with ways around the new legislation. As Bennett notes, 'companies blithely gave "raises" to their executives, who passed them along as personal contributions to politicians'.[15] When labour unions were banned from donating directly to campaigns in 1947, the AFL-CIO set up its own Political Action Committee, the Committee on Political Education (COPE), to channel funds indirectly. And, as we have already seen, when the 1974 Act was passed inventive electoral lawyers and politicians gradually began to find ways around this measure also, culminating with the current situation in which the original intent of the Act has mostly been circumvented through the 'soft money' loophole.

The Supreme Court was clearly aware of this problem in *Buckley* v. *Valeo*, even though it did not necessarily foresee the myriad ways in which the two main parties would manage to evade the 1974 legislation. It noted that it 'would naively underestimate the resourcefulness of persons and groups desiring to buy influence to believe that they would have much difficulty devising expenditures that skirted the restriction on express advocacy of election or defeat, but nevertheless benefited the candidate's campaign'.[16] Current reformers are aware of the problem also, which makes them rather sanguine about the possibilities of genuine reform. According to John McCain, 'I promise you that 20 or 30 years from now . . . a group of others will be standing here saying we've got to clean up the system again, because there'll be smart people that figure out loopholes in the system'.[17] On the admission of one of its own authors, then, the McCain–Feingold proposal – even in the event that it somehow overcomes current political obstacles and makes it on to the statute book – is unlikely to be the last word on campaign finance reform.

NOTES

1 Elizabeth Drew, *The Corruption of American Politics: What went Wrong and Why* (New York, Overlook Press, 2000), p. 50.
2 Elizabeth Drew, *Politics and Money: The New Road to Corruption* (New York, Macmillan, 1983), pp. 8–9.
3 See Gary Jacobson, *The Politics of Congressional Elections*, fourth edition (New York, Longman, 1997), pp. 55–6.
4 Quoted in Ruth Marcus and Sarah Cohen, 'The loophole lesson in "soft money": campaign reformers confront history of unintended results', *Washington Post*, 18 March 2001.
5 Marcus and Cohen, 'The loophole lesson in "soft money"'.
6 Quoted in Drew, *The Corruption of American Politics*, p. 50.
7 Thomas Mann, 'Funding is poisoning our elections', *Newsday*, 29 July 1997.
8 Thomas Mann, 'Not a danger to free speech', *Washington Post*, 14 July 1998.
9 Drew, *The Corruption of American Politics*, p. 45.
10 Apart from the work of Drew and Mann, already cited, see also Brooks Jackson, *Honest Graft* (New York, Knopf, 1988).
11 Janet Grenzke, 'Shopping in the congressional supermarket: the currency is complex', *American Journal of Political Science*, 33 (1989), pp. 1–24.
12 Lance Bennett, *The Governing Crisis: Media, Money and Marketing in American Elections* (New York, St Martin's Press, 1992), p. 55.
13 Richard Hall and Frank Wayman, 'Buying time: moneyed interests and the

mobilization of bias in congressional committees', *American Political Science Review*, 84 (1990), pp. 797–820.

14   On intensity and passivity among the US public see V. O. Key, *Public Opinion and American Democracy* (New York, Knopf, 1961).

15   Bennett, *The Governing Crisis*, p. 51.

16   Quoted in Drew, *The Corruption of American Politics*, p. 52.

17   Quoted in Marcus and Cohen, 'The loophole lesson in "soft money"'.

5 Containing Presidential Power

- THE 'IMPERIAL PRESIDENCY' THESIS
- THE 'POST-IMPERIAL PRESIDENCY' AND THE 'IMPERIAL CONGRESS'
- THE WAR POWERS RESOLUTION
- THE IRAN-CONTRA SCANDAL
- CONCLUSION

During the late 1960s and early 1970s various commentators – most notably the historian Arthur Schlesinger – expressed concern about the existence of an 'imperial presidency' in America.[1] This widespread perception led to a resurgence of congressional power and prerogatives in the 1970s and 1980s. By the late 1980s the debate had turned full circle, however, to the point where 'congressional imperialism' had become the predominant concern. This chapter looks at both sides of the debate, examining, first of all, whether 'imperial presidency' or 'imperial Congress' is a more accurate label for the condition American political institutions find themselves in today. We also examine the 1973 War Powers Resolution (WPR) and the Iran-Contra scandal as case studies of attempts to contain presidential power. As we shall see, the general consensus among political scientists is that the WPR has not been successful in meeting this objective. However, the second case is a good deal more ambiguous in its meaning and lessons. Iran-Contra arguably represents both an instance of temporary systemic 'breakdown' in the American system and a demonstration of the importance of the separation of powers, but commentators differ on the question of what that scandal has meant for the balance of power between the president and Congress.

The formal powers of the presidency, as enumerated in the American constitution, have remained essentially the same as they were at the founding of the republic. What is beyond dispute, however, is that the *practical* powers of the presidency increased appreciably during the early part of the twentieth century. Some trace the beginnings of this development to the days of Theodore Roosevelt, Woodrow Wilson and the birth of the 'rhetorical presidency',[2] but there is broad agreement that it was Franklin Roosevelt who increased the power and prestige of the presidency most appreciably. Responding to the Great Depression and the Second World War, F.D.R. expanded the role of the White House in both domestic and foreign policy.

The basic attitude of political scientists and historians during this phase was essentially pro-presidential power. Richard Neustadt's *Presidential Power*, first published in 1960, was and still is a celebration of the institution. Its core thesis was that presidents are weak in comparison with chief executives elsewhere, and that they consequently must bargain with and persuade various audiences in order to get things done. (Hence the most famous phrase drawn from the book, that the power of the presidency is essentially the 'power to persuade'.) It takes a skilled president to get Washington moving, but the powers of the office must be used, Neustadt argued, to good effect. He celebrated those occupants of the Oval Office whom he viewed as having done this effectively (notably F.D.R. and Kennedy) and castigated those who he thought had not (Dwight Eisenhower, for instance).[3]

This pro-presidency position reigned supreme during the 1940s, 1950s and early 1960s, a period which has been described as that of the 'textbook presidency' and the 'heroic presidency'. Clinton Rossiter's book *The American Presidency* and James McGregor Burns's *Presidential Government* also appeared around the same time.[4] As Thomas, Pika and Watson note, Rossiter's book 'clearly glorifies the office and the "great" presidents who have shaped it – George Washington, Thomas Jefferson, Andrew Jackson, Abraham Lincoln, Theodore Roosevelt, Woodrow Wilson, Franklin D. Roosevelt, and Harry Truman'.[5] The emphasis on the inherent desirability of a powerful presidency is perhaps made most explicit in James McGregor Burns's work, however. In *The Deadlock of Democracy*, for instance, Burns argued that the paradox of American democracy is that 'we can choose bold and creative national leaders without giving them the means to make their leadership effective'.[6] America had been 'captured' by the Madisonian model, 'which requires us to await a wide consensus before acting, while we have neglected, except furtively and sporadically, the Jeffersonian strategy of strong leadership, majority rule, party responsibility, and competitive elections'.[7] In all these works presidential power is assumed to be inherently desirable, the only way in which American government can be expected to function effectively. As Thomas, Pika and Watson put it, 'the authors of these books . . . were political liberals who saw the office as the only institution in the political system that can understand the needs of all Americans, including the disadvantaged, and that has a nation-wide constituency providing the political support to meet those needs'.[8] Given that Dwight Eisenhower did not have an especially ambitious policy agenda and John Kennedy was very much constrained by his own party, most presidency scholars until the 1960s would not have thought of the *containment* of presidential power as something at all desirable. The president, in Neustadt's view and that of Burns especially, was already contained enough. All this was to change, however, with Vietnam and Watergate.

THE 'IMPERIAL PRESIDENCY' THESIS

In the late 1960s and early 1970s many began to complain about the supposed existence of an 'imperial presidency'. In 1973 the distinguished American historian Arthur Schlesinger published a book of that name in which he argued that the presidency had taken on far too many powers, particularly in foreign policy. The founding fathers, Schlesinger notes, intended the power to make foreign

policy to be shared between the two main branches of government. The US constitution is notoriously vague on questions of foreign policy: Article 1, s. 8, gives
Congress the power to declare war and raise an army to fight it, while Article 2,
s. 2, gives the president the power of 'Commander-in-chief'. This is one of the
prime demonstrations of how vaguely worded and non-specific the constitutional
document is. As former Attorney General Archibald Cox has noted, this is a huge
'grey area' at the heart of the document, and it is therefore hardly surprising that
it has long been an area of rivalry and conflict between the two branches. Writing towards the end of the Vietnam War, though, Schlesinger argued that the
president had seized the power to make war from the Congress. After the Second
World War, he said, American presidents began to make foreign policy without
reference to the legislature. This culminated in the disaster of Vietnam, an im-
mensely destructive and wasteful conflict which the president had effectively decided to wage on his own without getting a declaration of war. Johnson took
advantage of an acquiescent Congress quietly to increase American involvement,
and did so without telling the people what he was doing. L.B.J.'s time in office,
then, saw the emergence of presidential 'imperialism'.

As Schlesinger sees it, L.B.J.'s successor, Richard Nixon, took this process one
step further, because he expanded the imperial presidency into the domestic policy
realm. Nixon was ruthless in dealing with his domestic opponents: he impounded
funds that had been appropriated by Congress, he sought to withhold information from Congress, and he authorized covert surveillance of his enemies, including tapping the phones of his opponents and harassing the liberal Brookings
Institution. This culminated in the scandal of Watergate – initiated by a break-in
at the Democratic Party's headquarters and followed by a presidential cover-up –
which eventually brought Nixon down and led to his resignation in 1974 before
he could be impeached.

THE 'POST-IMPERIAL PRESIDENCY' AND THE 'IMPERIAL CONGRESS'

Congress reasserted its political and constitutional prerogatives in the 1970s,
and a number of 'weak' presidencies resulted. Not unnaturally, the steady encroachment of presidential power during the Vietnam War and Watergate produced a reaction in Washington DC, and as a result many scholars began to talk
about the emergence of a 'post-imperial presidency'. Between 1978 and 1980
Fred Greenstein, Godfrey Hodgson and Thomas Cronin all published work which
variously described the presidency as 'post-imperial', 'powerless' and 'imperilled'.[9]
Writing in the late 1980s, Richard Rose's *The Postmodern President* also emphasized the weakness of the office in the face of relative American economic
decline and the growth of global interdependence.[10]

Towards the end of the Vietnam War Congress became a good deal less deferential towards the president on many policy questions. This increasing assertion
of congressional power helped to produce the now more fashionable counter-
claim that Congress has encroached upon powers constitutionally reserved for
the president: the 'imperial Congress' thesis. Its advocates contend that this

reassertion of congressional authority has gone a good deal too far in the other direction. In the late 1980s – when the Democrats still appeared to possess a kind of 'lock' on the House and the Senate, and the Republicans appeared to be a permanent fixture in the White House – a number of voices in the Republican Party (including the future House Speaker, Newt Gingrich) began to claim that congressional reassertion had gone too far. In 1988 Gordon Jones and John Marini published an edited volume entitled *Imperial Congress: Crisis in the Separation of Powers* which set forth this thesis.[11]

The book was the very mirror image of Schlesinger's. In essence, it argued that since the 1970s Congress had created a crisis in the separation of powers, engaging in a number of actions which extended the power of the legislative branch in a way that the founding fathers never envisaged. Congress, they argued, has started to encroach upon powers rightly reserved by the framers of the constitution for the presidency and the Supreme Court. One way in which Congress has done so is to begin 'micro-managing' what the executive branch does, both in domestic and in foreign policy. Congressional committees have imposed endless rules and regulations on executive agencies. Even the Speaker of the House has dabbled in foreign policy, while House members make constant trips abroad, grandstanding and undercutting the president's prerogatives and the national interest as well. Rather than simply making laws – as the constitution says it ought to do – the Congress has begun administering the laws, which is properly an executive function. To make things worse, the Congress has stopped the president appointing the people he wants in his Cabinet and on the Supreme Court, refusing to approve candidates it does not like on ideological grounds. Cabinet officials spend all their time testifying on Capitol Hill rather than advising the president. The end result of all this, the authors say, is nothing less than a threat to the separation of powers itself.

An especially worrying trend, the authors say, is that Congressmen who are unable to win the policy debate with the president have resorted to launching criminal investigations against the White House, using the legal process to resolve what are properly political debates. For instance, Gordon Crovitz argues that 'the criminalization of politics' has occurred.[12] In 1978 Congress passed the Ethics in Government Act, which established the office of the independent counsel. The office was intended as a means of enhancing its ability to oversee and correct executive branch wrongdoing. Under the legislation Congress can petition the Attorney General to appoint an independent prosecutor to investigate suspicions of executive criminality. Kenneth Starr, for example, was appointed to investigate the Whitewater affair during the Clinton administration, and in the 1980s Lawrence Walsh played a similar role in relation to the Iran-Contra scandal. In the wake of the Watergate investigation – during which Richard Nixon had actually sacked the special prosecutor appointed to investigate him – it is clear why Congress should want to create such a facility. But Crovitz argues that independent counsels can quite simply destroy people's lives, showering indictments on the innocent and landing them with huge legal bills that they inevitably spend the rest of their lives paying off.

It is not only conservative or Republican figures who have used the 'imperial

Congress' argument. In an article in the *New York Times* magazine published in 1994, when the Democrats still controlled the House, former presidential aide Joe Califano claimed that:

> Congress has become the King Kong of Washington's political jungle, dominating an executive branch that can no longer claim the coequal status that the Founding Fathers saw as crucial. Those who blame Bill Clinton for this sorry imbalance of power fail to take into account the stunning ascendancy of Congressional clout since the years of Lyndon Johnson.[13]

Since 1994 – when the Republicans took control of the House and the Senate – it is mostly Democrats who have been heard to claim that Congress has 'gone too far'. The controversy over Ken Starr's investigation of Bill Clinton – and the attempt by Congress to impeach the president – fuelled claims that the Republicans were using the powers of Congress to shrink those of the presidency. During the impeachment hearings of 1998 we began to hear a good many allegations that the Republicans in Congress were using the Independent Counsel law and the impeachment process as political tools to bring down the Clinton presidency. Congressman John Conyers, a vigorous opponent of Bill Clinton's impeachment by the House, described the impeachment process as 'almost a *coup*' by the Republican Congress. According to these critics, there were so many congressional investigations of the executive during the 1990s that the presidency was seriously hampered in its ability to function. The Clinton administration had to face investigations not only of Whitewater but also of the Paula Jones affair, 'filegate', the Vince Foster affair, 'travelgate' and charges of criminal wrongdoing by former Agriculture Secretary Mike Espy and former Housing Secretary Henry Cisneros.

The merits of these arguments are difficult to assess. Before attempting the exercise, however, we will examine two attempts by Congress to try to contain presidential power during the 1970s and 1980s: the 1973 War Powers Resolution and the Iran-Contra scandal of 1986–7. The former was an attempt by the legislature to ensure that there would be 'no more Vietnams', an effort to wrest back the control of the war-making power from the presidency; the second involved a partial attempt to take control of American foreign policy towards Nicaragua during the 1980s. These cases are worth examining in detail, for both provide us with an example of the difficulty of containing presidential power, on the one hand, and of the ultimate reassertion of legislative power, on the other.

THE WAR POWERS RESOLUTION

Many constitutional analysts believe that the grey area in the constitution referred to by Archibald Cox can be filled only by using congressional legislation. The War Powers Resolution (WPR) of 1973 was an attempt to do this in a way that prevents the president from waging war unilaterally. It was primarily intended to clarify what the constitution confuses; the advocates of the resolution knew that it would take a constitutional amendment to actually change the constitution, and so they attempted to draft a form of words that would be consistent with the document as it already exists.

While there had been rumblings of discontent about presidential power in the area of war making for some years before, the War Powers Resolution essentially arose out of America's unsuccessful involvement in the Vietnam War. Although President Lyndon Johnson did seek a form of congressional approval at the very outset of the war – the 1964 Tonkin Gulf Resolution, which authorized the president to respond to a specific attack against US destroyers off the coast of Vietnam[14] – the president took the United States into the war in 1965 without obtaining a declaration of war from Congress. When the war ended in humiliation and disaster for the United States, Congress decided that it could never again permit the president unilaterally to commit US troops abroad. Congress therefore drafted the WPR, which was passed in 1973 over President Richard Nixon's veto.

The War Powers Resolution basically requires any president who sends US troops abroad to consult congressional leaders first, and then to submit a written report justifying the action to the leadership of both the House and the Senate within forty-eight hours of the troops' deployment. The president can then leave the troops where he has placed them for sixty days; this is the famous 'sixty-day clock'. If in that time Congress approves the commitment of troops – for instance, via a declaration of war – the president can continue the military initiative he has begun. The resolution also builds some flexibility into this rule, since it allows Congress to extend the sixty-day deadline by thirty days if it so wishes. If, on the other hand, Congress does *not* grant its approval, the president is required by law to withdraw the troops immediately.[15]

In practice the resolution has not worked and certainly does not operate as its framers intended. All presidents (with the exception of Jimmy Carter) have argued that it unconstitutionally binds their hands, and they have complied with it – where they have done so at all – in only a token fashion. For instance, presidents very rarely consult Congress before committing troops abroad. President George H. Bush did ask for congressional approval – which he received – before sending troops to fight in the Persian Gulf War in 1991, but by that time he had public opinion on his side and stated that even if such support was not forthcoming he would have sent troops anyway. Presidents have sometimes submitted a written report afterwards, perhaps because it is a relatively easy thing to do and does not act as a real constraint. Ronald Reagan, for instance, did this when sending marines to the Lebanon in 1982 and after bombing Libya in 1985, even as he denied that the constitution required him to do so. And, most tellingly, *in no instance* since the resolution came into effect has Congress actually forced the president to withdraw US troops from foreign soil. On no occasion has the sixty-day clock even been started.

There are a number of flaws in the WPR which in practice have limited its utility as a device for containing presidential power. One problem has been its imprecise language, which gives presidents sufficient 'wriggle room' to avoid invoking it. For instance, the text of the resolution states that it applies in situations where 'imminent involvement in hostilities is clearly indicated' and talks of the need to consult Congress 'regularly', but these phrases are open to different interpretations. Congress has often not asserted itself in situations where one could make the case that it should have, and the courts have refused to enforce the resolution, arguing that they lack the expertise to consider such issues. Most problematically, though, under the terms of the WPR it is the president who starts the sixty-day clock ticking, by submitting a report. If the president fails to submit a report the clock will not start. Alternatively, a president can submit a report without mentioning the provision of the resolution that starts the clock, and this is a course of action many presidents have taken.[16]

This is not to say, of course, that the WPR has no effect on presidential foreign policy making whatsoever, for it may have impacts that are hard to observe or measure. While the resolution does not stop presidents keeping troops overseas in a war or crisis *once* they have been committed – they almost always have public opinion on their side once US troops have been sent – it is conceivable that potential congressional opposition may sometimes have led presidents to rethink a decision to send troops. This proposition is not easily tested, however, and the preponderance of the evidence suggests that the WPR has been what Schlesinger calls 'a toy handcuff'.[17] The consensus in the political science literature is summed up well by James Lindsay – an *advocate* of the view that Congress is important in American foreign policy generally – who argues that 'by almost any measure, the War Powers resolution is a dead letter'.[18] In practice, the use by Congress of its budgetary powers has been a more forceful means of containing the presidency in matters of foreign policy.

THE IRAN-CONTRA SCANDAL

The Iran-Contra scandal involved a complex but rather ingenious series of secret moves through which the executive branch tried to continue a foreign policy initiative for which the legislative branch had cut off funding. At the heart of the scandal was Congress's constitutional power of the purse. Congress exercises ultimate control over the appropriations process (or the budget, as it is more often referred to), and presidents cannot spend a single cent without first obtaining authorization to do so from the Congress. So one technique Congress can use to influence policy is simply to write something into the budget or appropriations Bill which says, 'None of the funds appropriated herein shall be used for the purposes of X.'

This is what Congress did in relation to the Reagan administration's policies towards Nicaragua. Iran-Contra was really two scandals rolled into one, a scandal in US policy towards Iran and a scandal in US policy towards Nicaragua. The first stage involved the secret sale of arms to Iran, which violated the administration's own stated policy of not doing deals with terrorists and which was also rendered illegal by an executive order which Reagan himself had signed. During the early 1980s a number of American citizens were taken hostage in Lebanon. In its desperation to get the hostages back the Reagan administration agreed to sell arms to Iran in exchange for the latter using its influence to get the Americans out. The funds from this secret arms sale were then diverted to fund the Nicaraguan Contras, again without the knowledge of Congress.

In the early 1980s Nicaragua was ruled by a democratically elected but Marxist-inspired group called the Sandinistas. The Reagan administration came to office determined to stamp out communist influence in Central America and in Latin America generally, and the Sandinistas were therefore an obvious target. In keeping with the post-war policy of containment, Reagan sought to contain the spread of communism and Soviet influence throughout the world. In Nicaragua this translated into a policy of supporting the Contras, a group of armed rebels who were trying to overthrow the Sandinista government. The administration provided the Contras with military assistance in their fight against the Marxists.

A number of things led Congress effectively to 'pull the plug' on this strategy. In the wake of Vietnam there was relatively little support among the American public or in the Democratic House of Representatives for overthrowing the Sandinistas, who had, after all, been democratically elected. In order to restrain the administration, Congress passed a series of amendments known as the Boland amendments, named after Congressman Edward Boland of Massachusetts. They took the form of clauses, written into the text of the budget, which said in essence, 'None of the funds appropriated herein shall be used for the purpose of funding the Nicaraguan Contras.' The third Boland amendment, passed in October 1984, cut off all funds for military and paramilitary purposes. And since presidents cannot spend funds that have not been authorized by the Congress, this in theory ended the Reagan administration's policy of supporting the Contras.

If this swish of the congressional axe had worked, we would have heard no more about the matter. But it was at this stage that elements within the administration came up with an ingenious move: a linkage would be created between two problematic areas of the world, with the profits from the secret arms sale to Iran being used secretly to continue funding the Contras in Nicaragua. The Reagan administration also solicited contributions from wealthy private individuals in the United States and from foreign governments, which again violates the constitutional requirement that the money for government policies must come from Congress. It may never be known whether President Reagan personally authorized this plan, but CIA Director William Casey, National Security Advisers Admirals John Poindexter and Robert McFarlane and Oliver North, a colonel stationed in the National Security Council, are known to have played a major role in its development. We do know that Reagan instructed his staff to 'keep the Contras alive body and soul', but it is unclear whether he simply articulated the general principle and left others to decide what it meant in operational terms or whether he had a role in its development. Such knowledge as we have about this is consistent with different interpretations of his role. We can say with certainty, however, that someone within the executive branch decided that, legally or illegally, it was possible to 'get round' the will of Congress. The Iran-Contra policy was made public in a Lebanese magazine in November 1986, and during the summer of 1987 Congress held joint, televised hearings into the scandal. An independent counsel, Lawrence Walsh, was appointed to investigate allegations of wrongdoing, and as a result several indictments were brought against Reagan administration officials.

How are we to assess the constitutional and political meaning of Iran-Contra? This case is rather more ambiguous and open to competing interpretations than the WPR. On the one hand, the 'imperial presidency' school argues that with the Iran-Contra scandal Ronald Reagan partially re-established the practice of presidential imperialism (which had lain dormant under the weak leadership of Ford and Carter). According to Arthur Schlesinger, Reagan went two-thirds of the way towards restoring presidential imperialism. 'The critical tests of the imperial presidency,' Schlesinger argues in the 1989 edition of his book, 'are threefold: the war-making power; the secrecy system; and the employment against the American people of emergency authority acquired for use against foreign enemies.'[19] Asking these three questions of Reagan during Iran-Contra, Schlesinger concludes that he did the first two but not the third. He did wage a war that Congress was not told about and did withhold information about what his administration was doing behind the scenes, but he did not use the powers of the White House to try to silence his critics, as Nixon had done.

On the other hand, supporters of the 'imperial Congress' thesis have argued that the whole Iran-Contra scandal was caused by an unconstitutional encroachment of the legislature on to a domain constitutionally reserved for the presidency. According to Crovitz, this led to the 'criminalization' of what were actually legitimate policy differences between Reagan and the Democrats. Crouitz argues in the *Imperial Congress* volume that the disagreement between the Reagan administration and the Democrat Congress over funding for the Contras should never have been treated as a criminal issue. Congress should not in any case have been telling the president what American foreign policy should be. According to Michael Malbin, 'when Congress chose to investigate Iran Contra . . . it did so almost solely to portray the administration's behavior as illegal. The legal judgments underlying the investigation almost all involved assertions, made with unswerving confidence, that serious lawyers can and will debate'.[20] Hence supporters of both 'imperialist' theories find evidence in this case to support their positions.

One thing that Iran-Contra shows quite clearly is that there are ways, both legal and illegal, that a president (or at least, the presidential branch) can circumvent congressional control if he (or it) so chooses. However, the chief lesson of Iran-Contra is probably that such efforts generally fail in the end. As Theodore Draper notes:

> This is supposed to have been the era of the imperial presidency. It has turned out to be the era of presidencies that have tried to make themselves imperial – and failed. The attempt and the failure of the Reagan presidency in the Iran-Contra affair are only the latest of this kind.[21]

Although there may well be other 'Iran-Contras' which were never made public, both Watergate and Iran-Contra were exposed and led to a reassertion of legislative power. If Reagan was imperial, then, he was only so for a short period of time. At its root – when we cut through all the elaborate deception, complexity and detail – Iran-Contra was a struggle for power between the president and the Congress within a grey and ill specified area of the constitution. Although it was an attempt to escape the shackles of congressional control, it arguably demonstrates just how constrained presidents really are in the contemporary era.

CONCLUSION

The issue of presidential versus congressional power arguably matters a great deal in terms of democratic accountability and representation. In the Iran-Contra case, for instance, the presidential branch of government implemented what was effectively a *secret* policy which differed markedly from its publicly stated policy positions. If a democratic system is to function effectively, it must be clear what policies a government is pursuing. Voters must be given at least the opportunity to approve or reject the choices made by politicians. For the US separation of powers to function effectively, Congress also needs to be able to engage in effective oversight of what the executive is doing. However temporarily, Iran-Contra short-circuited these mechanisms.

How *desirable* is the containment or expansion of presidential power *vis-à-vis* Congress? As we noted earlier, the constitution gives no clear guidance on this question, and there is consequently ample room for different positions. This is also essentially a normative question and hence no definitive answer to it can be given. There are essentially two schools of thought on the question of presidential power and its limits. The first position sees the enhancement of the president's powers as a natural and inevitable response to the nature of the times. The second recognizes that Congress was intended by the founding fathers to be the premier branch of government, and views the encroachment of presidential power warily or as a positive evil, to be avoided at all costs. This issue inevitably gets mixed up with partisan biases and preferences, however. It is to the credit of Schlesinger that when *The Imperial Presidency* appeared he was attacking the presidency of a fellow Democrat, Lyndon Johnson, as well as the Republican Richard Nixon. It was also to Califano's credit that his own 'imperial Congress' thesis was directed in large measure at his own party in the House and Senate. (The article was written before the Gingrich revolution of November 1994.) However, other arguments carry more than a tinge of personal political preference. The 'heroic presidency' advocates of the 1950s and 1960s wanted powerful presidential leadership in part because it was a means to the pursuit of an activist, liberal Democratic agenda. In the 1980s conservative commentators had inherited the presidential leadership position, in part because they wanted to prevent the then Democrat Congress from obstructing the anti-governmental agendas of Reagan and Bush senior.

Understandably, once the Republicans took control of the House of Representatives in 1994 – the first time that it had happened in forty years – they fell largely silent on the question of congressional imperialism. The Republican Congress failed to pass a Bill that would have limited the terms of members of Congress – a measure included in Newt Gingrich's *Contract with America* and widely seen as partial remedy for congressional power – but it did pass the Line Item Veto Act of 1996. This was intended to increase the president's power *vis-à-vis*

Congress by allowing him to strike out lines in the budget that he viewed as wasteful or motivated by 'pork barrel' politics. It was subsequently ruled unconstitutional by the Supreme Court. But it at least represented a principled effort to restore the power of the presidency at the expense of Congress. (After all, the Bill was passed by a Republican Congress at a time when the White House was controlled by Bill Clinton, a popular Democrat president.)

Although Arthur Schlesinger continues to argue for the relevance of his imperial presidency thesis, one can potentially reconcile his approach with that of Jones and Marini by arguing that each is essentially a time-bound 'snapshot' of a pattern of presidential–congressional relations at a particular moment in political time. Hence one could conclude that both positions are (or were) correct but that neither should be taken as a timeless theory of presidential or congressional power. Historically the relationship between the president and Congress has been a cyclical one; periods of dominance have been followed by periods of congressional reassertion, which in turn tend to usher in periods of presidential power.

Not unnaturally, under conditions of 'divided government', where the presidency and Congress are controlled by opposing political parties, members of the president's party have tended to criticize the behaviour of Congress as 'imperial', while similar claims have long been heard about presidential power. Under contemporary conditions the 'imperial Congress' position probably comes closest to describing the American political landscape, but there is no guarantee that it will do so in the longer term. Scholars of American politics need also to strike a balance between the two rather extreme positions described in this chapter. As James Lindsay has noted in relation to foreign policy, Congress should not be taken to be impotent, but neither should it be seen as all-powerful or imperial. As the framers intended, the executive and the legislative branches continue to enjoy the exercise of formidable powers in relation to one another.

NOTES

1 Arthur Schlesinger, *The Imperial Presidency* (Boston MA, Houghton Mifflin, 1973).
2 Jeffrey Tulis, *The Rhetorical Presidency* (Princeton NJ, Princeton University Press, 1987).
3 Richard Neustadt, *Presidential Power: The Politics of Leadership* (New York, Wiley, 1960).
4 Clinton Rossiter, *The American Presidency*, revised edition (New York, Mentor, 1960); James McGregor Burns, *Presidential Government: The Crucible of Leadership* (New York, Avon, 1965).
5 Norman Thomas, Joseph Pika and Richard Watson, *The Politics of the Presidency*, third edition (Washington DC, CQ Press, 1993), p. 4.
6 James McGregor Burns, *The Deadlock of Democracy: Four-party Politics in America* (Englewood Cliffs NJ, Prentice-Hall, 1963), p. 325.
7 Ibid., p. 323.
8 Thomas *et al.*, *The Politics of the Presidency*, p. 6.
9 Fred Greenstein, 'Change and continuity in the modern presidency', in Anthony King (ed.), *The New American Political System* (Washington DC, American Enterprise

Institute, 1978); Godfrey Hodgson, *All Things to all Men: The False Promise of the Modern American Presidency* (London, Weidenfeld & Nicolson, 1980); Thomas Cronin, 'An imperilled presidency?', in Vincent Davis (ed.), *The Post-imperial Presidency* (London, Transaction Books, 1980).

10   Richard Rose, *The Postmodern President: The White House meets the World* (London, Chatham House, 1988).

11   Gordon Jones and John Marini (eds), *Imperial Congress: Crisis in the Separation of Powers* (New York, Pharos Books, 1988). See also Gordon Crovitz and Jeremy Rabkin (eds), *The Fettered Presidency* (Washington DC, American Enterprise Institute, 1989).

12   Gordon Crovitz, 'The criminalization of politics', in Jones and Marini, *Imperial Congress*. The independent counsel statute was allowed to lapse by Congress in 2000.

13   Joe Califano, 'Imperial Congress', *New York Times* magazine, 23 January 1994. See also George Szamuely, 'The imperial Congress', in Jerel Rosati (ed.), *Readings in the Politics of United States Foreign Policy* (London, Harcourt Brace, 1998).

14   It is fair to say that members of Congress never intended the Tonkin Gulf Resolution as an authorization of full-scale war, although the administration and Johnson's successor Nixon were to use it as such until Congress repealed the resolution in 1970.

15   Note that it does not matter what function the troops have been sent abroad to perform. The reporting and consultation requirements are intended to apply where a president sends troops as part of a collective peace-keeping effort, for instance.

16   See James Lindsay, *Congress and the Politics of US Foreign Policy* (London, Johns Hopkins University Press, 1994), pp. 147–51.

17   Arthur Schlesinger, *The Imperial Presidency*, second edition (Boston MA, Houghton Mifflin, 1989), p. 433.

18   Ibid., p. 110.

19   Schlesinger, *The Imperial Presidency*, second edition, p. 441.

20   Michael Malbin, 'Legalism versus political checks and balances: legislative–executive relations in the wake of Iran-Contra', in Crovitz and Rabkin, *The Fettered Presidency*, p. 273.

21   Theodore Draper, 'Reagan's junta: the institutional sources of the Iran-Contra affair', in Charles Kegley and Eugene Wittkopf (eds), *The Domestic Sources of American Foreign Policy: Insights and Evidence* (New York, St Martin's Press, 1988), p. 131.

6 The Supreme Court: the Politics of Judicial Activism

- **ACTIVISM, PASSIVITY AND INTERPRETING THE CONSTITUTION: THE ENDURING DEBATE**
- **THE BURGER COURT: CONFUSION IN THE FACE OF RAPID SOCIAL AND POLITICAL CHANGE?**
- **THE REHNQUIST COURT: CONSERVATISM REVIVED?**
- **CONCLUSION: SHOULD THE COURT CONTINUE ITS ACTIVIST ROLE?**

For most of American history the Supreme Court has played a major – and usually controversial – role in politics. The reasons for this are well known. Ever since the landmark *Marbury* v. *Madison* case in 1803 the Court has asserted the power of judicial review, or the capacity to declare unconstitutional any law passed in the United States, whether at the federal, state or local level. When exercising this function the Court not only assesses whether or not laws are compatible with the constitution, it also acts as the final arbiter between the state and the federal government and between the legislative and executive branches. As with all courts, America's highest court of appeal relies on compliance with its directives to maintain its legitimacy. Lacking the coercive means of enforcement (officials, police forces), courts have to ensure that their decisions are acceptable to the concerned parties. Non-compliance would not only undermine the legitimacy of the courts but also bring into question the status of the constitution itself. On two occasions in American history the Court came close to being in this position. In 1857 it declared that the constitution did not permit African Americans to become US citizens. In addition, it voided the Missouri Compromise that limited slavery to the southern states. The decision helped precipitate the Civil War and was eventually to be reversed by the Thirteenth, Fourteenth and Fifteenth Amendments. In the mid-1930s the Court struck down great swathes of the New Deal legislation designed to bring economic recovery from the Great Depression. President Roosevelt threatened to pack the Court in order to undermine its conservative majority. In the event, one justice changed his position to create a five–four liberal majority. Had this not occurred a serious constitutional crisis would have ensued.[1]

Although nothing equivalent to these events has occurred since, the Court has remained firmly in the political thicket. The purpose of this chapter is to provide an account of the main controversies surrounding Court decisions over the last thirty years, with an emphasis on the experience of the Rehnquist Court (1986). When the decisions of the Court are assessed two sorts of criteria are normally employed. First, there is the question of the political or social importance of the decision. Some are of such importance that they set the agenda in a particular policy area for years. Such was the case with the 1954 *Brown* v. *Board* decision, which established that separate educational facilities for blacks were inherently unequal, and with the 1973 *Roe* v. *Wade* decision, which voided state laws banning abortion. In other instances the decisions of the Court can help determine the fate of a president (several Supreme Court judgements at the time of the Watergate scandal helped seal Richard Nixon's fate) or even who will become president, as with *Gore* v. *Bush* in December 2000.

Second, decisions are judged in terms of their intellectual coherence. Have the justices made a proper use of precedent? Have they argued the case in ways that are consistent, coherent and convincing? Before discussing the experience of the Rehnquist Court some background on the jurisprudence of the Court is necessary.

ACTIVISM, PASSIVITY AND INTERPRETING THE CONSTITUTION: THE ENDURING DEBATE

Jurisprudence is the philosophical basis of the law, and as far as the Supreme Court is concerned the most significant jurisprudential divides align along two continua. One measures the level of activity of the Court. Hence there are those who believe that the Court should keep out of the political thicket and, if possible, defer to the political branches or to public opinion. If the Court plunges into highly controversial areas such as abortion and affirmative action it is in danger of deepening divides in society. Ultimately it may lose its legitimacy. Those who believe in an activist Court are convinced that because the Court is charged with the job of judicial review it has a duty to arbitrate between the branches and between the states and the federal government. If that means striking down laws that are incompatible with the constitution – for example, state laws restricting the freedom to vote – then so be it. The resulting political backlash may be fierce – as it was in the south during the 1960s – but that is a price that has to be paid for adhering to the rule of law.

A second jurisprudential divide exists that cuts across the first. It concerns those who believe in a strict interpretation of the constitution and those who do not. In short, *interpretivists* believe that the actual text of the constitution together with the meaning behind the actual words of the framers is what should guide judges when they make their decisions. *Non-interpretivists* believe that the meaning of the constitution changes through time as society's institutions and values change; it is, if you like, a living document that constantly has to be re-interpreted to reflect the spirit of the times. Interpretivists are sometimes called *positivists*, after the philosophical school that places great emphasis on scientific observation. Non-interpretivists are part of what used to be called the *sociological* school of jurisprudence, or those who think that if necessary the Court should invoke the experience of modern society to justify its decisions. It is very easy to assume that interpretivists favour an activist Court stance and non-interpretivists a passive stance. However, much depends on the particular historical context in which decisions are taken. For example, the Hughes Court which declared much of the New Deal legislation unconstitutional was interpretivist because it based its decision on a particular reading of the Interstate Commerce Clause. Yet the results of its conservative decisions were highly activist. Both the Vinson and the Stone Courts, which followed the Hughes years, were very self-constrained and set few precedents. Yet, in economic policy at least, they were regarded as liberal because they failed to challenge the prevailing philosophy of government intervention in the economy and society.

Today the so-called 'strict constructionists' believe that liberal Courts have misinterpreted the constitution. However, should they succeed in returning to the *status quo ante* in such areas as abortion or school prayer the outcome would also be highly activist. Similarly, liberal jurists may be (and indeed have been) highly positivist in their interpretation of the constitution but the results may maintain the *status quo* and thus be judged non-activist. For example, two of the leading jurists of the early twentieth century, Justices Oliver Wendell Holmes and Louis Brandeis, based some of their judicial opinions in civil liberties cases on a strict reading of the constitution. Sometimes this resulted in 'activist' decisions and sometimes not.[2]

It is easy to see why interpretivist and passivist stances are often conflated. Critics of the Court, especially those on the right, have resented the increase in the powers of the federal government over the last fifty years. When the Court has upheld these new powers, and invoked sociological reasons for doing so, conservatives have been quick to claim that this represents an 'illegitimate' incursion into what should be a strictly political matter. Where in the constitution, they ask, is there any reference to abortion or to the claim that separate educational and other facilities are inherently unequal? The Warren Court (1953–69) was constantly criticized in this way, as was the early Burger Court (1969–79). It so happened that sociological and other evidence *was* frequently invoked by successive Supreme Courts, and a number of legal scholars both liberal and conservative were uncertain as to the wisdom of this course.

In recent years conservative interpretivists have also favoured state over federal power, and indeed much of the current debate on the role of the Court relates to this question. This is apparent from a brief review of the main controversies that have surrounded the Burger and the Rehnquist Courts. Let us look at these in more detail.

THE BURGER COURT: CONFUSION IN THE FACE OF RAPID SOCIAL AND POLITICAL CHANGE?

In 1969 Warren Burger replaced Earl Warren as Chief Justice. At first Burger was outnumbered by a liberal majority of the other justices who had been appointed by Kennedy and Johnson. Over the next fifteen years, however, Presidents Nixon, Ford and Reagan had the opportunity to replace many of the liberals with conservatives. (No deaths or resignations occurred during Jimmy Carter's presidency.) Of course, changing the Court's ideological complexion through the appointment process does not always work. Warren Burger was considered a conservative when appointed by Eisenhower, but turned out to be a liberal. John Paul Stevens was appointed by Ford but is now part of the liberal minority on the Court.

None the less, the Court did change considerably during the Burger years, and in a decidedly conservative direction. Because of this transition it is difficult to characterize the Burger Court in terms of a single philosophy, but by the 1980s it was very different indeed from the Warren Court. The changes can be summarized in terms of three broad areas. In the three areas most associated with the Warren Court – apportionment, civil liberties and civil rights/affirmative action – there was a general retreat from a liberal position. As far as apportionment is concerned the Burger Court generally endorsed the principle of mathematical equality between federal and state voting districts established in the famous Warren Court decisions.[3] However, in *Mahan* v. *Howell* it conceded that state districts could vary up to 16.4 per cent in size from one another. Later the Court shifted the burden of proof to those challenging population inequality between districts, and thus implicitly deferred to the judgement of the legislatures responsible for reapportionment.

Much more significant shifts in policy were imposed in the general area of criminal procedural rights. Warren had transformed the legal status of arrested persons. *Gideon* v. *Wainwright* (1963) established the right to legal representation irrespective of ability to pay. *Mapp* v. *Ohio* (1961) placed strict limits on the police power of search and seizure. In effect, the decision made it very difficult for the police to use any evidence culled in a search that was not the specific subject of a search warrant. Thus the justices strengthened what is known as the 'exclusionary rule'. Finally *Miranda* v. *Arizona* (1966) established the right of suspects to remain silent when read their rights. The actual implementation of these decisions had caused great concern among police and public alike. Many arrested persons, and in particular those with knowledge and resources, found that they could manipulate the system and win cases because the police had failed to follow procedures.

The Burger Court gradually weakened many of these rights, although it never actually voided any of the landmark Warren cases, and it did nothing to undermine the principle that every arrested person should have the right to counsel.

Hence the reading of 'Miranda rights' could be omitted in dangerous circumstances and the exclusionary rule has gradually been weakened. In a succession of cases during the 1980s the Court decided that illegally found evidence could be used against a defendant during cross-examination in court, that the rule did not apply to prison cells, that illegally culled evidence could be used if the police *could* have used legal ways to find it. In addition, police could search automobiles without a warrant. Perhaps the greatest challenge the principle established in *Mapp* came in 1984 in *Nix* v. *Williams*, when the court established that evidence could be used if the police would eventually have found it anyway. This 'inevitable discovery' rule greatly strengthened police powers.[4]

Much more controversy surrounds the stance of the Burger Court in the general area of affirmative action and civil rights. As Paul Brest noted in a 1983 article:

> The Warren Court really had it pretty easy. By 1953, when the new chief justice assumed office, the overt racism of the Deep South was no longer an American Dilemma, but was widely perceived as a national moral disaster. *Brown* v. *Board of Education* was a decision whose time was long overdue ... it was the egregious nature of the discrimination in the 1950s and 1960s that made life so easy for the Warren Court. The underlying claim in almost every case was that someone ... was currently and intentionally discriminating against blacks for no other reason than that they were black.[5]

As far as civil rights are concerned, the Burger Court had to deal with the sometimes subtle distinction between *de facto* and *de jure* segregation. Warren had outlawed segregation sanctioned by law (*de jure*) but had not addressed the question of segregation that had evolved as a result of other factors, including choice and poverty. In many northern cities, for example, schools were segregated because of segregated residential patterns. These in turn resulted from a wide variety of factors, many of them discriminatory, but not from the law as such. If, as had been established, separate facilities were inherently unequal, then surely a case existed for the desegregation of northern as well as southern schools? In the event, the Burger Court imposed no blanket ban on *de facto* discrimination but did outlaw it when there was a long-established history of conscious separation by race. Hence in *Swann* v. *Charlotte Mecklenberg* (1971) the Court ordered the bussing of children within the school district to reverse a long-standing pattern of separation. The key issue in this and subsequent cases became the 'purpose or intent' to segregate. Where this was evident, desegregation would be ordered. Unlike the south, where typically segregated schools were close by one another, large areas of northern cities were segregated. The remedies, including bussing, were, therefore, more complicated. Two issues dominated. Should desegregation orders include districts adjacent to the segregated areas and, once desegregated, should schools be required to maintain a particular racial balance? In both cases the Court decided on conservative interpretations. So in *Milliken* v. *Bradley* the desegregation of the predominantly black Detroit school district could not be facilitated by bussing children in to adjacent, suburban white school districts. In *Pasadena Board of Education* v. *Spangler* the Court found that there was no need to make annual adjustments to the ratio of whites to blacks once the aims of the initial desegregation order had been met.

These cases raise the issue of affirmative action, of course, a question that was to be specifically addressed in one of the most celebrated cases of the period. In *Regents of the University of California* v. *Bakke* (1978) the Court dealt a blow to the use of quotas in affirmative action programmes. Bakke had applied for one of eighty-four places in the Davis Medical School at the University of California. He was rejected even though his grade point average was higher than most of the seventeen places reserved for blacks and other minorities. The Court struck down the provision as a violation of Bakke's Fourteenth Amendment right to equal protection before the law. In spite of dire predictions that the decision would greatly reduce minority admissions to universities, it actually had little effect, because it was argued on the specifics of the case rather than establishing a broad judicial precedent. As is shown in chapter 10, it was not until 1997 that by upholding California's Proposition 209 banning affirmative action in state employment, education and contracting that the Court effectively sounded the death knell of affirmative action.

As chapters 14 and 12 show, the Burger Court was responsible both for the *Roe* v. *Wade* (1973) decision permitting abortion and for *Furman* v. *Georgia* (1972), which put a temporary stop to capital punishment in the American states. Later in the same decade the Court restricted the availability of abortion by declaring that states had no obligation to provide medical assistance to women wanting an abortion. *Gregg* v. *Georgia* effectively reinstated the death penalty. Note that in the former two cases the Court restricted the states' freedom to act while in the latter it returned some discretion to them. As we will see, favouring state over federal law was to become the hallmark of the Rehnquist Court.

As earlier implied, the Burger Court was often criticized for failing to adopt a consistent judicial philosophy. It seemed to be constantly asking not 'Is it right?', the guiding principle of the Warren Court, but 'Will it work?' or 'Is it acceptable to society?' By the late 1970s it was also apparent that the Court was becoming increasingly ideologically polarized. On the right, William Rehnquist was adopting a consistently conservative stance, and Chief Justice Burger and Sandra Day O'Connor often joined him. On the left, Justices Marshall and Brennan were consistently liberal and were frequently supported by Justices Blackmun, White and Stevens. In one case, *Garcia* v. *San Antonio Metropolitan Transit Authority* (1985), the liberal wing succeeded in establishing the precedent that the states could be regulated by the federal government or that what they did or did not do inhered not in the constitution but 'in the workings of the national government itself'. In other words, federal–state relations were politically rather than constitutionally defined. This was a remarkable decision, given that the Reagan administration was at the time devolving power to the states. In a blistering dissent Justice Rehnquist vowed that he would strive to reverse it as soon as he could.

THE REHNQUIST COURT: CONSERVATISM REVIVED?

William Rehnquist replaced Warren Burger in 1986. He was replaced on the bench by fellow conservative Antonin Scalia. With this personnel change the balance of opinion in the Court therefore tilted to the right. Between 1986 and 1993 three more Republican appointees, Anthony Kennedy, David Souter and Clarence Thomas, assured a permanent majority for the Republican camp. This was unaffected by the two Clinton appointees, Ruth Bader Ginsburg and Stephen Bryer, who replaced fellow liberals Byron White and Harry Blackmun. A great deal of controversy surrounded the appointment process during the 1980s and early 1990s. Two of Reagan's nominees, Robert Bork and Benjamin Ginsberg, did not survive the nomination process. Bork's record on First Amendment rights and the right to privacy (which includes the abortion issue) proved unpalatable to the Democrat-dominated Senate and his nomination was rejected by a vote of fifty-eight to forty-two. Unusually, he was rejected not on grounds of competence or bigotry (as had two of Nixon's appointees) but because he was a committed conservative. Ginsberg withdrew from the process when it was revealed that he had smoked marihuana at college. Controversy also surrounded the nomination of Clarence Thomas, who was accused by a past employee, Anita Hill, of sexual harassment. Thomas's nomination was none the less approved.

As time has passed so the Rehnquist Court has become more activist and in many respects more conservative. It also developed into a Court divided between liberal and conservative wings. Some of the more celebrated cases are as follows.

United States v. *Lopez* (1995). In this case the Court argued by five to four that the Interstate Commerce clause of the constitution did not extend to a federal law creating gun-free zones in public schools. Lopez, a student in Edison High School in San Antonio, Texas, had been found to be carrying a 0.38 revolver and four bullets. He was subsequently convicted under the Gun-free School Zones Act and appealed on the grounds that the federal government had no constitutional right to interfere in the affairs of public schools. The Court agreed and struck the conviction down as an improper use of the Interstate Commerce clause. This was highly significant because since the late 1930s the Court had effectively conceded that the Commerce clause could be interpreted in ways that allowed the federal government to do pretty much anything. Critics argued that should this assumption be challenged a wide range of federal social policies could be invalidated.

Printz v. *United States* (1997). Just this happened in the *Printz* case, where, in another five-to-four decision, the Court argued that the requirement in the Brady gun control Bill for local law enforcement officers to conduct background checks on would-be gun purchasers was a violation of the Commerce clause and the Tenth Amendment.[6] Although the actual effect of the decision was minimal – the local background checks were due to be replaced by a federal register of gun dealer transactions in 1998 – it set a precedent. Indeed, the opinion of the Court was written by Justice Scalia, who argued fiercely in favour of the assertion of states' rights. He even went so far as to claim that federal officials could no more order state officials to administer state law than state officials could order federal officials to implement federal law. If this principle was to be extended to other areas, whole swathes of federal environmental, social and economic regulation would be invalidated.

Adarand Constructors v. *Pena* (1995). In this case the Court held by a five–four majority that federal programmes designed to reserve business to minority contractors were constitutional only if they met strict guidelines. In the words of Justice O'Connor, who wrote the opinion of the Court, all government classifications by race 'should be subjected to detailed judicial inquiry to ensure that the personal right to the equal protection of the laws has not been infringed'.[7] In other words, the Court favoured a very restricted use of affirmative action where the individuals concerned could be shown to be past victims of discrimination. The general stance of the Court in this area was reinforced in 1997 when it refused to hear an appeal court case challenging the constitutionality of

California's Proposition 209, which eliminated affirmative action in state education and employment.

Bush v. *Gore* (2000). Of course, this case helped decide the outcome of the very close 2000 presidential election. The Court argued that the Florida Supreme Court's procedures for conducting recounts in some counties violated the Equal Protection clause of the Fourteenth Amendment. The state's procedures, the Court argued, were arbitrary, and there was no guarantee that hand recounts could be conducted fairly by the 12 December deadline. In a *per curiam* (collective) decision the five conservatives on the Court concurred in this judgement while the four liberals dissented. The decision was remarkable in a number of ways. First, the conservatives on the Court almost never invoked the Equal Protection clause to strike down state law. Instead they tended to argue federalism cases invoking the Tenth Amendment or the Commerce clause. Second, the decision challenged the right of a state high court to decide the electoral rules operating within that state. In contrast to most other federalism cases, therefore, the Court favoured federal over state rules. Third, the Court was clearly divided along ideological lines and the majority was a very narrow one. Most legal scholars agree that such an outcome was bad for the Court's reputation as an impartial arbiter between the states and the federal government. All the majority justices were Republican appointees, Bush was, of course, the Republican candidate, and the majority on the Florida Supreme Court had been appointed by Democrats. *Bush* v. *Gore* looked like a highly partisan decision. Recognizing this, Justice John Paul Stevens chastised his colleagues with the remark 'Although we may never know with complete certainty the identity of the winner of this year's presidential election, the identity of the loser is perfectly clear. It is the nation's confidence in the judge as an impartial guardian of the law.'[8] While it is too early to judge the full impact of this decision on the reputation and indeed the legitimacy of the Court, it did have the advantage of bringing to an abrupt end the long and bitter dispute over the election result in the state of Florida.

One of the more interesting features of the Rehnquist Court is that by no means all its decisions have been conservative. In fact the Court has occasionally stunned its conservative supporters by failing to make definitive judgements in such areas as abortion, affirmative action and gay rights. Indeed, in some instances it has favoured a liberal or libertarian stance. Hence it has struck down government attempts to limit pornography on the Internet as a violation of freedom of speech and has forced the Virginia Military Academy and the Citadel Military Academy to open their doors to women. It has also voided a Colorado law that prevented local governments from passing laws banning discrimination against gays.

Perhaps the most emotive recent case in the 1999–2000 session was *Stenberg* v. *Carhart*, which struck down a Nebraska law that had banned 'partial birth abortions'. Some thirty states had passed laws that limited the right to abortion in 'late term' cases. Often these laws were a cover to ban abortions early in term. In the more extreme cases they placed the life of the foetus over that of the mother. Four justices (Scalia, Rehnquist, Kennedy and Thomas) dissented. In this case the liberal side won because of the vote cast by Sandra Day O'Connor.

Summing up on the Rehnquist years, it is clear that the Court is highly activist.

Unlike the Burger Court, it is not reluctant to enter the 'political thicket' and establish broad precedents. This has been clearly demonstrated in the federalism cases and in the *Bush* v. *Gore* decision. Some scholars have argued that it is one of the most positivist or interpretivist Courts in recent history. One commentator has labelled its stance 'judicial supremacy', or the assumption that 'We are going to tell you. We are going to tell you, the Congress, you, the states.'[9] On the right Justices Rehnquist and Scalia have very clear views on the meaning of the constitution and are determined to see them established in case law. Since the departure of Justices Brennan and Marshall liberal opinion is much less well formed. Indeed, one of the remaining liberal stalwarts, Paul Stevens, is over eighty and will likely be replaced during the Bush term by an ideological conservative. A second feature of the Court is, of course, that it is deeply divided. Indeed, it is more divided on a range of issues than any Court since the 1930s. This ideological division is centred on the questions of federalism and the extent to which the federal government has the right to standardize social and economic policy across the whole country. There is no doubt that the position of the conservatives on this issue (and notwithstanding the *Bush* v. *Gore* decision) is coherent and jurisprudentially sound. If, as seems likely, President Bush appoints additional like-minded jurists to the bench we could witness some of the most momentous decisions in such areas as abortion and environmental protection in the last hundred years.

CONCLUSION: SHOULD THE COURT CONTINUE ITS ACTIVIST ROLE?

History tells us that activist Courts are often regarded as dangerous Courts. Prior to the Civil War it was an activist Taney Court that handed down the infamous *Dred Scott* decision that helped precipitate war. During the 1930s the Hughes Court, convinced that the New Deal was an unconstitutional incursion into the affairs of the states, very nearly caused a major constitutional crisis by invalidating much of the Roosevelt administration's programme. The Warren Court also moved ahead of public opinion in such areas as criminal procedural rights, and the early Burger Court reinforced this activism in capital punishment, abortion and affirmative action. Later the Burger Court adopted a more sociological or non-interpretivist stance and seemed content to go along with public opinion.

By the early 1990s, however, it was clear that the Rehnquist Court had developed into a very different animal indeed. It is activist and conservative and promises to become more so over time. Walter Dellinger, a former Solicitor General in the Clinton administration, has noted that:

> This is a Court that is confident of its capacity to make decisions, and when it comes to interpreting the Constitution, this is a Court that believes state governments, Congress and the lower courts should take a back seat to its interpretations. I think John Marshall, who established the tradition of judicial review in *Marbury* v. *Madison*, would be proud of this Court, even if he disagreed with some of its . . . decisions.[10]

With the notable exception of the *Bush* v. *Gore* case, the Rehnquist Court has not handed down any one decision that has caused widespread political controversy. In the next few years, however, this is likely to change as the composition of the Court moves in a more conservative direction. Justices Rehnquist, Scalia and Thomas are committed conservative activists. Should they be joined by one or two newly appointed like-minded associates the scene will be set for some highly controversial reversals, including *Roe* v. *Wade* and *Miranda* v. *Arizona*. Reversing *Roe* would, of course, return to the states the right to ban or limit abortions. Up to thirty states would likely do so. Such a move would aggravate what is already a deep divide in American society (see chapter 14), which would take some time to heal.

Arguably, the Court is at its most dangerous when it arbitrates between societal interests that are already deeply divided. Such was the case with *Dred Scott*, which helped precipitate the Civil War. When the Court clearly moves against the balance of opinion, as did the Hughes Court in the 1930s, it is less dangerous, because it is unlikely that the Court will remain out of line for long. Indeed, in the Hughes case the Court reversed itself before any serious harm (the voiding of vital New Deal laws) could be done. Herein lies the greatest danger to the legitimacy of the Court. Possibly this danger is of a different order at the beginning of the twenty-first century, when society is less divided by region or by class but more divided on single issues such as abortion, prayers in public schools, environmental protection and affirmative action.

In this context the Court will become more rather than less important as an interpreter of the constitution and as an arbiter between the states and the federal government. With an incumbent president elected by a minority of the voters and with the balance of power in Congress very finely balanced, a case could be made for a moderate and cautious Court. Instead we have the exact opposite. How this situation plays out with the American people remains to be seen.

NOTES

1   For a general discussion of this and other issues relating to the limits of the Court's power see Lawrence Baum, *The Supreme Court* (Washington DC, Congressional Quarterly Press, 1995).

2   On the role of these famous justices see Henry J. Abraham and Barbara A. Perry, *Freedom and the Court: Civil Rights and Liberties in the United States* (Oxford and New York, Oxford University Press, 1994), chapter 5.

3   The key case was *Baker* v. *Carr* (1962), which established that the federal courts could look into the size of legislative districts. Later, in *Reynolds* v. *Sims*, the Court argued the 'one person, one vote' principle that underpins equality in district size.

4   For a full discussion of these cases see Abraham and Perry, *Freedom and the Court*, chapters 3 and 4.

5   Paul Brest, 'Racial discrimination', in Vincent Blasi (ed.), *The Burger Court: The Counter-revolution that Wasn't* (New Haven CT, Yale University Press, 1986), p. 113.

6   The Tenth Amendment is usually interpreted as a guarantee of state rights, as it

states that the powers not given to the federal government in the constitution are reserved to the state and to the people.

7   Quoted in Kermit L. Hall (ed.), *The Oxford Guide to United States Supreme Court Decisions* (New York and Oxford, Oxford University Press, 1999), p. 6.
8   *George W. Bush* v. *Al Gore Jr* (2000).
9   Cited by Edward Walsh, 'An activist Court makes its high-profile messages', http://www.washingtonpost.com/wp-dyn/articles/A33611-2000Jul1.html, p. 2.
10 Ibid., p. 3.

7 Direct Democracy: Power to the People?

- ■ THE THEORETICAL AND HISTORICAL DEBATE IN BRIEF
- ■ THE CONTEMPORARY DEBATE
- ■ RESPONSIVE OR RESPONSIBLE LAWS, OR BOTH?
- ■ CONCLUSION

The traditional policy-making process in the United States involves elected representatives in federal, state and local legislatures writing and passing laws. The participation of the citizenry in this process – usually called representative democracy – is limited and indirect: voters elect representatives who in turn make the laws. But in some states and many cities and towns an alternative and additional way to make policy exists. Utilizing direct democracy procedures, voters can bypass the traditional law-making institutions and make laws themselves. Supporters of direct democracy argue that it is inherently more democratic than representative democracy because voters' opinions and choices are not mediated and distorted by the shenanigans of interest groups and elected representatives wheeling and dealing behind closed doors. Direct democracy, they argue, is a 'purer' form of democracy because the voters get what they want, not what others think they should get. What's more, voters themselves seem genuinely enamoured of the process. They like it, they use it, and they don't want anyone to take it away.[1] However, as the number of laws made through the direct democracy process has steadily increased over the past twenty years, critics' voices have grown louder and sterner. The core of their argument is that, while direct democracy sounds like a good idea in theory, it actually doesn't work very well in practice. They point to ill-conceived laws producing unintended policy outcomes, to incompatible laws resulting in fragmented and often contradictory regulatory systems, to laws that violate minority rights, to laws that benefit special interests rather than the wider community, and to laws that usurp the role of legislators and pervert and demean the traditional policy-making process. This chapter will review and examine the arguments promulgated by both supporters and critics of direct democracy, and it will seek to determine whether it is good or bad for the United States.

Caught in the spirit of the Progressive reform movement, many western, Midwestern and southern states introduced direct democracy procedures in the early decades of the twentieth century. The Progressives wanted to challenge and reverse what they perceived to be the corruption of the 'democratic' process. Legislators, they argued, were in the pocket of special interests, beholden to their

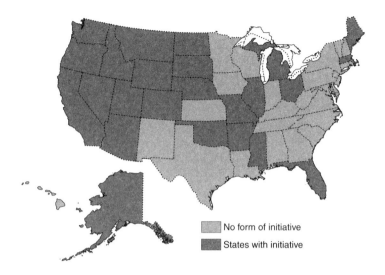

Figure 7.1 The geographical distribution of states using the initiative.
Source: Bowler *et al., Citizens as Legislators,* figure 1.1, p. 6

wishes, mere pawns in the policy process. In California the Southern Pacific Railroad dominated the legislature, cajoling and bribing its members, and generally pulling strings behind the scenes. In Oregon legislators auctioned off their votes to the banks, utility companies, logging interests and, again, the railroads, to produce a legislature with 'an unenviable reputation as the best that money could buy'.[2]

The Progressives' solution to the corruption of democracy was more and better democracy. They introduced a host of reforms, including secret ballots, women's suffrage, direct election of US Senators and direct primaries as well as three direct democracy procedures: the recall, the referendum and the initiative. Recalls allow voters to remove an elected official from office before his or her usual re-election date. They may want to do so because the official broke his or her election promises, because s/he was corrupt or perhaps because s/he was simply not very good at the job. Referendums permit a legislature to solicit the opinion – sometimes binding, sometimes not – of the whole electorate on an issue or question. A legislature may do so if it regards the issue as crucially important, politically sensitive, or if it is mandated to do so by the state constitution. Initiatives are similar to referendums in that the electorate makes a simple yes/no decision on a public policy question. However, they differ in that the question derives from, and is placed before the electorate by, voters themselves. Thus the people bypass the traditional law-making institutions by making laws directly. For this reason, initiatives are often described as 'tools of the people'. Figure 7.1 maps the states with the initiative device and table 7.1 shows the frequency with which those states use it. Because it is the most controversial of the three direct

Table 7.1 Initiative use, by the number on the ballot, 1898–1998

Rank	State	Year process adopted	Total no. on ballot	Average no. per year	No. adopted	No. rejected	% adopted
1	Oregon	1902	300	3.13	110	190	37
2	California	1911	263	3.02	90	173	34
3	Colorado	1912	195	2.27	74	121	38
4	North Dakota	1914	167	1.99	75	92	45
5	Arizona	1912	144	1.67	58	86	40
6	Washington	1912	124	1.44	60	64	48
7	Oklahoma	1907	82	0.90	40	42	49
8	Arkansas	1909	77	0.87	46	31	60
9	Missouri	1906	66	0.72	26	40	39
10	Montana	1904	64	0.68	32	32	50
11	Ohio	1912	62	0.72	16	46	26
12	Michigan	1908	58	0.64	20	38	34
13	Massachusetts	1918	54	0.68	29	25	54
14	South Dakota	1898	45	0.45	14	31	31
15	Nebraska	1912	39	0.45	13	26	33
16	Nevada	1904	37	0.44	24	13	65
17	Maine	1908	32	0.36	13	19	41
18	Alaska	1959	31	0.79	18	13	58
19	Idaho	1912	25	0.29	13	12	52
20	Utah	1900	15	0.15	3	12	20
21	Florida	1972	14	0.54	9	5	64
22	Wyoming	1968	6	0.20	3	3	50
23	Illinois	1970	1	0.04	1	0	10
24	Mississippi	1992	1	0.17	0	1	0
	Total		1,902	19.02	787	1,115	41

Source: Initiative and Referendum Institute at http://www.iandrinstitute.org/.

democracy procedures this chapter will focus on its use and abuse. First, what is the process by which an initiative becomes law?

While the details of the initiative process are different in every one of the twenty-four states that permit it, in most it looks something like this. Someone must first decide that the law should be changed. Anyone can do so, and the motivation will be different in every case. It could be that an individual feels strongly about a certain issue, an interest group or large corporation wants to amend the law in its favour, or a politician's pet project has failed in the legislature. Although the Progressives did not intend or foresee that special interests or politicians would use the initiative, no rules exist to prevent them from doing so. And, as we shall see, their use of the process has caused much controversy. The next step is to draft the proposed law, which is a complex process often done by lawyers. A poorly written law is less likely to be approved by the electorate and unlikely to pass constitutional muster. As well as lawyers, proponents of a nascent initiative will often hire a professional initiative firm to help frame the proposal. The firm may conduct opinion polls and use focus groups to test the message and language of the proposed law. The initiative's proponents must get it right, because they will not be able to make changes later, even if it is shown to be fundamentally flawed.

After drafting, the initiative is submitted to state election officials, who give it a title and provide a summary of the measure, both of which are placed on the petition forms that voters sign during the qualification phase.[3] After titling, the initiative must next be 'qualified' for the ballot. This is usually the toughest test, and the point at which most fail. For example, in California in the 1980s, over 250 initiatives were titled but only about one-fifth of them qualified for the ballot.[4] The biggest obstacle to qualification is the large number of signatures that must be collected within a specified time, often about three to five months. In California, for example, an initiative that proposes a change in the statute law must receive within 150 days a number of verifiable signatures equivalent to 5 per cent of the number of persons who voted in the preceding governor's election. One that proposes a change in the state constitution must receive 8 per cent. In real terms, this means about 400,000 verified signatures for a statute initiative and about 650,000 for a constitutional initiative. These imposing totals are rarely met without help from a professional signature-gathering firm. Firms employ people to go out on to the streets to collect signatures on behalf of the proponents of an initiative proposition. Anyone can sign the petition to qualify an initiative, but his or her signature will count only if s/he is a registered voter and it matches state records. Although it would also be foolish for anyone to sign the petition if they disagreed with the proposed law, research suggests that sometimes they do. When the requisite signatures have been collected and verified the initiative officially qualifies for the ballot. Most are placed on the November general election ballot in the year they qualify, although some appear on the earlier primary election ballot instead.

Now the real campaign can begin. Proponents and opponents of the initiative try to get their message across while rebutting and ridiculing the other side. The favourite media are television (especially), radio and newspaper advertising and tailored direct-mail hits. The campaign finishes on election day, when a state's voters will decide the fate of the initiative. A simple yes/no choice is made. Voters cannot choose to support one part and reject another part of the initiative. It is all or nothing. If a simple majority of the electorate approve, it becomes law, unless challenged in the courts. Successful initiatives often face court challenges, which can drag on for years.

THE THEORETICAL AND HISTORICAL DEBATE IN BRIEF

Democracy means different things to different people. Advocates of direct democracy – whose intellectual heritage can be traced back to the ancient Athenian polity, New England's seventeenth-century town meetings, Rousseau's early eighteenth-century writings and the Progressives' early twentieth-century reforms – argue that 'true' or 'pure' democracy requires that the people rule themselves directly. If institutions such as legislatures and individuals such as politicians mediate their opinions and desires, they will never be truly represented. The people must decide which issues require attention, discuss the alternatives, and choose the policy to meet the objectives. In this way, direct democracy is populist or participatory democracy because everybody participates directly.

Advocates of representative democracy criticize the direct democracy vision presented above as idealized. It is simply unrealistic to expect or indeed hope that citizens can become well enough informed to make wise decisions on complex policy issues. Even assuming that everybody has the potential to be wise, there simply isn't the time in practice. The obvious solution is a division of labour between a political class and the citizenry or electorate. Politicians are routinely accountable to their constituents on election day, and represent their views and wishes between elections. If they fail to do so to an acceptable standard, they are removed from office and replaced by someone who will.

THE CONTEMPORARY DEBATE

A THREAT TO MINORITY RIGHTS?

Probably the most serious criticism levelled at direct democracy today echoes that posited by Madison over 200 years ago: it promotes majority tyranny and threatens minority rights. A cursory glance at some initiatives approved by Californians over the years seems to bear this out. It has been used to prevent Asians owning land (Proposition 1 of 1920), to repeal anti-discriminatory state housing law (Proposition 14 of 1964), to establish English as the official language (Proposition 63 of 1986), to make illegal immigrants ineligible for welfare, health care and education services (Proposition 187 of 1994) and to abolish affirmative action (Proposition 209 of 1996). All these initiatives targeted minorities, and they all passed. However, some initiatives targeting minorities failed to win voter approval. In 1978 Californians voted against Proposition 6, which threatened the rights of gay teachers and could have led to the sacking of any who promoted homosexuality. And in 1986 they defeated Proposition 64, which could have led to the quarantining of people with AIDS.

It appears, then, that the evidence is mixed. Voters have both rejected and approved initiatives threatening minority rights. However, the evidence presented above is rather anecdotal and unsystematic. What is the 'scientific' evidence?

Barbara Gamble, utilizing more rigorous statistical methods to analyse seventy-four civil rights-related ballot measures between 1959 and 1993, found:

> strong evidence that the majority has indeed used its direct legislative powers to deprive political minorities of their civil rights. . . . Citizen initiatives that restrict civil rights experience extraordinary electoral success: voters have approved over three-quarters of these, while endorsing only a third of *all* initiatives and popular referenda.[5]

What's more, say direct democracy's critics, the courts are reluctant to protect minority rights when those rights have been violated as a result of a popular vote.[6] This is because many state judges are themselves elected, and going against public opinion could result in their removal from office. To these, critics add further opprobrium. Not only do initiatives threaten minorities directly, but they also engender an anti-minority climate. For example, gay rights advocates often complain that the incidence of anti-gay assaults increases when there is a gay-related initiative on the ballot. Minorities thus face a triple whammy from the initiative process: (1) anti-minority initiatives are more likely to pass than initiatives not targeting such groups; (2) law making by initiative reduces the chance of using the courts as a means of redress; (3) an anti-minority climate may be engendered by initiative proposals.

The prognosis for direct democracy indeed looks dire. However, its proponents are not disheartened. Regarding the first triple whammy allegation, Thomas Cronin has shown that civil rights-oriented initiatives make up only a small proportion of all measures put before the people. And, of those that do make it on to the ballot, 'most of those have been defeated'.[7] Although he provides no systematic evidence for this, two respected scholars of direct democracy, Todd Donovan and Shaun Bowler, have.[8] Using the same anti-minority categories as Gamble, but looking only at state-level initiatives, Donovan and Bowler found that 52 per cent passed (well below Gamble's 82 per cent) but that only 44 per cent actually posed a threat to minority rights. Furthermore, only 27 per cent of the anti-gay statewide initiatives on the ballot between 1978 and 1995 were approved, and only 18 per cent posed a real threat to gay rights. How can these results be reconciled with those of Gamble? The answer, say Donovan and Bowler, is in the data. They argue that Gamble's data set is non-random and biased towards local rather than state-level initiatives. And, given the opportunity, smaller, homogeneous local communities will be more likely to pass anti-minority legislation than larger, heterogeneous statewide populations. The problem, then, is not direct democracy *per se* but rather the size of the constituency. Indeed, the founding fathers were well aware of the potential for majority tyranny in small jurisdictions and thus desired an 'extended' republic or national constituencies to guard against it.

In response to the second of the allegations, supporters of direct democracy point out quite rightly that there is no rigorous evidence supporting the claim that the courts are less willing to strike down initiative laws than they are those passed by legislatures. The evidence, they say, is purely anecdotal. And anyway,

there are plenty of cases where the courts have struck down anti-minority legislation – Proposition 187 being the most notable recent example. What's more, the
argument that direct democracy elections encourage anti-minority sentiment is
also unproved. One study by respected scholars concludes that the 'Results . . .
are decidedly mixed. They neither wholly relieve direct democracy from the critique that anti-minority initiatives stigmatize targeted groups, nor do they totally
acquit direct democracy of these charges.'[9] In fact, advocates argue, direct democracy campaigns can actually have a positive educational effect on the electorate. Issues are raised, evidence is debated, consequences are discussed, and people
thus acquire information that can challenge 'initial responses to outgroups, [. . .
which] are almost universally intolerant'.[10]

Finally, and strangely, other proponents of direct democracy freely admit that
the direct democracy process can result in bad laws and anti-minority laws. But,
they point out, so can representative democracy:

> A cumulative list of these might well dishearten even the most optimistic Jeffersonian.
> Censorship laws, anti-evolution laws, flag-salute laws, red-flag laws, anti-syndicalists,
> anti-socialist, anti-communist laws, sedition and criminal anarchy laws, anti-con-
> traceptive information laws–these and others come all too readily to mind. The
> New York legislature purged itself of socialists; the Massachusetts legislature im-
> posed loyalty oaths on teachers; the Oregon legislature outlawed private schools
> and the Nebraska legislature forbade the teaching of German in public schools; the
> Tennessee legislature prohibited the teaching of evolution; the Pennsylvania legisla-
> ture authorized the requirement of a flag salute from schoolchildren; the Louisiana
> legislature imposed a discriminatory tax upon newspapers . . . The list could be
> extended indefinitely.[11]

In sum, there is little evidence to support the claims that minorities suffer a diminished recourse to judicial review and that initiative proposals engender an
anti-minority climate. However, while most initiative propositions do not threaten
minority rights, social science research has shown that those that do are more
likely to pass than those that do not. There is, though, one important caveat: this
finding applies only at the local level, where constituencies are small and homogeneous. The conclusion, then, is that direct democracy does not directly threaten
minority rights, although the process may well indirectly threaten them because
it exists at the local level. It is worth noting that this may be a semantic academic
distinction. The real point is that small local communities may generally dis-
criminate against minorities, whether by direct democratic or traditional representative mechanisms.

SPECIAL INTERESTS AND BIG MONEY

One of the Progressives' most persuasive arguments in favour of introducing
direct democracy was that legislatures and politicians were corrupt. The corruption was a product of the undue influence wielded over the legislative process by
special interests, usually giant corporations such as the Southern Pacific Railroad

in California. The interests' great wealth allowed them to buy political favours from politicians, and their economic importance allowed them to blackmail individual states – 'If you don't give us what we want, we'll go elsewhere.' Today the Progressives' arguments are, ironically, more likely to be used against direct democracy. This is because direct democracy is often beyond the reach of ordinary citizens and grass-roots community organizations, who simply do not have the financial resources to qualify an initiative and run a successful campaign. Only the wealthy can use it, and they do so to further their own narrow interests. Indeed, the influence of wealthy special interests greatly worries even some advocates of direct democracy. Are they right to be concerned?

While the idea of launching an initiative may be free, nothing else is. There are three main areas of expenditure: (1) the lawyers used to draft the initiative and defend it in court if it passes; (2) the campaign professionals or 'hired guns' of the 'initiative industry' who organize the collection of signatures and run the campaign; and (3) getting the message across to voters through advertising. While there are strict limits on contributions to, and spending by, politicians running for elective office, strangely no limits exist in direct democracy campaigns.[12] Consequently the money involved can be quite simply staggering. For example, the proponents and opponents of California's Proposition 226 – a 1998 contest between conservative groups and labour unions over unions' use of members' dues for political purposes – spent a combined $29.6 million. And in another 1998 contest, this one about gambling on Indian reservations in California, both sides spent an astonishing $92 million, over $11 per vote. In total, spending on initiative campaigns in 1998 broke the $¼ billion mark.[13]

These few anecdotal examples, however, do not prove the case. In order to judge rigorously whether the initiative process is a tool of the people (as it was designed to be) or of wealthy special interests, three related questions must be answered. (1) Are wealthy special interests advantaged *vis-à-vis* non-special ones in qualifying an initiative for the ballot? (2) Once qualified, do initiatives backed or opposed by wealthy special interests enjoy an advantage over those championed or opposed by non-special interests? (3) What effect does campaign spending have on the election outcome?

A simple answer to the first question is yes, the wealthy are advantaged in qualifying initiatives, because the right amount of money can virtually guarantee qualification. In fact some petition consultants (i.e. signature-gathering firms) will guarantee it – at a price. But the price can be very high, and it is one that few groups, even moderately well-off ones, can afford. And even the wealthiest groups may balk at the $1 million to $3 million needed to qualify a constitutional initiative in California, especially when there is no guarantee that it will be approved by voters on election day. But at least the wealthiest groups can make a choice about whether they want to pay the price and take the risk or not. It is, of course, a price that many poorly resourced grass-roots groups cannot pay. What's more, they rarely have the organizational structures in place, or the critical number of volunteers required, to collect enough signatures themselves.

One way to address the second question about whether special interests enjoy campaign advantages is to utilize an approach adopted by Donovan, Bowler,

Table 7.2 Success of California initiatives, by nature of inter-group conflict, 1986–96

Type of contest	No. of cases	Mean yes vote (%)	% passed
Type 1 Narrow proponent *v.* narrow opposition	7	40.5	14
Type 2 Diffuse proponent *v.* narrow opposition	14	44.4	35
Type 3 Narrow proponent *v.* diffuse opposition	7	28.1	14
Type 4 Diffuse proponent *v.* diffuse opposition	25	51.7	58
Totals	53	44.5	41.5

Source: Todd Donovan, Shaun Bowler, David McCuan and Ken Fernandez, 'Contending players and strategies: opposition advantages in initiative campaigns', in Shaun Bowler, Todd Donovan and Caroline J. Tolbert (eds), *Citizens as Legislators: Direct Democracy in the United States* (Columbus OH, Ohio State University Press, 1998), table 4.1, p. 90.

McCuan and Fernandez.[14] These scholars divide opponents and proponents of an initiative into two categories based on the breadth of the coalition involved on either side of the campaign: broadly based, diffuse coalitions and narrowly based coalitions. They hypothesize that diffuse coalitions will be more likely to represent the wider public interest and narrow coalitions will be more likely to represent special interests. Using this narrow–diffuse dichotomy, they categorized each of the fifty-three initiatives on the California ballot between 1986 and 1996 into one of four types: narrow proponent *v.* narrow opposition (type 1; seven cases), diffuse proponent *v.* narrow opposition (type 2; fourteen cases), narrow proponent *v.* diffuse opposition (type 3; seven cases) and diffuse proponent *v.* diffuse opposition (type 4; twenty-five cases). The results of their analysis are presented in table 7.2.

While this typology does not directly address the questions in hand, it does provide some leverage.[15] Two results are immediately striking. First, of the fifty-three contests, only fourteen (or a quarter) involved narrowly based coalitions trying to change the law for their own advantage. Second, narrow proponents are successful only 14 per cent of the time, whether facing narrow or diffuse opposition. Conversely, diffuse proponents have a 35 per cent success rate when facing narrow opposition and a 58 per cent success rate when facing diffuse opposition. These results suggest, contrary to many people's perceptions and much anecdotal evidence, that (1) special interests do not dominate the initiative process and that (2) they are not especially successful when they do qualify for the ballot. Put differently, initiatives sponsored by diffuse coalitions are more likely to be on the ballot, to receive a higher share of the vote and to pass than those sponsored by narrow coalitions.

On the third question, the effect of campaign spending on the election outcome, the evidence is mixed. Recent research has shown that '"yes" spending appears to buy more "yes" votes'.[16] And a respected scholar of direct democracy has estimated that if an initiative's proponents significantly outspend their opponents 'their chance of success climbs from roughly one in three to one in two'.[17] However, most political scientists agree that campaign spending is not the most significant factor in determining the election result. They are also of the opinion that, while spending and votes may be positively correlated in some cases, money cannot guarantee victory on election day. For example, of the sixteen initiatives on the California ballot between 1972 and 1976, the biggest spending side won on only eight occasions. And of the eight initiatives on which the proponents outspent their opponents, only two were successful.[18]

Indeed, there is evidence to suggest that higher spending in favour of an initiative is actually correlated with election failure.[19] How can this counterintuitive result be explained? First, it is usually the narrowly based coalitions that spend more, and they are less likely to win voter approval, perhaps because voters are conditioned to reject their special interest claims. Second, and related to the first point, high spending by an initiative's proponents makes them more visible to the voters, who may be turned off by 'big money' sponsors. A classic case of this was in 1994 when Philip Morris, the makers of Marlboro cigarettes, spent over $20 million promoting Proposition 186. The initiative ostensibly sought to tighten smoking regulations in California. When Californians learned that Philip Morris were funding the campaign, they quite rightly realized the initiative would have liberalized the state's onerous anti-smoking laws and that a corporate giant was trying to dupe them. The initiative lost. Finally, spending could be correlated with the closeness of the election. Close contests are more likely to attract higher spending (by both sides) than those where the result is a formality, yet in such contests the initiative stands a good chance of being defeated.

While the impact of money on the 'yes' campaign is contested, political scientists are confident that 'big money' is more important when used in opposition to an initiative than in support of it.[20] Cronin has shown that the big-spending proponents are successful only about a quarter of the time, while big-spending opponents manage to defeat the initiative about three-quarters of the time.[21] And table 7.1 shows that narrow (potentially bigger-spending) opponents are slightly more successful in defeating initiatives than are broad coalitions. Opponents of an initiative enjoy a significant advantage over the proponents because they do not have to spend their resources qualifying it for the ballot. Furthermore, negative spending may be effective because it reinforces voters' natural inclination to support the *status quo* by voting 'no' or because it causes confusion in voters' minds, and in such cases they will be more likely to vote 'no'.

In sum, then, big money cannot buy an election victory, but it can more often than not ensure the defeat of an initiative. Thus wealthy special interests may not be able to use the direct democracy process to write laws in their favour, but by spending large amounts of money in opposition to a measure they can usually prevent the process from harming their interests.

Responsive or Responsible Laws, or Both?

Theoretically, public policy outcomes achieved through direct democracy should be responsive to public opinion, because there is a direct and unmediated link between the voter and the policy. This may not be the case in the normal legislative process, because voter preferences are mediated by elected representatives who are additionally responsive to interest-group lobbying and liable to log-roll and trade votes with other representatives. Indeed, at least partly for these reasons, Americans are increasingly suspicious and untrusting of legislatures and their members. If the theory is correct, policy outcomes in states with direct democracy should represent the views of the median voter better than in states without it. Not surprisingly, critics of direct democracy argue the theory is flawed.

Edward Lascher and his colleagues examined a range of policies and found that 'the presence or absence of the initiative process has very little effect on the correspondence of public policy with public opinion. Policy outcomes are as strongly related to the desires of citizens in non-initiative states as in states that provide for initiatives.'[22] But Caroline Tolbert has shown that direct democracy states are more likely than non-direct democracy states to adopt term limits, taxing and spending restrictions, and supermajority rules for tax increases – yet such policies are popular across all states.[23] She calls these 'governance' policies, because they change the rules about the way a state is governed.[24] How can Tolbert's results be reconciled with those of Lascher? As Donovan and Bowler point out, because direct democracy states are responsive to voters' demands for lower taxes and/or supermajority rules concerning tax increases, the same states are also less responsive when it comes to those spending programmes analysed by Lascher. Responsiveness in one area (taxes) produces unresponsiveness in another (spending) because the first constrains the second. Furthermore, it is easy to see why legislators would be unwilling to introduce term limits (turkeys don't vote for Christmas) and to understand why these would be introduced through the initiative process. In sum, then, research on the responsiveness question seems to suggest that public policy in direct democracy states is responsive to public opinion but only on 'governance' issues where elected representatives are reluctant to act.

There is, however, a world of difference between responsive laws and responsible laws. The founding fathers rejected direct democracy at the federal level precisely because it threatened to be too responsive to tyrannical factions. Only if the passions are mediated by representative institutions could responsible laws be made. Although what constitutes a responsible law is almost impossible to determine scientifically, anecdotal evidence from many observers of direct democracy suggests that it is anything but responsible. Two of its most ferocious critics are the respected journalists David Broder and Peter Schrag. Broder argues that direct democracy 'has given the United States something that seems unthinkable – not a government of laws, but laws without government'.[25] By this he means that direct democracy produces a series of narrow, unconnected laws, many of which may be incompatible with, even contradictory to, each other. Elected politicians, meanwhile, especially under unified government, are better able to write coherent laws that seek to address problems in a more holistic manner.

Schrag is even more scathing than Broder about direct democracy. In a deeply passionate and highly readable book he argues that there has been a dramatic deterioration of the quality of life in California – in its progressive institutions, generous social welfare structure, liberal attitudes and once revered education system. This 'paradise lost' is directly attributable to a series of direct democracy measures beginning with Proposition 13 of 1978, which changed fundamentally the state's property tax law and sparked the new interest in government by initiative.

> The recent history of the California initiative system has demonstrated the essential irony of that process: that as the public trusts the system less and less, it becomes ever more susceptible to untested quick-fix remedies that, instead of resolving the problems of the moment, limit public choice and make long-term solutions even more difficult. But it has hardly deterred it . . . [Instead,] the *ad hoc* nature of the initiative process tends to elude anything resembling a consistent pursuit of policy.[26]

Moreover, as the initiative process has increased the complexity of policy making it has become increasingly difficult to determine who should be held accountable. This in turn reduces the need to make responsible policy because individuals are less likely to be held to account for their actions and decisions.

Broder's and Schrag's anecdotal evidence is supported to some extent by more robust social science analysis, which demonstrates that direct democracy states, with their lower taxes and/or supermajorities for tax increases, tend to adopt irresponsible budgetary measures.[27] With the exception of fiscally responsible spending cuts – which are rarely electorally popular – members of the state legislature may resort to 'creative' accounting to balance the budget, or they may issue government bonds (i.e. go into debt) to cover spending that would otherwise have been funded by taxes. And, even if the proponents of a tax-cutting initiative wanted to constrain spending on certain programmes, single-subject rules in some states prevent them from doing so. These rules force initiatives to address only one issue, and thus produce myopic and one-sided policy making. California's Proposition 13 – the 1978 initiative that drastically limited property taxes and hence state and county revenue-raising ability – is a classic case of irresponsible policy, according to direct democracy's critics. However, it would not be fair to single out direct democracy as the root of all irresponsible policies. In the past elected representatives have hardly been paragons of virtue when it comes to balancing the budget. Furthermore, as Bowler and Donovan point out, when it comes to anti-minority laws it is not direct democracy that is at fault but policy making in small homogeneous areas. The larger the constituency the less chance there is of anti-minority measures succeeding (whether through the legislative or the direct democracy route).

CONCLUSION

Having examined the arguments for and against direct democracy, we can now return to the central question posited at the beginning: is it good or bad for the United States? The evidence presented above is undoubtedly mixed. While proponents of direct democracy may be right to suggest that it does not threaten minority rights to the extent suggested by the critics, direct democracy has unquestionably been used to pass some pretty unsavoury laws. While the money spent on initiative campaigns is sometimes large, and while research has shown that it is particularly effective when used in defeating a measure, it is also apparent that money cannot always buy victory. While special interests do not wholly dominate the initiative process, neither is it truly open to ordinary citizens. While direct democracy is responsive to public opinion on 'governance' issues such as term limits and tax reductions, it is not particularly responsive when it comes to spending priorities and programmes. And while it is easy to point to direct democracy laws that are less than responsible, similar laws are often passed by legislatures.

Can we interpret or evaluate such mixed evidence to provide a more concrete answer to the question? Doing so is problematic because it involves making normative judgements. For example, should each of the five elements (minority rights, special interests, money, responsiveness and responsibility) be weighted equally, or is one or are some more important than others? Ultimately normative judgements have to be made because different people often have different priorities. For example, if I think that making responsible law is of the utmost importance and I distrust the public to do what is right most of the time, I would probably be more suspicious of direct democracy than of representative democracy. However, if I think that laws should be responsive to public opinion and that the majority are right most of the time, I would probably favour direct democracy over representative democracy.

It is probably fair to say that most politicians, journalists and academics – what we could call the establishment or the elite – distrust direct democracy because they do not trust the collective judgement of the mass of voters. But the evidence above suggests that the judgement of the voters is often as good as that of legislators. Most ordinary Americans, while probably unaware of the social science debates and evidence presented in this chapter, believe that they can and should make decisions directly, at least in part because they are increasingly distrustful of their elected representatives' ability to do so – with some justification. While there are many reasons why Americans are angry with their government – some real, some imaginary – direct democracy acts as a safety valve. It allows them to send a warning shot across the bows of the government and, if the government continues to ignore the warnings, actually to make the law themselves. And who is to say they should not? It would be a brave politician who tried to repeal or seriously reform (downgrade) direct democracy in the United States.

NOTES

1 Opinion polls consistently put public support for direct democracy at between 70 per cent and 80 per cent.
2 David S. Broder, *Democracy Derailed: Initiative Campaigns and the Power of Money* (New York, Harcourt Brace, 2000), pp. 34–5.
3 The title and summary also appear on the ballot pamphlet accompanying the election. At each election voters may have to make decisions about dozens of candidate races and several more direct democracy contests. Even if they could understand the original legalese of the proposed law, it is unlikely voters would have time to read the initiative in full. Research has shown that they do not, and thus the summary provides a quick and easy guide in the face of election and information overload. Sometimes the summary is accompanied in the ballot pamphlet by proponents' and opponents' arguments for and against the initiative, and sometimes by a fiscal impact study done by state officials.
4 David B. Magleby, 'Direct legislation in the American states', in David Butler and Austin Ranney (eds), *Referendums around the World: The Growing Use of Direct Democracy* (Washington DC, AEI Press, 1994), figure 7.3, p. 233.
5 Barbara S. Gamble, 'Putting civil rights to a popular vote', *American Journal of Political Science*, 41 (1997), pp. 246–7.
6 Julian N. Eule, 'Checking California's plebiscite', *Hastings Constitutional Law Quarterly*, 17 (1989), pp. 151–8.
7 Thomas E. Cronin, *Direct Democracy: The Politics of Initiative, Referendum, and Recall* (Cambridge MA, Harvard University Press, 1989), p. 92.
8 Todd Donovan and Shaun Bowler, 'Responsive or responsible government?', in Shaun Bowler, Todd Donovan and Caroline J. Tolbert (eds), *Citizens as Legislators: Direct Democracy in the United States* (Columbus OH, Ohio State University Press, 1998).
9 James Wenzel, Todd Donovan and Shaun Bowler, 'Direct democracy and minorities: changing attitudes about minorities targeted by initiatives', in Bowler *et al.*, *Citizens as Legislators*, p. 241.
10 Ibid., p. 229.
11 Henry Steele Commager, quoted in Cronin, *Direct Democracy*, pp. 91–2.
12 The Supreme Court ruled invalid most state laws limiting contributions and spending in *First National Bank of Boston* et al. v. *Bellotti*, 1978.
13 Figures from Broder, *Democracy Derailed*, pp. 17, 141, 163–4.
14 'Contending players and strategies: opposition advantages in initiative campaigns', in Bowler *et al.*, *Citizens as Legislators*.
15 It is not ideal because the narrow versus broad categorization does not mirror perfectly the special interest versus non-special interest categorization that we wish to test. It does not do so because not all narrow coalitions are seeking material benefits for themselves and not all broad coalitions are seeking to promote the wider public good, and because not all narrow coalitions are wealthy and not all broad coalitions are poverty-stricken. It is also worth noting that these categories are flexible across initiatives; on one initiative a group may be classified as a narrow interest and on another as a member of a diffuse coalition.
16 Susan A. Banducci, 'Direct legislation: when is it used and when does it pass?', in Bowler *et al.*, *Citizens as Legislators*, pp. 126–8.
17 David B. Magleby, 'Direct legislation in the American states', in Butler and Ranney, *Referendums around the World*, p. 250.

18   Eugene C. Lee, 'The American experience, 1778–1978', in Austin Ranney (ed.), *The Referendum Device* (Washington DC, AEI Press, 1981), p. 54.

19   See Banducci, 'Direct legislation', pp. 119–29.

20   Ibid., pp. 127–8.

21   Cronin, *Direct Democracy*, p. 109.

22   Edward L. Lascher junior, Michael G. Hagen and Stephen A. Rochlin, 'Gun behind the door: ballot initiatives, state policies and public opinion', *Journal of Politics*, 58 (1996), pp. 760–75, at p. 761.

23   Caroline J. Tolbert, 'Changing rules for state legislatures: direct democracy and governance policies', in Bowler et al. (eds), *Citizens as Legislators*.

24   Most of the reforms introduced by the Progressives – including direct democracy – can also be regarded as governance policies because they changed the rules of the game.

25   Broder, *Democracy Derailed*, p. 1.

26   Peter Schrag, *Paradise Lost: California's Experience, America's Future* (New York, New Press, 1998), pp. 19 and 22.

27   See Donovan and Bowler, 'Responsive or responsible government?' in Bowler, Donovan and Tolbert (eds), *Citizens as Legislators*.

Part II
Policies

■ GUN CONTROL: THE RIGHT TO BEAR ARMS   *Andrew Wroe*
■ IMMIGRATION: A NATION STATE OR A STATE OF NATIONS?   *Andrew Wroe*
■ AFFIRMATIVE ACTION: THE CONTINUING DILEMMA   *Andrew Wroe*
■ THE POLITICS OF HEALTH CARE: ANXIETY AMID PLENTY   *David McKay*
■ CAPITAL PUNISHMENT: THE POLITICS OF RETRIBUTION   *David McKay*
■ WELFARE REFORM: PROVIDING FOR THE OLD BUT NOT FOR THE POOR?
  David McKay
■ ABORTION: THE RIGHT TO LIFE DEBATE   *Andrew Wroe*
■ MANIFEST DESTINY AND *REALPOLITIK*: REALISM VERSUS IDEALISM IN FOREIGN
  POLICY   *David Houghton*
■ AMERICA AS A GLOBAL ECONOMIC PLAYER: FREE TRADE VERSUS PROTECTIONISM
  David Houghton

8 Gun Control: the Right to Bear Arms

- **ARGUMENTS FOR GUNS AND AGAINST CONTROL**
- **ARGUMENTS AGAINST GUNS AND FOR CONTROL**
- **CONCLUSION**

The long-running debate over gun control is one of several 'hot button' issues in American politics, a controversy that provokes strong and impassioned sentiments on both sides. As of early 2001 a spate of shootings in schools across America had heightened awareness of gun control issues. Foreigners often express amazement that the availability and use of guns is so widespread. And yet there are powerful constitutional and civil libertarian arguments on the other side of the debate. Well established lobbying groups like the National Rifle Association (NRA) oppose significant gun legislation on the grounds that it infringes what it sees as the legitimate right of every American to carry firearms.

There has in recent years been some significant legislation aimed at controlling the supply of guns. In 1981 there was an attempt on the life of President Ronald Reagan by would-be assassin John Hinckley. While Reagan survived, his press secretary, James Brady, was badly wounded and was left disabled by the attack. The incident evoked memories of the assassination of John F. Kennedy and led to renewed calls for reform of gun legislation in Congress. Sarah Brady, the wife of James Brady, spearheaded these efforts. Although it took many years to achieve, Congress finally passed the Brady Bill in 1993. The Bill required a five-day waiting period and background checks on the purchase of a handgun.[1] The following year Congress also passed Bill Clinton's anti-crime legislation, the Violent Crime Control and Law Enforcement Act. Among other things, it banned the sale and manufacture of nineteen different kinds of semi-automatic assault weapon.

And yet the anti-gun lobby contends that such legislation is nothing more than a start, as much stronger legislation is needed. Why is significant gun control legislation so difficult to come by in the United States? In part, the answer must relate to the sheer political and financial clout of the NRA, compared with the far less organized and cohesive nature of the anti-gun lobby. The NRA was founded in the 1870s as a body which offered training and instruction in how to use firearms – specifically as a response to the poor marksmanship of Union soldiers in the Civil War – and later represented the interests of those using guns in sports and hunting. Since the late 1960s and early 1970s, however, the NRA has increasingly come to focus its efforts on fighting legislation that would limit citizens' access to guns. As the anti-gun lobby has grown in strength the NRA has countered with massive lobbying activity of its own. It spends substantial sums of money on the defeat of congressional incumbents who favour gun control measures. While these efforts are not always successful, the gun lobby can claim some significant scalps. In 1994, for example, the Democratic Speaker of the House of Representatives, Tom Foley, lost his seat in his home state of Washington. It was the first time that a sitting Speaker had been defeated since 1862. While the reasons for his defeat are complex – it was in part a reflection of the national anti-Democrat, anti-Clinton trend at that year's mid-term congressional elections – the fact that Foley had voted for Clinton's anti-crime Bill alienated the powerful gun lobby in the rural areas of Washington state.

Public opinion polls have consistently shown that most Americans favour some sort of gun control. On average, about 9 per cent say that there should be at least minor restrictions on gun ownership, and around 6 per cent favour major restrictions. While a majority are against taking away the right to own a gun altogether, substantial majorities favour the Brady Bill, the registration of all handguns and limits on the sale and manufacture of semi-automatic weapons. In a Gallup poll conducted in January 2001, for instance, 54 per cent of Americans favoured making gun laws stricter, and only 14 per cent wanted the existing laws weakened.[2] If there are strong and consistent majorities for extending current legislation, why is the gun lobby able to prevail in the policy-making process? The answer probably lies in an understanding of V. O. Key's concepts of issue 'intensity' and 'passivity'.[3] While a majority of Americans favour some form of legislation to control firearms, that majority is essentially inert and 'passive'. It is composed of individuals who, while concerned about the spread of guns in general, are not so passionate about the issue that it would (say) determine the way they voted in federal and local elections. NRA members and the anti-gun lobbyists generally, on the other hand, are an 'intense minority'. Though they represent a minority numerically, they are mostly composed of individuals who *do* care passionately about their access to firearms. Charlton Heston sums up this intensity well when he issues the traditional NRA battle cry, 'You can have my gun when you pry it from my cold, dead hands.' Where the minority 'win out' over the majority, then, the victory is sometimes attributable to the fact that elected politicians care about the quality or intensity of public opinion as much as they do about its quantity.

We now turn to the arguments for and against gun control. The following sections of the text of this chapter explicitly abandon the 'neutral' language thus far adopted here, using the 'voices' of the pro- and anti-gun lobby. We begin with the arguments of those who oppose significant gun control legislation. In the concluding section we assess the prospects of a major change in gun legislation in the medium to long term.

ARGUMENTS FOR GUNS AND AGAINST CONTROL

In a major speech to the National Press Club on 11 February 1997 the President of the National Rifle Association, the veteran actor Charlton Heston, outlined the major reasons why guns are essential to the American way of life. The principal reason, he pointed out, is quite simply that every American has the right to own a gun. The Bill of Rights – specifically, the Second Amendment to the Constitution – gives individual Americans the *right to bear arms*. The language of the documents is clear on this, since the Second Amendment states explicitly that 'the right of the people to keep and bear Arms, shall not be infringed'. And as Heston notes:

> The right to keep and bear arms is not archaic. It's not an outdated, dusty idea some old dead white guys dreamed up in fear of the Redcoats. No, it is just as essential to liberty today as it was in 1776. These words may not play well at the Press Club, but it's still the gospel down at the corner bar and grill.

The possession of guns is a basic human right. The founding fathers were concerned about the tyranny of governmental power, and they therefore ensured that ordinary citizens would have the right to arm themselves against Washington DC if the need arose. Guns, then, are effectively an additional safeguard within the American system against the infringement of basic political liberties. As Heston notes:

> the beauty of the Constitution can be found in the way it takes human nature into consideration. We are not a docile species capable of coexisting within a perfect society under everlasting benevolent rule. We are what we are. Egotistical, corruptible, vengeful, sometimes even a bit power-mad. The Bill of Rights recognizes this and builds the barricades that need to be in place to protect the individual.

He argues that the Second Amendment is in fact more important than the First, for the right to free speech cannot be defended without the right to own a gun. The Second Amendment, Heston argues, is 'America's first freedom'.

Another reason for opposing gun legislation is that it misattributes the real causes of crime. People kill people, not guns. Logically, rises in violent crime cannot be attributed to the existence of guns, for guns have been a part of American life since the founding of the republic. The solution to rising crime must begin not with draconian infringements of the right to own a gun but with action to reverse the tide of violent crime. As George W. Bush emphasized during the 2000 presidential campaign, school shootings would not happen if were not for parental neglect and the culture of violence popularized by Hollywood. Film makers and television company owners must act far more responsibly than they have hitherto; more specifically, they must stop glamorizing violence, and must recognize the impact that the entertainment industry has on impressionable young minds.

Apart from their other advantages, guns also deter crime and protect those who respect the law from those who do not. If an armed attacker breaks into my house in the middle of the night I cannot be expected to defend myself with a rolled-up newspaper. On the other hand, violent crime is deterred where the law breaker knows that the law abider can defend himself or herself. Wayne LaPierre provides an especially telling example of this. In 1993 local juveniles in different cities in Florida murdered two foreign tourists. When asked why they had targeted the tourists specifically, they said that they had picked on them because they knew that they would not be carrying a gun. The likelihood that the tourists would be carrying firearms was low, and this was something that differentiated them from the local population. The latter could potentially fight back, while the former could not. As LaPierre notes:

> Self-defense works – criminals fear armed citizens. Self-defense, the most basic of all human reactions, is triggered by the threat or fear of harm. The survival instinct is not exclusive to law-abiding people, it is just as basic to criminals. As many as 2.45 million crimes are thwarted each year in the United States by average citizens using firearms, and in most cases the potential victim never has to fire a shot.

There is empirical evidence for the argument that guns deter crime. LaPierre cites the work of Gary Kleck, a Florida State University criminologist whose research – in common with a variety of other studies – shows that 'criminals flee when confronted with a firearm'.[4] If guns were not available for ordinary people to defend themselves from crime, LaPierre estimates, there might be as many as 2.5 million more crimes a year. Gun control measures work, if they work at all, by restricting the right of citizens to protect themselves against crime. As Jeffrey Snyder notes, they focus on punishing those who respect the law, not on capturing and punishing those who commit crimes.[5]

As George W. Bush argued in the presidential debate with Al Gore on 17 October 2000, 'law-abiding citizens ought to be allowed to protect their families'. New gun legislation is mostly not necessary, for there are already background checks in place to stop criminals getting access to guns. What is needed is full and proper enforcement of the *existing* laws. As Bush put it in a debate between the Republican candidates on 13 December 1999, 'I'm in favour of keeping guns out of the hands of people who shouldn't have them, like felons and juveniles. I'm for enforcing the laws on the books . . . the best accountability for someone who breaks the law with a gun is called jail, certain jail.'

All citizens have a basic right to defend themselves against attack, and they should therefore have the right to carry a concealed weapon. This is something which George Bush supported as Governor of Texas and a measure which the NRA has pushed for at the state level generally. The basic idea behind concealed weapons legislation is simple: law-abiding citizens can be issued with permits that allow them to carry concealed firearms for the purpose of self-defence. As Jeffrey Snyder notes, a good example of this is Florida's 1987 law, which grants a permit to carry such a weapon to anyone who satisfies certain objective criteria. For example, the person applying for the permit must be at least twenty-one, have no criminal record or history of mental illness and have attended a certified course in firearms safety. Opponents of the law in Florida claimed that it would lead to an increase in crime, prompting minor crimes and minor neighbourhood disputes to escalate into gun violence. In fact, however, the opposite has happened. 'Despite the fact that Miami and Dade County have severe problems with the drug trade, the homicide rate fell in Florida following enactment of this law, as it did in Oregon following enactment of similar legislation there,' Snyder points out.[6] A number of other states (notably Idaho, Montana and Mississippi) have now passed similar legislation with similar results. Across America such laws are being used to strengthen the arm of the law-abiding citizen against the criminal, since permits are, of course, denied to those with a record of criminality or mental instability.

Finally, many guns in circulation are used simply for recreational and sporting purposes, especially for hunting and target shooting. Gun control legislation presents a threat to the rights of these gun owners. It also threatens to do away with the traditional rural values on which America has always been based. Theodore Roosevelt summed up these values in relation to hunting when he said, 'The chase is among the best of all national pastimes; it cultivates that vigorous manliness for the lack of which, in a nation, as in an individual, the possession of no other qualities can possibly atone.'[7]

However, modern opponents of guns often have a hidden social agenda. They want not only to do away with the right to own a gun but to stop the practice of hunting on 'moral' grounds. As James Jay Baker, Executive Director of the NRA's Institute for Legislative Action, has noted, Animal Rights extremists are waging a war against the whole culture of hunting. The right to hunt, however, is a basic freedom and a part of America's heritage. Guns are part of the hardware of hunting, and it is not for government to micro-manage the kinds of tools which hunters and sportsmen will be 'permitted' to use.

As defenders of the *status quo*, the strategy and tactics of the NRA and pro-gun lobby generally differ from the approach taken by those who want to change the political landscape. The NRA's strategy is essentially negative, in the sense that it aims to preserve what already exists and to obstruct the development of legislation reducing access to guns. As a matter of strategy it concentrates on making a handful of arguments forcefully, especially those relating to the Second Amendment and the right to self-defence. Different tactics, however, are required of groups seeking to overturn the established order. The onus of the argument is on the anti-gun lobby to demonstrate, through sifting the empirical evidence, that positive change is necessary. This is reflected in the following section.

Arguments against Guns and for Control

The first, most obvious, most effective argument against firearms is very simple: guns kill people. The statistics prove it. Consider the number of Americans killed in the revolutionary war against England, in the Civil War, in the First and Second World Wars, and in the Korean and Vietnam Wars. Now consider that more Americans have died of gun-related incidents since 1933 than were killed in all these wars *combined*.[8] Also consider that the current death toll runs at about 35,000 gun-related fatalities per year.[9] Perhaps this should not surprise, given that it is more difficult to get a driving licence than it is to purchase a handgun licence and that consumer safety standards for toy guns are more rigorous than for the real thing.[10] The Department of Justice estimates that the United States suffers nearly a million handgun crimes every year.[11]

Guns have been used in the most high-profile political assassinations of recent years. John F. Kennedy, his younger brother Robert, Martin Luther King and Malcolm X all died at the hands of gunmen. Gun massacres, especially in the nation's high schools, are becoming shockingly familiar stories on television. In January 1989 Patrick Edward Purdy, a mentally unsound twenty-four-year-old drifter obsessed with guns, killed five students in the playground of the Cleveland Elementary School in Stockton, California, when he opened fire with his AK-47 semi-automatic assault rifle. In a similar incident in March 1998 eleven-year-old Andrew Golden and thirteen-year-old Mitchell Johnson shot dead four fellow pupils and one teacher from woods overlooking their school in Jonesboro, Arkansas. They were armed with ten handguns and rifles, including a semi-automatic, and 500 rounds of ammunition stolen from Golden's grandfather. The attack was wholly premeditated. The boys set off a fire alarm in the school and opened fire as their classmates evacuated the building. April 1999 saw the self-styled Trenchcoat Mafia of eighteen-year-old Eric Harris and seventeen-year-old Dylan Klebold murder twelve of their schoolmates and a teacher before turning their semi-automatic weapons on themselves at the Columbine High School in Littleton, Colorado. There has been no let-up in this shocking spate of school massacres as copycat killers continue to target fellow pupils. In March 2001, for example, a further two were murdered at Santana High School in Santee, California. In the light of such events, metal detectors and armed guards are now a familiar sight at many schools. The massacres have not been restricted to the schoolhouse, however: many disgruntled employees, unable to deal with redundancy, losing money on share deals, or even having child maintenance docked from their wage packet, have turned their guns on co-workers and employers with deadly consequences. All this is to say nothing of the daily threat of injury and death that faces residents of the inner cities, where crime, drugs and guns are natural and deadly complements.[12]

It is simply wrong to suggest that it is not guns that are the problem but the people that use them. The National Rifle Association's argument that 'guns don't kill people, people kill people' is evidentially incorrect. The US experiences similar levels of violent crime as other developed countries, but the ubiquitous presence of guns raises the ante, 'frequently transform[ing] violent situations into lethal ones'.[13] The figures bear this out. Handguns were used in 13,220 murders in the United States in 1992, compared with just 128 in Canada, ninety-seven in Switzerland, sixty in Japan, thirty-six in Sweden, thirty-three in Britain and only thirteen in Australia.[14]

The extraordinary and frightening death rate persists despite legislative efforts to control and regulate gun ownership. The passage of the Brady Bill in 1993 and the semi-automatic assault weapons ban in 1994 seem to have had little effect on the death toll. In part this is because the ban didn't really ban semi-automatic weapons; what was banned was the ownership, domestic manufacture and importation of *new* semi-automatic assault (or military-style) rifles. Most semi-automatic hunting rifles and old (pre-1994) assault rifles were exempted from the ban. Millions are still owned and traded legally. Another small part of the story is that the Supreme Court ruled unconstitutional the Brady Bill-mandated background check by local officials on gun purchasers.[15] It, and the Brady-mandated five-day waiting period between buying a gun and taking it home, have been replaced by the National Instant Check System (NICS) – a far from comprehensive and effective alternative. Much more relevant to the continuing gun violence, however, are the quarter of a billion guns already in the hands of American citizens – on average, a gun for every American. In fact, many states are actually liberalizing their gun laws. For example, more than half the states now permit their citizens to carry concealed weapons in their vehicle and/or on their person. Official data show that almost every other American home owns one or more guns. Another striking statistic is that several hundred agents from the Bureau of Alcohol, Tobacco and Firearms (BATF) are responsible for monitoring 28,000 federally licensed firearms dealers.[16]

Contrary to the claims of the pro-gun lobby, the Second Amendment does not guarantee an *individual* right to bear arms. Taken as a whole, the amendment states that 'a well regulated Militia, being necessary to the security of a free State, the right of the people to keep and bear Arms, shall not be infringed'. Supporters of the gun lobby frequently give a selective reading of this sentence that ignores the first critical clause. However, the first section is crucial because it shows that Americans are allowed to keep and bear arms *only* as part of a 'well regulated Militia' established to protect the security of the individual states against internal rebellion and oppression by the federal government. In other words, a collective but historically anachronistic right to bear arms exists, not an individual, private right. Moreover, because it has never been incorporated via the due process or 'liberty' clause of the Fourteenth Amendment, the Second Amendment does not apply to the state governments. This means that even if the federal government could not constitutionally violate an individual right to bear arms, there is nothing to stop state governments from doing so. Indeed, the existence of a constitutional guarantee to bear arms would not render gun control laws unconstitutional, because none of Americans' constitutional rights is absolute. For example, the freedom of speech guaranteed in the First Amendment is not absolute, although it is regarded as a 'fundamental' right. The Supreme Court has long held that no citizen has a right to cry 'fire' in a crowded theatre absent a fire; Congress can regulate speech that threatens a 'clear and present danger'.[17] Similarly, Congress could regulate gun ownership and use, even if a fundamental individual right to bear arms existed.

In spite of these legal and historical truths, the NRA has been very successful in creating a myth about the right to bear arms. It has done so through 'carefully worded misinformation about the text and history of the Second Amendment and a systematic distortion of judicial rulings interpreting the Amendment'.[18] It ignores cases such as the Supreme Court's 1939 ruling, in *United States v. Miller*, that the 'obvious purpose' of the Second Amendment was to assure the effectiveness of the state militia.[19] Many years later the former Chief Justice of the Supreme Court, Warren Burger, argued that the Second Amendment is:

> the subject of one of the greatest pieces of fraud, I repeat the word fraud, on the American public by special interest groups that I have ever seen in my lifetime . . .

The NRA has misled the American people and they, I regret to say, have had far too much influence on the Congress of the United States than as a citizen I would like to see – and I am a gun man.

The very language of the Second Amendment refutes any argument that it was intended to guarantee every citizen an unfettered right to any kind of weapon ... Surely the Second Amendment does not remotely guarantee every person the constitutional right to have a 'Saturday Night Special' or a machine gun without any regulation whatever. There is no support in the Constitution for the argument that federal and state governments are powerless to regulate the purchase of such firearms.[20]

There is little question that the NRA, which is the main pro-gun group, is an extremely effective lobbying force. It uses its huge financial resources to mobilize its large and often fanatical membership against members of Congress who seek to regulate firearms. Scared by the prospect of electoral defeat, and reckoning that such powerful organizations are not to be confronted, members may abandon their regulatory position. In this way the power of money is distorting the political process and leading to the loss of even more lives. While it is undoubtedly an effective inside player in the political process, the NRA has become a radical, absolutist lobbying group unable to recognize the importance of compromise and moderate language. During the late 1970s and 1980s it became increasingly political and intransigent over any reform of the gun laws. For example, whereas in the early 1970s the NRA had favoured a Brady Bill-style waiting period between buying a firearm and taking it home, it fought tooth and nail in the 1980s and 1990s against such reform. Its battle against the regulation of military-style assault weapons during the same period re-emphasizes the point. Extremist aims have been matched, moreover, by extremist language. The NRA's president claimed, for example, that banning assault weapons 'gives jackbooted government thugs more power to take away our constitutional rights, break in our doors, seize our guns, destroy our property, and even injure and kill us'.[21] Such strident anti-government rhetoric legitimizes and fuels the fire that burns in the bellies of many modern-day extremists. Characters such as Timothy McVeigh, his accomplice, Terry Nichols, and their ideological soul mates in the militia movement have murdered in the belief that the government is conspiring to take away their guns and enslave them.

Surprisingly, given the strong legal and moral arguments against the right to bear arms, none of the mainstream groups in opposition to the NRA actively lobbies for repeal of the Second Amendment. The most 'hard-line' mainstream organization is the Coalition to Stop Gun Violence (CSGV).[22] However, while it supports the existing assault weapon ban and advocates a similar ban on handguns, there would be 'reasonable exceptions for police, military, security personnel, gun clubs, and antique and collectable firearms stored in inoperable conditions. Hunting weapons, such as shotguns and rifles, would be unaffected by these bans.'[23] Recognizing that such perhaps moderate reforms are hopeful rather than realistic, its short-term goals include such minor reforms as 'establishing a national one-handgun-a-month purchase limit'.[24] Most gun control groups can usually be found proclaiming that they do not seek to ban guns and are not against guns *per se;* their aims are much more modest. For example, a relatively new organization called Americans for Gun Safety (AGS) wants 'a national dialogue on sensible solutions to improve gun safety',[25] and Handgun Control, America's largest and most important gun control group, led by Sarah Brady, wife of James Brady, aims 'to prevent gun crime and reduce gun violence'.[26] They position themselves as centrist promoters of reform and gun safety in part because an all-out challenge to the powerful NRA is unfeasible. Political reality forces gun control groups to seek incremental reforms. Another part of the story, though, is that many reformers genuinely believe that law-abiding Americans should be allowed to own firearms, especially for protection against crime and for sporting and hunting purposes. It is the nexus of guns and crime, and especially of guns, crime and youth, that is of concern to most Americans, and it is this that reform groups focus on.

Gun control groups seek to close various loopholes in current laws, such as those that allow 'private' collectors to sell firearms at gun shows and over the Internet without doing a background check on the buyer. Others seek to ensure that current laws are properly implemented – something even the NRA agrees with. And Handgun Control, for example, seeks 'commonsense measures to reduce the accessibility of firearms to kids', such as closing the loophole that allows eighteen-to-twenty-year-olds to buy weapons at gun shows, making it illegal for under-twenty-ones to own or carry weapons, ensuring that adults store their guns responsibly in the presence of children, and fitting childproof safety catches on triggers. Such laws, Handgun Control argues, would help reduce the 5,000 American children killed every year by firearms. Surely it is absurd that it is harder for an eighteen-year-old to get an alcoholic drink or a drivers' licence than a gun?

Gun control groups have recently put considerable resources into defeating what are known as Carrying Concealed Weapons (or CCW) laws. The thinking of the NRA is that CCW laws, which allow citizens to carry weapons on their person or in their car, reduce crime because criminals are likely to think twice about committing, for example, a robbery if the potential victim may be carrying a gun to defend himself or herself. The NRA's opponents respond that arming undertrained civilians exacerbates already volatile situations. Police officers and other armed officials are highly trained and subject to strict regulations and rules of engagement regarding the use of their firearms – and with very good reason. Guns are deadly, and guns in undertrained hands will result in unnecessary deaths, perhaps even of innocent bystanders. Reform groups also point to research that shows violent crime rates have fallen more in states that do not have CCW laws than in those that do. Their interpretation is that more guns means more crime, not less, at least in part because CCW laws are lax enough that criminals and potential criminals are able legally to arm themselves.

Sometimes poor manufacturing standards and safety features increase the inherent danger posed by firearms. For example, most guns have no indicator light showing the gun is loaded and no 'personalized' trigger lock ensuring that only the user can fire it. Moreover, firearms are exempt from Consumer Product Safety Commission regulation. There are, gun control groups maintain, more

regulations governing the manufacture of toy guns than real ones.[27] Gun manu-
facturers are also too little concerned about the identity and character of the 'end
user'. Lax documentation procedures and sales regulation – especially at gun
shows and of private resales – as well as the ease with which guns can be
'anonymized' by removing identity numbers, ensure that they fall easily into criminal hands – and with little concern on the part of the manufacturer. Manufactur-
ers have further demonstrated their negligence by designing guns squarely aimed
at the criminal market. Cheap, small, easily concealed 'Saturday night specials',
fingerprint-resistant finishes, self-assembly guns and 'cop killer' bullets which
can piece bulletproof vests, all service no legitimate user.

CONCLUSION

The prospects for additional gun control legislation through the executive and
legislative branches seem rather remote. The concern about crime that helped to
propel anti-gun legislation in the early 1990s has slightly abated in the decade
since, and the leadership on the gun question provided by President Clinton is no
longer there. His Republican successor, George W. Bush, appears unlikely to
push for more than minor changes in existing legislation. As a presidential candidate Bush supported the core precepts of the NRA position. While he supports
voluntary trigger safety locks on handguns, the outlawing of some high-capacity
ammunition clips and raising the legal age for purchasing a handgun from eighteen to twenty-one, he seems unlikely to be proactive in pushing these changes of
existing laws.

The judicial branch may provide an alternative avenue of change, however.
Recognizing the power of the NRA in the Congress and state legislatures, groups
seeking tougher firearms regulation have turned their attention to the courts. Just
as the anti-tobacco lobby sued tobacco companies for covering up research showing their products' ill effects, lawsuits have sought to make gun makers liable for
negligence. Those in favour of tighter regulation are quite open about the object
of such lawsuits, which 'is not to recover money . . . but to change the industry
itself'.[28] The suits have met with some success, although it remains to be seen
what the longer-term impact of judicial activity on the gun control issue will be.

NOTES

1   The Supreme Court later ruled the background checks unconstitutional in *Prinz* v.
    United States (1987).
2   See www.gallup.com/poll/indicators/indGuns.asp.
3   See especially V.O. Key, *Public Opinion and American Democracy* (New York, Knopf,
    1961), pp. 207–33.
4   Wayne LaPierre, 'Self-defense: the right and the deterrent', in Jan E. Dizard, Robert
    Merrill Muth and Stephen P. Andrews (eds), *Guns in America: A Reader* (London,
    New York University Press, 1999), pp. 173–4.
5   Jeffrey Snyder, 'A nation of cowards', in Dizard *et al.*, *Guns in America*, p. 187.

6 Ibid., p. 189.
7 Quoted in James Jay Baker, 'To save hunting in the twenty-first century', on the NRA's website atwww.nraila.org/reasearch/20000103-HuntingConservation-001.shtml.
8 Robert Singh, 'Gun control in America', *Political Quarterly*, 69 (1998), p. 288.
9 Robert Spitzer, *The Politics of Gun Control* (Chatham NJ, Chatham House, 1995), p. 7. Others have put the number as low as 3, and still others as high as 38,000. Most, though, are agreed that about half the fatalities are murders and half are suicides.
10 Singh, 'Gun control in America', pp. 289–90.
11 Jeremy Putley, 'The moral vacuum and the American constitution', *Political Quarterly*, 1 (1997), p. 69.
12 Less than one year after the March 1996 massacre of sixteen pupils and their teacher at Dunblane Primary School in Scotland by Thomas Hamilton, handguns were banned in the United Kingdom. Such swift and decisive action, as this chapter will show, is impossible in the United States.
13 Singh, 'Gun control in America', p. 290.
14 Jeremy Putley, 'The moral vacuum and the American constitution', p. 72.
15 As already noted, the Court struck down the background check in *Printz* v. *United States* (1997) in any case. The Court also struck down in *United States* v. *Lopez* the main provision of the Gun-free School Zones Act of 1990, which would have created a 1,000-ft gun-free zone around schools. The Court struck these provisions down not because of any dubious right to bear arms but because the federal government was impinging on states' rights in policy execution and education. While Handgun Control made much of the 'success' of the Brady Bill, in effect it is a minor reform, even pre-*Printz*.
16 Spitzer, *The Politics of Gun Control*, p. 165.
17 *Schenck* v. *United States* (1919).
18 Handgun Control at http://www.handguncontrol.org/facts/ib/second/asp.
19 Spitzer, *The Politics of Gun Control*, p. 41.
20 Quoted by Handgun Control at http://www.handguncontrol.org/facts/ib/second/asp.
21 President Bush senior resigned his NRA membership in 1992 after this outburst.
22 Until 1990 the CSGV was named the National Coalition to Ban Handguns.
23 CSGV at http://www.csgv.org/content/coalition/coal_aboutus.html.
24 Ibid.
25 Americans for Gun Safety at http://www.americansforgunsafety.com/solutions.html.
26 Handgun Control's letter to members of Congress, 21 February 2001, at http://www.handguncontrol.org/press/related_documents/022101.pdf. Sarah Brady also heads the Center to Prevent Handgun Violence, which is affiliated with Handgun Control. While Handgun Control is the largest gun control group, it is still only about one-tenth the size of the NRA.
27 Handgun Control at http://www.handguncontrol.org/fact/ib/reform.asp.
28 Ibid.

9 Immigration: a Nation State or a State of Nations?

- ■ THE IMMIGRATION DEBATE: ENVIRONMENTAL ARGUMENTS
- ■ THE IMMIGRATION DEBATE: ECONOMIC ARGUMENTS
- ■ THE IMMIGRATION DEBATE: CULTURAL ARGUMENTS
- ■ CONCLUSION

The United States is often and correctly described as a 'nation of immigrants' or even as a 'state of nations'. Ask Americans about their family history and the variety of the replies is bewildering. Nearly 58 million claim German ancestry, 33 million English ancestry, 24 million African ancestry, 18 million Mexican ancestry, 1.5 million Chinese ancestry and 1 million Japanese ancestry. Astonishingly, given that the Republic of Ireland's population is less than 4 million, 39 million Americans report having Irish roots. Millions more descend from Italy, Poland, Russia, Greece, Sweden, the Caribbean, Canada and the Philippines. Furthermore, over 17 million people speak Spanish at home, and French, German, Italian and Chinese are each spoken in more than a million homes.[1]

With the important exception of Africans who were forcibly transported as slaves and of the already resident Native Americans, most people came to the United States for one of two reasons: to escape persecution in their home country or to fulfil the American dream of improving their economic lot. Between 1820 and 1998 a staggering 64.6 million immigrants arrived. (See table 9.1.) Despite the number admitted, and while it is broadly the case that immigrants have been welcomed, the story of immigration to the United States has not always been a happy one. German and Irish immigrants arriving in the nineteenth century were viewed with suspicion by white Anglo-Saxon Protestants (WASPs). In the late nineteenth century Americans began to worry about the increasing number of arrivals from China and Japan. After putting a stop to Asian immigration in 1917, attention turned to the 'hordes' 'flooding' in from eastern and southern Europe. Professor Edward Ross, a distinguished sociologist at the University of Wisconsin, reported to Congress:

> that the Mediterranean peoples are morally below the races of northern Europe is as certain as any social fact. . . . It is unthinkable that so many persons with crooked faces, coarse mouths, bad noses, heavy jaws, and low foreheads can mingle their heredity with ours without making personal beauty yet more rare among us than it actually is. So much ugliness is at least bound to work to the surface.[2]

Such racist concern led Congress to restrict severely the immigration of southern and eastern Europeans in the 1920s. The door to non-northern Europeans was

Table 9.1   Immigration to the United States, 1800–1998

Year	No.	Year	No.
1801–10	–	1901–10	8,795,386
1811–20	–	1911–20	5,735,811
1820–30	151,824	1921–30	4,107,209
1931–40	599,125	1931–40	528,431
1841–50	1,713,251	1941–50	1,035,039
1851–60	2,598,214	1951–60	2,515,479
1861–70	2,314,824	1961–70	3,321,677
1871–80	2,812,191	1971–80	4,493,314
1881–90	5,246,613	1981–90	7,338,062
1891–1900	3,687,564	1991–98	7,605,068

– indicates data not available. The federal government made no systematic attempt to count
  the number of arrivals before 1820.
Source: US Immigration and Naturalization Service, *1998 Statistical Yearbook*, p. 7,
available on-line at http://www.ins.us.doj.glov/graphics/aboutins/statistics/imm98.pdf

opened slightly in the 1950s, but the welcome mat was not rolled out again until
1965, when Congress repealed these racially motivated immigration laws. Despite repeal, the number of visas offered to some countries was not enough to cope
with demand. The result was high levels of illegal immigration, most visibly from
Mexico, which shares a 3,000-mile border with the United States. When the
Immigration Reform and Control Act (IRCA) of 1986 offered an amnesty, about
2 million 'undocumented' immigrants took up legal residence and later citizenship. However, large-scale undocumented immigration continued and does so to
this day. The Immigration and Naturalization Service (INS), the government
agency responsible for admitting legal entrants and keeping illegal ones out, estimated that about 5 million were illegally resident in 1996. While the INS's
estimates that the illegal population grows annually by about 275,000 – putting
the number of undocumented persons at over 6 million in 2001 – early indications
from the 2000 census suggest that this figure could be a gross underestimate.

   A national debate about immigration generally and illegal immigration specifically was sparked by the passage of Proposition 187 in California in 1994. This
direct democracy initiative proposed to bar illegal immigrants from receiving
health care and welfare services and public education. It also mandated that those
'reasonably suspected' of being in the country illegally should be reported to the
authorities for possible deportation. Although Proposition 187 was struck down
by the courts, anti-immigrant sentiment remains, as a number of measures, including the denial of welfare benefits to non-citizens, shows. The rest of this
chapter explores the contemporary issues and arguments put forward by those
seeking to restrict immigration today and the responses of those who believe that
immigration is good for America.

The arguments for restricting, or, more accurately, reducing, the number of immigrants allowed to enter the United States fall broadly into three categories: environmental, economic and cultural. Restrictionists have long used economic and cultural arguments; environmental ones, however, are relatively modern. It is to these we turn first.

THE IMMIGRATION DEBATE: ENVIRONMENTAL ARGUMENTS

The number of, and membership in, American environmental groups, increased rapidly in the 1960s and 1970s. Unsurprisingly they were mainly concerned with protecting wildlife and its habitat; they worried that industrialization and the increasing use of agricultural pesticides would destroy delicate ecosystems. Some environmentalists also began to make the connection between environmental degradation and population growth. They argued that finite natural resources – such as mineral deposits, oil, water and land – were threatened by rapid economic and population growth.

In response to these concerns, some, but by no means all, environmentalists began to argue that the United States had to control its population growth. One way this could be achieved, they suggested, was by reducing the birth rate (by changing expectations about family size or by widening access to contraception and abortion). Others suggested that immigration should be restricted; after all, by their estimates, it accounted for about 40 per cent of the country's population increase.[3] However, most mainstream environmental groups, even those whose *raison d'être* was population control, were reluctant to promulgate and endorse an anti-immigrant message. Many, probably most, environmentalists consider themselves liberal on a range of issues, yet immigration control was and is widely regarded as a conservative, right-wing, even racist position.

Some environmentalists broke away from the mainstream movement, however, and formed their own groups to push the restrictionist message. The most important group today is the Federation for American Immigration Reform (FAIR). Led by the articulate and media-savvy Dan Stein, FAIR rejects accusations that it is a racist organization. It argues that its concern is with immigrant numbers, not immigrant type. How can this 'colour-blind' position be labelled racist? FAIR's critics make two points. First, because the vast majority of contemporary immigrants are 'people of colour', restricting immigration is one insidious way of maintaining white Americans' majority status. Second, FAIR receives funding from the Pioneer Fund, an organization its opponents believe is racist because it promotes white culture and identity.[4] Critics of the environmental restrictionists also contest the argument that the United States is overpopulated. This seems justified. In 1998 the population density was 73.5 persons per square mile, compared with, for example, 627.3 in the United Kingdom and 15,793.3 in Hong Kong![5]

Ultimately the environmental arguments in favour of restricting immigration have not been especially influential.[6] In part this is because the post-1995 Republican majority in Congress is more pro-business and less receptive to environmental concerns than its Democratic predecessors. There is also the division within the environmental movement over the politically charged issue of population control. While the mainstream environmental organizations (such as Friends of the Earth, the Audubon Society and the Sierra Club) refuse to endorse restrictionist arguments, the environmentalist message remains confused and disunited, and the costs and benefits for legislators ignoring it remain limited. Also, the population 'time bomb' message of doom promulgated by environmental restrictionists looks overly alarmist, given the progress the environmental movement has made in creating safe wildlife habitats, cleaning up lakes and rivers and reducing air pollution. Finally, on an academic level, research into the environmental impact of immigration is inconclusive. Those who argue that an increased population must necessarily increase the consumption of resources and the amount of waste society produces are countered by those who argue that 'immigration increases the base of technical knowledge. That speeds the current positive trends in both greater availability of natural resources and cleaner air and water'.[7]

While the environmental arguments alone have had little impact politically, they are often promulgated by anti-immigrant groups who use them in conjunction with economic and cultural arguments. In this sense, the 'package' of arguments against immigration has increased in size. It is to the economic part of the package that we now turn.

THE IMMIGRATION DEBATE: ECONOMIC ARGUMENTS

The arguments surrounding the economic effects of immigration are complex and contested, but they can be simplified somewhat by breaking them down into three interconnected subcategories: taxes, growth, and jobs and wages.

At the heart of the restrictionists' argument regarding jobs lies the premise that immigrants take the jobs of the native population. In particular, because they are often ill educated and lack English-language skills and thus do low-paid, unskilled work, immigrants take the jobs of America's least skilled and most vulnerable workers – or they at least increase competition for such jobs and thus drive wages down. Moreover they do so at a time when there is no shortage of native-born unskilled workers. The restrictionists supplement their jobs-and-wages argument with a poverty argument. Because immigrants drive down wages of the already poor, they produce an adverse, negative effect on the nation's income distribution. In other words, the poor get poorer.

Immigration also has a negative effect on the United States' human capital resources and hence the flow of tax revenue, the restrictionists argue. Because immigrants are likely to be unskilled and uneducated, there is a greater chance that they will be unemployed and on welfare. Additional demands are also placed on the school system, which must educate immigrant children, including the provision of special and expensive bilingual education classes. Somebody must pay for these, and the burden falls on the native-born population in the form of increased taxes. Taken one stage further, increased taxes have a negative effect on economic production, therefore driving down further the standard of living of native-born Americans.

Not all the economic arguments focus on the low-skilled sector of the labour market. There is increasing concern about the effects that highly skilled immigrants have on jobs and wages, especially in Silicon Valley, where thousands of non-native computer programmers are employed. IT bosses argue that they need skilled foreign labour, much of it from India, because not enough Americans have the technical ability to fill all the highly specialized posts available. Their critics reply that the problem is not supply; foreign workers are employed because they are cheaper.

It is important to recognize that the above arguments are promulgated by some respected economists, such as Vernon Briggs junior at Cornell University and George Borjas at Harvard. Nor is Briggs against unskilled immigrants *per se*. He argues that the wave of unskilled workers entering the United States in the pre-1920 period suited the needs of the labour market. His position is that today's immigrants continue in the main to be low-skilled when the economy requires highly skilled workers. He also argues that the costs of today's immigration fall unfairly on African Americans because they are most likely to be competing with the new immigrants for the low-skilled jobs. Using similar reasoning, Roy Beck has suggested that in the south-west – where many legal and illegal immigrants, especially Mexican ones, settle – the group most likely to be affected is Mexican Americans. Interestingly, Borjas has suggested that the group most likely to suffer economically is the immigrants themselves. This is because they get stuck in low-paying jobs with little chance of progress. One result is the creation of a semi-permanent underclass, which in turn burdens the taxpayer.

None of these anti-immigration arguments should be considered racist. In fact, part of their attraction results from the contention that the consequences/costs of immigration fall mostly on the already disadvantaged. These sober-minded economic assessments do not, however, stop pro-immigration activists suggesting that their authors are mean-spirited, even racist. This is because the immigration debate is highly charged politically, and rational debate, even in the academy, is difficult to achieve. Pro-immigration activists are also suspicious of the above arguments because of the way in which the anti-immigration forces use them. For example, in his highly controversial book *Alien Nation* the journalist Peter Brimelow utilizes the economists' arguments in a pseudo-rational attempt to argue for restricting 'Third World' immigration, while defending white Anglo-Saxon immigration. (Interestingly, he is a white Englishman living in New York.)

Unsurprisingly, proponents of immigration reject the economic arguments outlined above. Instead, they argue that immigrants usually do jobs that Americans are unwilling to do – for example, as dishwashers, hotel maids and porters, janitors, gardeners and fruit pickers, among other low-paid, often menial, repetitive and unpleasant jobs. They also argue that immigrants fill labour market shortages at the highly skilled level. For instance, in addition to the example of computer programmers noted above, they point to the large numbers of immigrant nurses and doctors performing crucial tasks in inner-city hospitals where posts might go unfilled were it not for immigrant labour. Furthermore, supporters of immigration suggest that immigrants create more jobs for natives than they take away. They may do so directly by employing native-born workers or indirectly by increasing both the demand for private and public services and the amount of money in circulation. Additionally, because they are prepared to accept lower wages, immigrants (especially illegal ones) have ensured the survival of many American industries – such as garment manufacturing in Los Angeles and New York – which would not be able to compete with producers in developing countries because of lower overhead costs there. Agriculture, and particularly fruit picking, is another example offered by supporters of immigration. Without cheap and mobile (again, often illegal) immigrant labour California farmers would not be able to sell their produce at competitive prices.

Proponents of immigration also challenge the claim that immigrants force up taxes. Because immigrants are more likely to be of working age than the native population, they contribute more to the tax base than they take away in pensions, for example. Furthermore, many immigrants arrive on the United States' shores already trained, often highly so. The American taxpayer effectively gets an educated and trained individual without having to shoulder the cost; the unfortunate country that educated the immigrant bears the cost and receives none of the benefits. For example, 'One estimate is that $500 million was saved by the prior education and training of physicians, engineers, and others . . . in 1971.'[8]

Proponents of immigration also suggest that immigrants act as a rejuvenating force in the inner cities. The trend of 'white flight' to suburbia, most would agree, causes serious problems for the inner cities. It curtails employment opportunities for those who remain (often African Americans), reduces the tax base, with a corrosive effect on schools, results in loss of services and helps create poverty-stricken ghettoes with their attendant social pathologies. Immigration proponents argue that immigrants rejuvenate the inner cities and thus help alleviate some of these problems. They add to, or at least slow the shrinking of, the city population, establish businesses, employ and provide labour, spend money, pay taxes and generally give the local economy a much needed boost. This in turn helps revitalize the local community.

In sum, many argue that immigration increases prosperity while others argue that it does not. At the micro-level both positions can be shown to be right. For example, even those in favour of liberalizing immigration policy admit that some native-born, low-paid, low-skilled workers may lose their jobs as a result of competition from immigrants, especially illegal ones. And even restrictionists concede that immigrants who set up businesses help rejuvenate inner cities and provide employment opportunities for others. At the macro-level – 'Does immigration benefit the United States as a whole?' – no conclusive judgement can be made. In part this is because the costs and benefits are just very difficult to measure. For example, while Briggs claims that 'it is . . . the least skilled segment of the labour force . . . who are bearing the burnt of the direct job competition with immigrant workers', he admits on the very next page that 'the issue of job competition . . . is the hardest to prove . . . developing a methodology to measure displacement has proven to be an insurmountable feat'.[9] It is also very difficult to determine whether economic growth should be attributed to immigration, increased competition, technological improvements or a combination of some or all of these factors.

Another part of the problem is that there is disagreement about what measures should be used: should we look at GNP, *per capita* GNP or *per capita* GNP of native-born people alone? Most economists agree that GNP itself is too simplistic a measure because it will automatically increase if the work force grows by just one person/immigrant. It tells us nothing about increases in efficiency or productivity or the distribution of resources. However, it is undoubtedly the case that America's military and diplomatic power and its cultural significance in the world are largely a product of its economic might. Regardless of the efficiency or distribution questions at home, the United States would not enjoy such might without its large population, which itself is in part a product of liberal immigration policies over the years.

It is probably fair to say that a majority of economists believe that immigration is a good thing. It dovetails neatly with a belief in free markets: if resources, goods and services are utilized and distributed most efficiently in a free market, it follows that labour also will. This belief finds its most articulate expression in the *Wall Street Journal*'s campaign for an amendment to the constitution: 'There shall be open borders.' While some economists' pro-immigration position may be founded on economic principles, it is less clear that it is also a product of their own or others' empirical scientific research. Some of the best brains in America's universities have tried to measure immigration's effects, but the dispute rages on. However, the pro-immigration position is also in part a belief that transcends purely economics-based arguments, whether theoretical or empirical. Even if it were shown conclusively that immigration had, for example, an overall negative effect on the economy, it does not follow that immigration should be restricted. A pro-immigration position is as likely to be founded on a personal political decision or a belief that immigration is good for cultural reasons. It is to the cultural arguments that we turn in the final section below.

THE IMMIGRATION DEBATE: CULTURAL ARGUMENTS

In the introductory section we saw how anti-immigrant campaigners in the nineteenth and early twentieth centuries argued that the 'new' wave of immigrants was less assimilable than previous ones. Many of these arguments were based on now unacceptable perceptions of the moral degeneracy and the physical and mental inferiority of the newcomers. Still, the assimilation debate rages on today, albeit in less race-specific terms. At the core of the debate are two interlinked questions: what does it mean to be an American, and who can be an American (and thus who should be allowed to immigrate)?

Restrictionists often posit one of two responses to these questions. (1) American culture is, at its core, white, English (or at least western European) and Protestant. Only people with these demographic characteristics should be allowed to immigrate, because only they will be able to assimilate or take on American ways and values. People without these characteristics will find it difficult or impossible to melt into American society. Their differences pose a threat to the established order, and their entry should therefore be curtailed. (2) Theoretically, anyone can become an American, whatever their religion, race, ethnicity or nationality.

However, they must be prepared to acculturate to American ways of doing things. This is generally understood to include subscribing to American ideals (believing in democracy, self-reliance, liberty, equality of opportunity and the rule of law) and learning and using the English language.

Only hard-line restrictionists are prepared to articulate the first contentious response, and until recently they included only those on the fringe of the political process. The publication of Peter Brimelow's *Alien Nation* – in which the hard-line position is repeated *ad nauseam* for some 300 pages – shocked many people because, although English, he is a member of the US establishment. (He has been a senior editor of *Forbes* and *National Review*.) The following quotations, all from *Alien Nation*, give a flavour of the racial animosity that underpins the arguments of the hard-liners

> [T]he American nation has always had a specific ethnic core. And that core has been white. [p. 10]

> [V]irtually all [today's] immigrants are racially distinct 'visible minorities' . . . from completely different, and arguably incompatible, cultural traditions. And, as we have seen, they are coming in such numbers that their impact on America is enormous – inevitably, within the foreseeable future, they will transform it. [p. 56]

> The American nation of 1965, nearly 90 percent white, was explicitly promised that the new immigration policy would not shift the country's racial balance. But it did . . . It is simply common sense that Americans have a legitimate interest in their country's racial balance. It is common sense that they have a right to insist that their government stop shifting it. Indeed, it seems to me that they have a right to insist it be shifted back. [p. 264]

Reading the above, it is easy to see why the first argument was rarely used: it relies on racially based conceptions about what America was, is and should be. However, while Brimelow's book created a great deal of controversy, it also highlights the changing nature of the immigration debate. Not many years ago, members of the establishment would rarely be heard expressing such views (although they may have held them in private). Today, as restrictionists have become bolder, they are more forthright (and perhaps more honest) in their public expressions against immigration. Still, for Brimelow's critics, his argument is simply summed up in one word: racist. To which he responds rather limply, 'I have indeed duly examined my own motives. And I am happy to report that they are pure.'[10]

Other hard-liners take a similar position, often focusing their attention on Mexicans and Arab Muslims. The latter are often associated with violence and terrorism, especially after the Gulf War and the 1993 bombing of the World Trade Center in New York, which was masterminded by a militant Islamic leader. The former attract attention in part because of the large number of Mexicans immigrating, both legally and illegally, each year. In part, though, it is also because of their colour, culture and language, which many restrictionists believe are incompatible with America's. Some of the arguments used against Mexican immigration are without question racist. Consider the following. Glenn Spencer, who heads an anti-immigrant pressure group called Voices of Citizens Together, believes:

> Mexico has declared war on the United States. It is purposefully sending drugs into our nation to destroy us. It is sending its people to occupy our land . . . The United States is being invaded by Mexico. Mexican gangs roam our streets. Mexican drugs destroy our children. Mexican politicians threaten White Americans with extinction.[11]

As with Brimelow, proponents of immigration have little difficulty labelling such outbursts as racist. The focus on one nationality as the source of all America's ills presents them with an easy target.

Less hard-line restrictionists reject Brimelow's argument that all new immigrants should demographically and culturally mirror 'white' America. Instead, they argue that immigrant numbers should be severely curtailed in order to facilitate a period of 'digestion' during which resident immigrants can be assimilated into American ways. They point out that immigration has always proceeded in waves, with large influxes followed by lulls as laws are tightened or events (such as war or depression) reduce the flow. They argue that there has been no lull in the post-1965 wave of immigration, but that one is now required. On its face, this argument appears sensible, and certainly not racist. Critics suggest, however, that it is actually an insidious argument. Because most contemporary immigrants are people of colour, curtailing their entry is actually an ostensibly race-neutral method of ensuring the political, demographic and cultural domination of the majority white population. The critics have history on their side. The Quota Acts of the 1920s did not specify that immigration from southern and eastern Europe should be curtailed. But, in basing each country's quota on the 1890 and 1910 censuses, when northern and western Europeans dominated the US population, legislators ensured the exclusion of southern and eastern Europeans by default. Immigration proponents, including some conservative commentators, have also pointed out that there is no need for an assimilist or digestive lull because the 'new' immigrants already subscribe to 'traditional' American values and pose no threat to the dominant culture. They are often deeply religious and family-oriented, and believe in getting ahead through hard work. Indeed, Francis Fukuyama, one of the United States' most famous academics, has pointed out that 'the real danger is not that [American] elites will become corrupted by the habits and practices of Third World immigrants, but rather that the immigrants will become corrupted by them.'[12]

In addition to imposing an immigration moratorium, restrictionists also believe that assimilation is aided by learning and speaking English. To this end, many favour designating English as America's official language. (It already is in many states, although this is usually more symbolic than effective.) Others are in favour of English-only laws, which would, for example, outlaw bilingual government publications and ballot papers in any language but English. More controversially, still others think that only English should be used in schools. At present, the individual states have a good deal of leeway in deciding how and in what language their pupils are taught. For example, until recently California's public schools practised what is known as bilingual education, meaning that children who had a poor or no command of English would be taught (maths, science, whatever) in their native tongue, usually Spanish. In addition to these lessons they would also receive English-language instruction. The aim was to ensure that they did not miss out on vital aspects of the curriculum, while improving their English to a level at which they could join other students in 'normal' classes. Many fear that bilingual instruction does nothing to encourage and facilitate the assimilation of immigrants into mainstream society. While they continue to be taught in their native tongue there is little incentive to learn English and, by association, American values and *mores*. The argument is that bilingual teaching could lead to the 'Babelization' of America, or to the growth of an ethnically and politically distinct group in society: only with a common language and culture can an ethnically heterogeneous population bond into a strong, homogenous society, they say.

Partly in response to these concerns, California voters passed Proposition 227 in 1998, a direct democracy initiative that abolished bilingual education in the state's schools. All non-English-speaking students now receive one year's intensive English-language instruction (and no teaching in their native tongue) before they are moved into mainstream classes with other English-speakers to continue their 'normal' education. The man behind the initiative was Ron Unz, a wealthy businessman and political maverick. While in no way could Unz be said to be a hard-line restrictionist, it is certainly the case that many supported his initiative.[13] Equally, though, many 'people of colour', including about 40 per cent of California Latinos, also supported it. Thus, while those in favour of bilingual education, such as the Mexican American Legal Defense Fund and the California Teachers' Association, try to label those who oppose it as racist, their charge simply cannot be sustained, or at least it cannot be sustained in all cases. Indeed, many proponents of immigration oppose bilingual education, although for different reasons than the restrictionists. Some worry that bilingual education 'promotes segregation more than it does integration'.[14] Others are less concerned about creating an integrated society and a homogenous culture than with ensuring that all students have an equal chance to succeed. They worry that success is not possible without a good command of English. One further factor confusing the bilingual debate is that the research into its effectiveness is inconclusive. As with the debates over the environmental and economic impact of immigration, both those pro and those anti bilingual education use empirical studies to support their view. One reason for the conflicting research results is that there are so many different types of bilingual education in operation across different states – some bad, some good, but most of mixed quality.

Proponents of bilingual education argue that the supposed English-language crisis is simply a myth. They point out that today's immigrants are much more likely to use and learn English than early generations of immigrants and that there are long waiting lists for English-language classes. Furthermore, considering the population is over 275 million, 6 million with limited English proficiency hardly constitute a significant figure.

Or to put it another way: more than 97 percent of Americans speak English well, a level of linguistic homogeneity unsurpassed by any other large nation in history. . . . Considered strictly in the light of the actualities, then, English-only is an irrelevant provocation. It is a bad cure for an imaginary disease, and moreover, one that encourages an unseemly hypochondria about the health of the dominant language and culture. . . . The irony of all this is that there was never a culture or a language so little in need of official support . . . and this at the very moment of the triumph of English as a world language of unprecedented currency.[15]

CONCLUSION

Just as there are many reasons for opposing bilingual education, some permissible, others not, there are many reasons for opposing immigration, not all of them racially suspect. Should not a nation state have the right to control its borders, to determine who and how many it should and should not admit, to prevent the entry of those it considers undesirable or deleterious to its health? Few would disagree with these sentiments in a rational moment. But the cultural debate is rarely rational, hardly considered and never calm. In fact the whole immigration issue is highly charged politically, and it is so because what is at stake is more than just a question of how many immigrants the United States should admit. It goes to the heart of the question about what sort of country America should be, and also what sort of people Americans should be. Perhaps more than any other people, Americans are concerned and fascinated by these questions; and, so long as they are, immigration will continue to be an issue that taxes their minds and arouses their passions.

NOTES

1   US Bureau of the Census, *Statistical Abstract of the United States, 1999*, 119th edition (Washington DC, US Bureau of the Census, 1999), tables 59 and 60, p. 56.
2   Quoted in David M. Reimers, *Unwelcome Strangers: American Identity and the Turn against Immigration* (New York, Columbia University Press, 1998), p. 16.
3   As late as 1790, around the time the United States became a nation, its population was under 4 million. At the end of the nineteenth century it was 76 million. Estimates put the population as of 22 August 2001 at 285 million. Middle-series projections estimate it will reach nearly 400 million by 2050. See Bureau of the Census, *Statistical Abstract of the United States, 1999*, pp. 8–9. For a day-by-day estimate of the US population size visit the US Census Bureau's home page at http://www.census.gov.
4   For a scathing critique of the Pioneer Fund and the research it funds see Adam Miller, 'Academia's dirty secret: professors of hate', *Rolling Stone*, 20 October 1994, pp. 106–14.
5   Statistics from the *Encyclopaedia Britannica*, available on line at http://www.britannica.com.
6   See Reimers, *Unwelcome Strangers*, chapter 3.
7   Julian Simon, quoted in Reimers, *Unwelcome Strangers*, p. 60.

8   Thomas Muller, 'The immigrant contribution to the revitalization of cities', in Stephen Steinberg (ed.), *Race and Ethnicity in the United States: Issues and Debates* (Oxford, Blackwell, 2000), p. 241.

9   Vernon M. Briggs junior, 'Immigration policy and the US economy: an institutional perspective', in Steinberg, *Race and Ethnicity in the United States*, pp. 260–1.

10 Peter Brimelow, *Alien Nation: Common Sense about America's Immigration Disaster* (New York, Random House, 1995), p. 11.

11 Quoted in Reimers, *Unwelcome Strangers*, p. 113.

12 Quoted in Reimers, *Unwelcome Strangers*, p. 114.

13 For example, Unz, although a Republican, came out strongly against Proposition 187 in 1994.

14 Arthur Schlesinger, quoted in Reimers, *Unwelcome Strangers*, p. 126.

15 Geoffrey Nunberg, 'Lingo jingo: English-only and the new nativism', in Steinberg, *Race and Ethnicity in the United States*, pp. 297, 299 and 303.

10 Affirmative Action: the Continuing Dilemma?

- ■ THE HISTORY OF AFFIRMATIVE ACTION
- ■ THE CASE FOR AFFIRMATIVE ACTION
- ■ THE CASE AGAINST AFFIRMATIVE ACTION
- ■ CLASS-BASED AFFIRMATIVE ACTION?
- ■ CONCLUSION

Affirmative action is a simple idea. African Americans have suffered several hundred years of racism. While it is no longer officially sanctioned, the legacy of racism still permeates American society. It can be witnessed, for example, in African Americans' high rates of unemployment, poverty and incarceration, and in inequalities of opportunity generally. One remedy is to offer a 'helping hand' to African Americans. Affirmative action, supporters argue, addresses racism's legacy of modern-day discrimination by providing a 'level playing field' in the 'race of life'. Somewhere along the way, however, this benign and simple idea has become one of the most contentious public policy questions in the United States. This chapter explains how it came to be, and examines the arguments of affirmative action's supporters and opponents. It then looks at some alternatives to race-based affirmative action programmes and discusses what the future may hold. Affirmative action has its roots in the history of the African American people. It is not a happy history, but it is one that needs to be told to make sense of affirmative action as an idea, a policy programme and a controversial issue in American politics and society. It is here that we begin.

THE HISTORY OF AFFIRMATIVE ACTION

BACKGROUND

African Americans are the only group of people to come to the United States involuntarily. Traders first imported slaves in the seventeenth century to fill the labour shortages of the English colonists. The slave trade was a very profitable business, and not only for American traders. The ports of Bristol and Liverpool, for example, grew rich in part on its unsavoury back. Despite its profitability, slavery was controversial even then. During the constitutional convention in Philadelphia in 1787 the slave states refused to allow slavery to be outlawed and they fought hard against restrictions on the trade. While the founding fathers representing the non-slave states wanted to outlaw slavery, being pragmatists they recognized that the successful ratification of the constitution required the assent of the slave states. Thus the 'Great Compromise' was struck. In its final form the constitution did not outlaw slavery and declared that Congress could not prohibit the importation of slaves before 1808, by which time 650,000 had been brought to American shores. Also, for purposes of a state's representation in the House, slaves were counted as three-fifths of a person, although they were not permitted to vote, of course.

Through the early nineteenth century, slavery remained a controversial issue. Congress's Missouri Compromise of 1820, which made slavery illegal north of the 36th parallel, failed to resolve the issue. When the US Supreme Court ruled the compromise unconstitutional in its infamous *Dred Scott* v. *Sandford* decision of 1857 the ground was prepared for civil war. In the same decision the Court established that slaves were property, and that no black person could be a citizen of the United States, even if s/he was born and lived in a non-slave state. *Scott* precipitated the onset of the Civil War. After the Republican and northern victory, Congress and the states passed the Civil War amendments to overturn *Scott*. The Thirteenth, of 1865, abolished slavery; the Fourteenth, of 1868, established birthright citizenship (automatically making all persons born in the United States American citizens) and prohibited the states from denying citizens due process and the equal protection of the law. Finally, the Fifteenth, of 1870, prohibited the states from denying citizens the right to vote because of their race or previous slavery.

Slavery was soon replaced, however, by a new form of oppression in the south: segregation. Jim Crow laws, granting segregation legal recognition, were given a constitutional boost by the Supreme Court's 1896 decision in *Plessy* v. *Ferguson*. Giving the *de jure* green light to segregation, the Court ruled that separate facilities for whites and blacks were permissible so long as the facilities were 'equal'. Predictably the southern states ignored the references to the 'equal' part of *Plessy* and instead used the decision to justify separate facilities.

The south remained segregated though to the 1960s. African Americans were second-class citizens, discriminated against at every turn. They drank from different water fountains, ate at different lunch counters, went to different schools, worked in menial jobs and lived in their own part of town. Not until *Brown* v. *Board of Education* in 1954 did the Supreme Court say what everybody knew: separate facilities were 'inherently unequal' and therefore unconstitutional. The next year the Court ordered local authorities to 'make a prompt and reasonable start' and district courts to 'proceed with all deliberate speed' towards desegregation. The Court's pronouncements were given additional weight by Congress's passage of the Civil Rights Act in 1964.[1] Using the power of the purse to good effect, Title VI of the Act denied federal monies to any organization, individual or policy programme practising racial discrimination. In addition, the Voting Rights Act of 1965 made illegal all laws denying (black) persons equal access to the ballot – such as literacy tests and poll taxes.

IMPLEMENTATION

Around the same time as Congress began to use its purse strings to outlaw discrimination, others began to realize that ending discrimination was simply not enough to eradicate the effects of several hundred years of racism. No high-profile individual articulated this more eloquently than President Johnson himself. In his famous June 1965 speech at Howard University he claimed that:

> Freedom is not enough. You do not wipe away the scars of centuries by saying: Now you are free to go where you want, do as you desire, choose the leaders you please. You do not take a person who, for years, has been hobbled by chains and liberate him, bring him to the starting line and then say, 'You are free to compete with all the others,' and still justly believe that you have been completely fair. We seek not just freedom but opportunity – not just equality as a right and a theory but equality as a fact and as a result. . . . Thus it is not enough just to open the gates of opportunity. All our citizens must have the ability to walk through those gates.[2]

Johnson's acknowledgement that outlawing discrimination would not result in equal opportunities for African Americans found its first policy expression in his Philadelphia Plan. The plan would have required the construction industry to employ certain numbers of black workers. As it stood, no African Americans were hired because the unions had negotiated closed-shop 'union members only' deals with the employers. Blacks were, in turn, refused union membership. This was partly due to the overt racism of the white working class, but it was also a way to keep the supply of workers down and wages high. Whatever the reasons, the effect was to prevent black workers accessing well paid jobs in the building trade.

The plan, however, was never put into effect by the Johnson administration. It appeared at the time that Johnson's decision not to seek re-election and the defeat of the Democrat Hubert Humphrey by the Republican Richard Nixon would result in the plan's death. To many people's surprise it did not. Indeed, it is 'one of the great ironies of racial politics in the post-civil rights era . . . that the Philadelphia Plan was implemented by Republicans over the opposition of the famed "liberal coalition" and without notable support from the civil rights establishment'.[3] Some scholars have attempted to explain this puzzle by suggesting that Nixon hoped the implementation of the plan would drive a wedge into the progressive Democratic coalition of labour unions and civil rights movement, thus splitting the powerful force of blacks and labour.[4] Others have suggested that its implementation was Nixon's crisis-management response to the sometimes violent, always tense demonstrations of 1969 in which African Americans protested at their exclusion from construction industry jobs. Whatever the original reasons for its implementation, the scope of the plan was soon expanded when the Department of Labor extended its reach to all federal contractors and higher education establishments. At this point the Nixon administration cooled towards the whole idea of affirmative action quotas.[5]

RETRENCHMENT

Retrenchment on affirmative action began almost as soon as the first programmes were implemented. Nixon's attacks led the way. More significant, however, was the Supreme Court's intervention in 1978. Under its affirmative-action programme, the medical school of the University of California at Davis had reserved sixteen of its 100 places for racial minority groups (African Americans, Latinos, Asians and Native Americans). A legal challenge to this 'quota' of sixteen began in 1974 and finally reached the Court four years later. Justice Powell's deciding opinion in *Regents of the University of California* v. *Bakke* ruled the quota unconstitutional. He interpreted Title VI of the 1964 Civil Rights Act to mean that 'race cannot be the basis of excluding anyone from participation in a federally funded program'. Because they set aside a fixed number of places based solely on race, quotas exclude others from competing for those places solely because of their race. Powell, however, did *not* rule affirmative action unconstitutional. He said that race could be considered *a* factor in the admissions process (but not the sole factor) so long as the university aimed to create a 'diverse student body'. Diversity was considered desirable because it facilitates the 'robust exchange of ideas', which is a valid First Amendment interest.[6] In short, what the Court did in this complex opinion was (1) abandon quotas but not affirmative action and (2) abandon the simple idea upon which affirmative action was founded. The remedying of past injustice was replaced by a new idea: encouraging diversity.

Since *Bakke* retrenchment has continued. While the Supreme Court continues to restrict the use of affirmative action programmes, it has not yet ruled them unconstitutional. Federal and state governments, schools and colleges, and private and public organizations have all joined the Court in backing away from affirmative action programmes.

President Clinton's 'don't end it, mend it' pledge and his constant reminders that he was against quotas reinforced in people's minds the practical problems inherent in affirmative action. In June 1995 California Governor Pete Wilson issued executive order W-124-95 to 'End Preferential Treatment and to Promote Individual Opportunity based on Merit'; in July 1995 the University of California Board of Regents complied with Wilson's order by adopting resolution SP-1, 'Policy ensuring Equal Treatment – Admissions'. Effective from 1 January 1997, America's premier state university ruled it would 'not use race, religion, sex, color, ethnicity, or national origin' in its admission procedures. In the same year California voters approved by 56 per cent to 44 per cent Proposition 209, a direct democracy initiative that outlawed affirmative action in all state and local government contracts and in all the state's higher education establishments. In 1996 the US Fifth Circuit of Appeals ruled in *Hopwood* v. *Texas* that the University of Texas 'may not use race as a factor in law school admissions'. In other words, it banned preferences, just as the Supreme Court had outlawed quotas before it. By declining to review this case the Court has effectively accepted the constitutionality of Proposition 209.

While it is undoubtedly the case that affirmative action programmes have been significantly cut back over the past two decades, this does not mean that the opponents have won the battle. In fact the success of affirmative action's opponents has led affirmative action's supporters to fight their corner more doggedly than ever. We will examine the arguments of both below and, where possible, attempt to make some judgements about their 'truth' or quality.

THE CASE FOR AFFIRMATIVE ACTION

[Despite the existence of some race and gender preferences] white men make up 33 percent of the population. They are: 85 percent of tenured professors; 85 percent of partners in law firms; 80 percent of the US House of Representatives; 90 percent of the US Senate; 95 percent of all the Fortune 500 CEOs; 97 percent of all school superintendents; 99.9 per cent of athletic team owners; and 100 percent of all US presidents.[7]

The United States needs affirmative action today for exactly the same reasons it was first introduced in the 1960s: non-whites face significant barriers to entry in a range of professions and walks of life because of institutional racism. African Americans, especially, will not be able to compete equitably with fellow Americans until they can take advantage of affirmative action measures. The aim of affirmative action is not, as some critics claim, to privilege minorities over the majority. Nor is affirmation action 'reverse discrimination'. It actually seeks to create a colour-blind society, but it recognizes that in the short run programmes must be put in place that temporarily privilege minorities. Only that way can all groups in society enjoy equality of opportunity. Only then can America claim to be a colour-blind society. In the United States today, as the above quotation from Elizabeth Dole – no liberal, for sure – demonstrates, modern society discriminates *in favour* of white males on a daily basis. It is they who are privileged by positive discrimination, not minorities. But they seek to maintain their privileged position in society by denying to others the opportunity to fulfil their potential. All that supporters of affirmative action ask is that minorities and women are also given this opportunity.

Opponents of affirmative action respond that it has served its purpose. They argue that opinion polls show, and people's actions demonstrate, that racism is no longer a problem in the United States. There is thus no need to privilege certain minority groups. They point to the success of Asian Americans, who are the largest group at California's most prestigious universities and who out-perform and out-earn whites. If they can make it, so can other minority groups. Supporters of affirmative action respond that most Asian Americans are relatively recent arrivals who have not suffered hundreds of years of discrimination. The data, they say, show that African Americans and Latinos suffer from the remnants of historical oppression. For example, median income for whites in 1997 was nearly $47,000. For blacks and Latinos it was just $28,000. Just 8.6 per cent of whites live below the poverty line, compared with 26.5 per cent of blacks and 27.1 per cent of Latinos. Whites are not just richer, they're better educated too. In 1998 27.3 per cent of white males over the age of twenty-five had graduated from college, compared with 13.9 per cent of black males and just 11.1 per cent of Latino males.[8] Perhaps we should not be too surprised with these data, given the *de facto* racial segregation of most schools. White kids' schools in the suburbs are relatively well funded, especially compared with the predominantly black schools in the inner cities.[9]

Finally, say proponents of affirmative action, the United States is a multicultural society. Mass immigration in the twentieth century from all round the world has created a society that demographically is no longer predominantly white or Protestant. However, white Protestants remain economically and politically dominant. Their grip on power enables them to impose on other races and cultures a view of the world that they may not share, and it allows them to fight off challenges to their hegemonic position. Affirmative action programmes encourage other races and cultures to find their 'voice', help create a vigorous public debate about what type of nation America should be, and help dominated groups challenge the dominators. The programmes deliver a much-needed kick to a sluggish and unrepresentative polity, and encourage the cultural diversity lacking in much of American life.

THE CASE AGAINST AFFIRMATIVE ACTION

In the 1960s the Reverend Martin Luther King junior famously outlined his vision of a society where men would be judged not by the colour of their skin but by the content of their character. Affirmative action, because it takes account of, even classifies people by, the colour of their skin, can never produce the colour-blind society that the great civil rights leader envisaged. Only the end of racial preferences can do so. What in effect affirmative action does is heighten people's awareness of difference and by so doing actually aggravates racism and sexism. As an issue it exploits people's base, more selfish instincts. It is thus politically divisive and socially destructive.

A further dimension to the critique of affirmative action relates to its effects on the American values of capitalism, freedom and choice. Firms should be allowed to employ workers best suited to the job. Universities should be able to admit the brightest and best students. Government agencies should be permitted to contract with firms offering the most competitive tender. These are the principles on which America was founded and which made America great. Any deviation from these norms will undermine the efficiency of the market. This threatens not only America's dominant economic, political and military place in the world but also the very fabric of its meritocratic society. America is a country where individuals can fulfil their potential and where individuals rise to the top because of their talents, not because of their class, race or gender. Extremes of wealth exist, admittedly, but Americans do not strive for equality of outcome. Equalities of opportunity and esteem ensure that inequalities of condition are justified. Affirmative action will only stifle America's competitive edge as universities admit second-rate candidates, firms employ second-rate workers and government agencies award contracts to featherbedded and inefficient companies.

Related is the argument that affirmative action cares nothing for the individual, only groups. Opponents of affirmative action argue that this is deeply un-American. The United States is a country built on the liberty of the individual, and individual liberty is a core belief that should not be infringed lightly. Consider the following real-world example. The Boalt School of Law at UC Berkeley for many years offered places to Latino, African American and Native American students with lower SAT scores than were required of white and Asian students. Thus white and Asian students with demonstrably higher SAT scores were denied a place in the school, even though they were clearly not associated with any form of racism, past or present.[10] They were being discriminated against because of their colour. Surely that must be wrong? But the zero-sum game that is affirmative action ensures that, when a university place or a job is offered to a minority because they are a minority, someone better or equally qualified is denied that opening.

Another argument often used in tandem with the above is that affirmative action actually benefits already privileged members of minority groups. It is not African Americans from inner-city ghettoes who are selected for the prestigious universities but the children of the affluent black middle class who have never, or only very rarely, been the victims of racism themselves. Other beneficiaries include middle-class females and the children of other better-off and well educated minorities. Moreover, these children of privilege are preferenced over poor white males who have never benefited from the resource advantages of some of their minority peers.

At issue here is the question of who exactly can and should be able to access affirmative action programmes. To qualify for entry, minority or female status is usually the key, not demonstrable past discrimination. In part this is a result of the Supreme Court's *Bakke* decision that privileged diversity as a desired goal and downgraded previous injustice. In part, though, it is also a result of the practicalities of policy implementation. How is a programme to distinguish between the oppressed and non-oppressed? How do you judge and make distinctions between various levels of oppression? Does an African American woman trump an African American man, for example? What if we throw sexuality and disability into the pot? The combinations are frighteningly complex. The bureaucratic solution has been to treat all minorities equally, but that means privileging those who have never suffered discrimination. It also means including recent immigrants, even though they came to the United States willingly and have suffered no discrimination. Again, the justification for their inclusion is the advancement of 'diversity'.

The move from injustice to diversity has alienated many liberal supporters of affirmative action. While they recognized the logic of its early incarnations, contemporary affirmation action, in their eyes, has become yet another government programme where different groups fight for a slice of the pie even when its moral *raison d'être* no longer exists. The inequity of the process – where the well educated daughter of a rich black college professor living in the suburbs trumps the uneducated white son of a jobless single female subsisting in the trailer park – riles them. Race and class clashed, and race won. Liberals also worry about the political consequences of affirmative action. Supporters of affirmative action complain that Republicans and conservatives use it to divide and rule. There is little question that this has been an effective strategy. Many white blue-collar workers, antagonized by the Democrats' close association with affirmative action specifically and minority groups generally, have moved to the right politically. And these 'Reagan Democrats', as they are still sometimes called, form a significant voting bloc. Some liberals have made the calculation that the fight for affirmative action is simply not worth it politically. Other liberals, however, are not completely disheartened. For the abandonment of race- and gender-based affirmative action in California and the retrenchment occurring in the rest of the United States has possibly opened up the opportunity for a new form of affirmative action.

Class-based Affirmative Action?

There is little question that race-based affirmative action programmes are controversial. This has led some advocates of affirmative action to consider instead class-based programmes. If the same ends can be achieved through a less divisive process, doesn't it make sense to follow that route? What are these programmes, and do they work? Class-based affirmative action programmes would, as their name suggests, give preferential treatment to poor Americans, including poor whites previously excluded from race-based programmes. However, because many African Americans are poor – about a quarter live below the poverty line[11] – affirmative action programmes that target the poor directly will thus target many blacks indirectly. In this way the truly underprivileged African Americans receive a helping hand, and so do poor whites. And both need it. The data show that poor whites and poor blacks perform much worse than rich whites and rich blacks in SATs, for example. Proponents point out that Martin Luther King junior himself recognized the advantages of this approach in his 1964 book *Why we can't Wait*, in which he suggested a 'Bill of Rights for the Disadvantaged'. King argued that the approach was equitable and fair: 'It is a simple matter of justice that America, in dealing creatively with the task of raising the Negro from backwardness, should also be rescuing a large stratum of the forgotten white poor.'[12] And he recognized that the approach made good political sense. While racial preferences divide white and black, class-based preferences, he thought, could form the basis of a radical and sizeable multi-racial coalition.

A class-based programme, then, appears to solve all the liberal objections to race-based affirmative action programmes and even some of the conservative ones. Indeed, partly for these reasons, and partly because of Proposition 209, class-based programmes have replaced race-based ones in some California universities. However, closer analysis suggests that this 'solution' is not without its problems. On a practical level, because the pool of poor whites is much larger than the pool of poor blacks,[13] a class-based programme would benefit many more whites than blacks. In short, while under race-based programmes all African Americans are eligible, under class-based ones only around a quarter would be. And they would be competing against a very large pool of poor whites. Moreover, even controlling for class, African Americans still do less well in SATs, for example, than do whites. Put simply, poor blacks do worse than poor whites, and they do so because class and race are both causes of educational disadvantage. While African Americans thus face a double whammy – class and race – only one is considered a mitigating factor. But if class-based affirmative action is permissible, then why not race-based affirmative action too? It makes no sense to privilege class and not race. Both should be used, say some scholars, perhaps with justification.[14]

CONCLUSION

When judging a public policy, bureaucrats, academics and commentators always ask, 'Has it been a success?' The question is a difficult one to answer, whatever the programme. For affirmative action it is perhaps more difficult to answer than most. This is partly because it was not introduced as a coherent, cogent legislative programme. Instead, it was developed in a piecemeal fashion by various bureaucracies and public and private organisations. It differs in each state, and sometimes by county or city within a state, and it can differ between organizations even within the same city, for example. Affirmative action has also changed over time. The original aim was to provide a helping hand to address the historical injustices suffered by African Americans. Then other groups became eligible, such as women, the disabled, Latinos, Asians and Native Americans. Soon encouraging diversity became the main aim, largely replacing the earlier emphasis on positive discrimination.

All these factors hinder a straightforward but carefully weighted analysis of affirmative action's success. At least in part as a response to these difficulties, Arthur Schlesinger has proposed that it should be the participants in affirmative action (most notably African Americans) who decide whether it works or not. By this measure the programmes have had some successes. African Americans are more supportive of affirmative action than are white Americans. And, while many African Americans are still poor, it is unquestionably the case that the economic plight of black Americans has eased since the introduction of affirmative action. Also no one can dispute the existence of a sizeable and successful black middle class. It is difficult, however, to make clear causal links between affirmative action and such successes. Perhaps they are the result of Americans' changing attitudes on racial questions, of laws outlawing racism in the workplace, or of the end of *de jure* segregation in the nation's schools.

Moreover, even if affirmative action has demonstrably aided some minority groups, what have been the longer-term costs? The backlash against affirmative action and the ill will it engenders have done much to harm race relations. In the long run such hostility may do more to harm minorities' progress than the alleged benefits resulting from affirmative action. These considerations have led many liberals to abandon their support for affirmative action, at least in its race-based form. Yet clearly the class-based alternative is not wholly satisfactory, given the complex relationship between class and race. As diehard supporters point out, if affirmative action is defensible on class grounds, then it is so on race grounds too. The principle in both cases is the same, they say. And they are right. The conflict on affirmative action is actually not as simple as a conservative–liberal battle. Within the liberal camp a battle rages between those who cling to the core principles of race-based affirmative action and those who have abandoned them as too costly politically. And conservatives, recognizing full well a political opportunity when they see it, do everything in their power to stir the hornets' nest. It is little surprise, then, that affirmative action continues to be one of the most controversial and divisive policy issues in the United States today.

NOTES

1 It is unlikely that the Act would have passed had it not been for the sympathy engendered by the death of President Kennedy *and* the supreme political skill of his successor, Lyndon Johnson.

2 Quoted by Stephen Steinberg, 'Two steps forward and one step backward', p. 4, and 'The liberal retreat from race', p. 40, in Stephen Steinberg (ed.), *Race and Ethnicity in the United States: Issues and Debates* (Oxford, Blackwell, 2000).

3 Stephen Steinberg, 'Occupational apartheid and the origins of affirmative action', in Steinberg (ed.), *Race and Ethnicity in the United States*, p. 69.

4 Troy Duster, 'Individual fairness, group preferences, and the California strategy', in Robert Post and Michael Rogin (eds), *Race and Representation: Affirmative Action* (New York, Zone Books, 1998), p. 111.

5 Steinberg, 'Occupational apartheid', pp. 69–71.

6 Robert Post, 'Introduction: after *Bakke*', in Post and Rogin (eds), *Race and Representation*.

7 Elizabeth Dole, 'Glass Ceiling Commission Report', in Michael B. Preston and James S. Lai, 'The symbolic politics of affirmative action', in Michael B. Preston, Bruce E. Cain and Sandra Bass (eds), *Racial and Ethnic Politics in California*, II (Berkeley CA, IGS Press, 1988), pp. 181–2.

8 Harold W. Stanley and Richard G. Niemi, *Vital Statistics on American Politics, 1999–2000* (Washington DC, CQ Press, 2000), table 10.5.

9 In the United States schools have historically been funded mainly by local taxes. Therefore the more affluent the catchment area the more affluent the school.

10 See Duster, 'Individual fairness', for a convincing argument about why groups matter.

11 Stanley and Niemi, *Vital Statistics on American Politics*, table 10.5.

12 Quoted in Richard D. Kahlenberg, 'The case for class-based affirmative action', in Steinberg (ed.), *Race and Ethnicity in the United States*, p. 86.

13 Even though 26.5 per cent of African Americans and 27.1 per cent of Hispanics are poor compared with 8.6 per cent of (non-Hispanic) whites, whites constitute 46.4 per cent of all poor people, blacks 25.6 per cent and Hispanics 23.4 per cent. Stanley and Niemi, *Vital Statistics on American Politics*, table 10.5.

14 See, for example, Amy Gutmann, 'Should public policy be class conscious rather than color conscious?', in Steinberg, *Race and Ethnicity in the United States*.

11 The Politics of Health Care: Anxiety amid Plenty

- ■ SELF-RELIANCE, HEALTH CARE AND PUBLIC EXPECTATIONS
- ■ THE FAILURE OF THE CLINTON HEALTH CARE PLAN
- ■ THE HEALTH CARE CONTROVERSY: AN UNENDING STORY?
- ■ THE NEW FEDERALISM, GEORGE W. BUSH AND THE FUTURE OF HEALTH CARE REFORM

One of the greatest paradoxes in the modern United States is that although Americans spend more on health care than almost any other country on earth (around 14 per cent of total GDP, compared with just 6.7 per cent in the United Kingdom, see table 11.1), there is near universal acceptance that the health care sector is in a mess. Worse, this perception has increased over the years, even as the amount spent on health care has spiralled upwards. Indeed, in 1960 American health spending was only moderately more than in comparable countries such as Germany and France. By 1997 it was almost double that of the nearest country as measured in terms of purchasing power parity. (Table 11.1.) Surveys consistently show that the public are more concerned with health care issues than with almost any other, and health has been a major electoral issue in each of the last three presidential elections.[1] Add to this the fact that no major reform of the system has occurred since 1965 and the paradox is compounded. How is it that health spending is so high, the public so unhappy with the service and yet so little has been done to reform it? To answer these questions it is necessary to outline the historical development of the politics of health care in the United States.

SELF-RELIANCE, HEALTH CARE AND PUBLIC EXPECTATIONS

As is pointed out in chapter 13, the United States has generally lagged behind comparable countries in the provision of social welfare. Not until the passage of the 1935 Social Security Act did the federal government become involved in the provision of pensions and welfare for the poor, and unlike most European governments no system of universal health insurance was created in the two decades following the Second World War. However, the issue has certainly been on the political agenda for many years. Senator Robert Wagner sponsored a national health insurance bill in 1939 and a modified version of this bill remained in

Table 11.1 National expenditure on health, selected countries, 1960–97

| Country | Spending as % of GDP | | | Spending per capita ($)[a] |
	1960	1990	1997	1997
United States	5.3	12.2	13.5	3,927
Germany	4.9	8.7	10.4	2,339
France	4.3	8.9	9.9	2,103
Canada	5.3	9.2	9.3	2,095
Netherlands	4.0	8.3	8.5	1,825
Israel	1.0	7.3	8.4	1,511
Portugal	2.3	6.5	8.2	1,125
Denmark	3.6	8.2	7.7	1,848
Italy	3.6	8.1	7.6	1,589
Belgium	3.4	7.5	7.6	1,747
Norway	3.2	7.8	7.4	1,814
Spain	1.6	6.9	7.4	1,168
Japan	3.0	6.0	7.3	1,741
Greece	2.6	4.2	7.1	974
Ireland	3.8	6.7	7.0	1,324
United Kingdom	3.9	6.0	6.7	1,347

a   At purchasing power parity.
Source: various, including US Health Care Financing Administration.

Congress until 1950, when a coalition of conservative Republicans and southern Democrats finally killed it off. The American Medical Association (AMA), the main interest group representing doctors at the time, supported them in this endeavour. Convinced that any universal scheme was tantamount to 'socialized medicine', the AMA consistently argued that a federal medical programme would result in a reduction of consumer choice and, above all, a lowering of doctors' salaries and status as self-employed businesspeople.[2]

During the ensuing twelve years the focus of attention turned to helping the aged. Under the existing system most Americans subscribed to health insurance (either directly or through employers) via the nominally non-profit insurance schemes run by the Blue Cross and Blue Shield companies. As medical technology advanced, however, the demands on the system increased, and this was particularly so among the aged, whose insurance premiums rarely covered the true cost of care. Indeed, a survey from the early 1960s showed that only a quarter of the elderly's hospital costs were covered by insurance. Many had no insurance at all, and ill health often spelt financial catastrophe. Given that the old were already entitled to pensions under social security, it was a logical extension to add medical coverage.

By the early 1960s, therefore, the focus of reform had shifted to medical care for the old. This change was facilitated by the growth of older persons' interest groups such as the National Council of Senior Citizens, which, in turn, were supported by a broad coalition of liberal groups such as the AFL-CIO and the National Farmers' Union. The issue had grown sufficiently important to be included in President Kennedy's 'New Frontier' legislative programme of 1961. However, in that year, and again in the autumn of 1964, even amid all the enthusiasm for the Great Society, the Medicare Bill (as it came to be known) failed. It was not until after the autumn of 1965 and the election of the overwhelmingly Democratic Eighty-ninth Congress that the Bill passed. In its final form Medicare had a number of important features which were to have a crucial impact on the future development of health care in the United States:

1   Medicare was passed as an amendment to the 1935 Social Security Act. Eligibility was open to all those who paid the social security tax deducted from payrolls. In effect, therefore, all employed Americans would be covered.
2   The programme was exclusively *federal*. Unlike welfare (public assistance), the states would play no role. On the other hand, the Bill also included provision for Medicaid, or medical care for the poor, which would be provided on a means-tested basis mainly to the recipients of welfare and their dependants. In effect, Medicaid provided minimal cover for the very poor. Unlike Medicare, the programme would be shared between the federal government and the states, so some variations in benefit levels would prevail, depending on the willingness of individual states to fund the programme.
3   One of the main barriers to health care reform in the past had been the requirement that doctors and other providers should be paid according to a scale of fees determined by the government. Medicare was not subject to such restrictions. Instead the medical profession itself would negotiate its fee levels with the government. In other words, the creation of Medicare did not change the essential nature of health care provision. Older Americans would be able to use the existing hospital system, but the federal government would pick up the tab. This obviously left the door open to a rapid increase in fee levels.
4   Medicare was aimed specifically at the cost of hospital care and at outpatient diagnostic services. It included only limited coverage of the cost of prescription drugs. It was, therefore, designed to provide for the costs of 'catastrophic' circumstances or costs that could, in the absence of a health plan, end in bankruptcy for the person or persons affected.

In spite of these limitations the passage of Medicare and Medicaid was hailed as a major breakthrough. The two most needy groups – the old and the very poor – would be covered, although only the recipients of Medicare would enjoy something approaching comprehensive hospital coverage. At the same time it was assumed that this was a first step towards the introduction of a medical insurance system for all. Indeed, by the 1970s health care reform was firmly back on the agenda, and during that decade both the Nixon and the Carter administrations tried – and failed – to enact comprehensive reforms. Demands for reform grew, because the fundamental problem remained: health costs were soaring but the ability of many Americans to pay was increasingly limited. The 'solution' was a substantial extension of insurance programmes offered by employers. Between 1965 and 1989 health benefits increased from 2.2 per cent to 8.3 per cent of all wage costs and from 8.4 per cent to over 56 per cent of pre-tax profits.[3] At the same time health care accounted for a larger and larger share of gross domestic product. (Table 11.1.) Increasingly, companies were removing cover for employee family members and were screening potential employees for 'pre-existing conditions' to ensure that potentially 'expensive' workers would not be covered by company plans. In order to reduce costs further, large numbers of employers opted for 'managed care' provided by Health Maintenance Organizations (HMOs). Although originally HMOs were non-profit, the sector increasingly attracted profit-making private companies. In effect managed care is a form of rationing. Members are limited to those doctors, hospitals and other services provided by the scheme. The HMOs will in turn pay these providers only according to set scales of fees. As HMOs are often profit-making, there is enormous market pressure to keep these to a minimum. The best doctors and other medical professionals, as well as many hospitals, tend to opt to work exclusively for private patients who either pay as they go or subscribe to private insurance schemes. Doctors and hospitals paid by HMOs found themselves restricted in the amount of time and money they could spend on patients. As a result HMOs became increasingly unpopular. By the early 1990s more than 50 per cent of Americans received medical coverage through some form of managed health care plan. (A variation on HMOs is the preferred provider organization, or PPO, which typically is non-profit and provides care to assigned members of such organizations as unions and other associations.) Just how unpopular HMOs had become is well illustrated by the almost universal reaction of cinema audiences to Jack Nicholson's comment in the 1997 movie *As Good as it Gets*. When he calls them 'f – ng HMOs' audiences all over the country burst into spontaneous cheering.

Increasing health care costs had an even more damaging effect on those with limited resources who were not covered by managed care schemes. This group included many self-employed, the unemployed and the poor, some of whom could not afford medical insurance of any kind. As a result, they were obliged to fall back on charity or to seek hospital care at increasingly hard pressed public facilities, often funded at the municipal or county level. In some instances Medicaid coverage would be available, but the means test for Medicaid eligibility was set low enough to ensure that only those with virtually no financial assets would qualify. By the early 1990s the uninsured had increased to about 38 million; by the end of the century the figure was 42 million. So by the early 1990s the United States had acquired a four-tier medical care structure – the uninsured (around 15 per cent of the total), those in managed care (around 55 per cent), Medicare and Medicaid recipients (about 22 per cent) and the privately insured (a mere 8 per cent). As suggested, the vast bulk of these people (the uninsured and those in managed care) were unhappy with the *status quo*. But so, arguably, were Medicaid recipients who were eligible only if close to destitution and who automatically lost coverage if their economic circumstances improved.

Moreover, many of the elderly became increasingly unhappy at the spiralling cost of prescription drugs, the full price of which was not covered by Medicare. Even the privately insured had cause to complain at their ever-increasing insurance premiums.

In sum, the country that spent more on medical care than anywhere else on earth and also provided some of the finest – if most expensive – treatment available had acquired a system that satisfied almost nobody. It was in this context that the Clinton administration when first elected in 1992 proposed a major reform of the system and in particular the introduction of universal health insurance. Given the disquiet with the existing system, how was it that this plan failed?

The Failure of the Clinton Health Care Plan

The immediate context in which the plan was hatched was, of course, Bill Clinton's electoral victory in 1992. Clinton had made health care reform the centrepiece of his campaign. Public support for the introduction of universal insurance cover was high, particularly so given the effects of the 1991/2 economic recession. By 1992 the number of uninsured had reached 39 million and this figure does not include the 40 million underinsured whose coverage was so limited that it would be of little use in the event of a serious illness.[4] Another group (often including the underinsured) critical of the existing system were those who felt insecure in their job and whose coverage would go should they lose it.

Expectations of the Clinton initiative were high. Around two-thirds of the public supported comprehensive reform, the Congress remained in the hands of the Democrats and the president had set up a task force led by his wife Hillary Rodham Clinton and the policy analyst Ira Magaziner to hammer out the details. The task force's work was done by September 1993. Yet almost exactly one year later the plan was dead. What went wrong?

Undoubtedly the main impediment to health care reform in the early 1990s was the fact that the country was experiencing a massive budget deficit. All parties agreed that reform could not be at the price of increasing the deficit, or indeed of compromising the plans in place to reduce it. At the same time, the anti-big government mood of the 1980s persisted: Americans were not prepared to pay higher taxes in order to pay for health care reform. Add to this the enormous complexity of the existing health delivery system, and the problems facing the reformers become apparent. One of the main constraints facing the task force was that Congress would not accept a specific new tax – and the president favoured a payroll tax – to finance the project. In other countries, and notably in Canada, this had been the main vehicle used to finance the universal health insurance scheme introduced in the 1970s. In the event the task force, which at its greatest numbered some 500 individuals, opted for a complex combination of initiatives organized around three main themes:

1   *Employee mandates.* All large companies (with more than 5,000 employees) would have to share the cost of insurance with employees. The split would be

80 per cent/20 per cent. Smaller companies would have their costs capped at between 3.5 per cent and 7.9 per cent of their total payroll bills.

2 *Purchasing alliances.* Workers in companies covered by the scheme as well as the self-employed and non-employed would obtain health care through Regional Health Alliances. Small employers and the self-employed would pay into these organizations, which in turn would receive federal subsidies. The alliances would 'buy' services from health professionals on a competitive basis.

3 *Statutory limits* would be placed on private health insurance premiums in order to keep costs down.

Some of the increased cost of the programme would be financed through a large hike in the federal tax on cigarettes, some through proposed savings in the Medicaid programme and some through general taxation.

President Clinton called the reforms the Health Security Act (HSA), mimicking the language of the Social Security Act. Although when first announced the plan enjoyed the support of around 80 per cent of the public, by February 1994 less than 50 per cent supported it. What went wrong? Three main factors can be identified:

1 *Opposition from many interests, limited support from others.* Perhaps the strangest aspect of the politics surrounding the plan was that the two most powerful organizations that traditionally had opposed universal health care actually supported the HSA. But the support of the American Medical Association and the Health Insurance Association of America (HIAA) was lukewarm at best. They supported the *principle* of universal care and employee mandates but were critical of the *specifics* of the Bill. Moreover many smaller insurance companies strongly opposed it, fearing that the creation of large purchasing alliances would favour larger insurers. More seriously, most members of the public either did not understand the scheme or were suspicious that the Health Alliances would come to resemble the managed care provided by HMOs. America's highly organized senior citizens were also suspicious of the plan, thinking that it might threaten their generous and increasingly expensive Medicare benefits. Without strong support from the lead players the Bill would require clear leadership and direction in order to succeed. This it failed to get.

2 *Absence of clear political leadership and direction.* There were many dimensions to this problem. Within Congress a number of lead players had their own health care agendas. This showed itself in the presence of several competing Bills, which tended to confuse the issue even further. The president himself seemed to lose interest. He appeared preoccupied first with trying to win the passage of NAFTA (see chapter 16) and second with the Whitewater real estate allegations that broke in early 1994. The less than wholehearted support of the president may account for his failure to win over Senator Robert Byrd, who was the key player in guiding the Bill through the complexities of the Senate's parliamentary rules. Clinton also almost certainly suffered from the fact that the Bill was closely associated with the *Clintons* as a couple. Hillary was, of course, intimately involved and the Bill came to be known as the *Clinton*

Health Care Plan. A more bipartisan emphasis might have pre-empted what eventually became a highly partisan affair, with the Senate Republicans, led by the minority leader, Bob Dole, condemning the scheme as unworkable. Part of the problem related to the inordinate amount of secrecy surrounding the work of the task force. It took eight months to produce the plan, during which no effort was made to build political bridges with Congress and the main interests affected. As Paul Starr put it, 'On health care, the administration ignored the first rule of political co-operation, "in on the take-off, in on the landing", which underlay other quieter and more successful legislation.'[5] As a result, by the time the Bill was being considered by Congress the mid-term elections were just a year away. The critical first 100 days of the new administration that historically have been used by presidents to drive their programmes through Congress had been wasted.

3   *The economic circumstances were inauspicious.* At least during his first year in office, Bill Clinton made the mistake of believing that the anti-big government mood that had dominated the Reagan years was over. But antipathy to government in general, and to the federal government in particular, remained strong throughout. This was reflected in the congressional mood and, as the economy recovered rapidly during 1993 and 1994, also among the public. As employment opportunities improved so the health care 'crisis' receded – at least in the public perception – and the costs of what looked like mandatory managed care, albeit combined with some consumer choice, increased. Indeed, the health care reform issue slipped from the political agenda after the 1994 mid-term elections, when the Republicans won their famous victories in both the House and the Senate.

Health care reform was officially pronounced dead in September 1994, just two months before the mid terms, when Senate majority leader George Mitchell declared that further progress on the Bill was impossible. Although the salience of the issue receded during 1995 and 1996, none of the problems associated with health provision went away. On the contrary, health care costs continued to rise, so that by 1997 they had reached $4,000 for every man, woman and child in the country. (Table 11.1.) The number of uninsured also continued to rise – even amid the longest economic boom of the twentieth century – and disquiet at the ways in which HMOs operated continued unabated. Table 11.2 shows the projected costs of health care through to 2007. The actual cost increases did, in fact, exceed these projections. For example, in 2000 overall medical costs increased by 8.1 per cent and were expected to escalate further to 12.2 per cent in 2001.[6] In spite of these developments, comprehensive health reform is as far away as ever. Why is this?

THE HEALTH CARE CONTROVERSY: AN UNENDING STORY?

As is pointed out in chapter 13, with the notable exception of education, it is much more difficult to establish comprehensive social programmes in the United States than in other countries. Indeed, only the elderly enjoy generous pension

Table 11.2   US health expenditure, actual and projected, 1970–2007

Expenditure	1970	1980	1990	1997	2000	2003	2007
Value ($ billion)	73.2	247.3	699.4	1,092	1,316	1,519	2,043
As % of GDP	7.1	8.9	12.2	13.5	14.3	15.2	16.0
Per capita ($)	341	1,052	2,689	3,927	4,877	5,439	6,780

Figures for 2000–7 projected.
Source: Health Care Financing Administration at http://www.hcfa.gov/stats/NHE-Proj/proj/
1998/tables/table1.htm.

and health benefits – and even they came late compared with other countries. (Social security dates from 1935, but coverage for all workers was not established until the 1960s.) An ideology of self-reliance and the complexity of federal political arrangements have combined to act as veto points on reforms proposing comprehensive income support, unemployment insurance and other benefits. *A priori*, health should be different. Few people are themselves directly responsible for their ill health, and children in poorer families are particularly vulnerable. Yet even in 2001 and 2002 the prospects of reform seem as far away as ever. Indeed, it may actually be *more* difficult to achieve reform today than ten or twenty years ago. There are two main reasons. First, the economics of health care make its provision ever more expensive. Unlike the production of consumer goods such as cars, higher standards in health can be achieved only through increased spending on equipment *and* on labour. In a car factory the use of robots will typically reduce the demand for labour and thus increase productivity. In a hospital expensive new equipment not only increases the demand for medical staff to use it but also typically requires increased skill levels for its use. Staff costs therefore rise rather than fall. Of course, this applies in all health systems in all countries, but it is particularly problematical in the United States because so many Americans have high expectations of health care delivery.

Most, and especially the elderly, have grown accustomed to high standards and assume that the sort of consumer choice available for cars or homes should also be available for doctors and hospitals. They are naturally reluctant to support any reform that threatens to *reduce* choice. Yet because health services, including the number of doctors and hospitals, are finite, reforms are likely to alter the existing distribution of resources. Put another way, at present health care is rationed by price and by age. Reforms designed to extend coverage to the uninsured and to improve coverage for those in HMOs are bound to affect the already advantaged groups through higher charges and insurance premiums, increased taxation or reduced choice.

Of course, voters do sometimes choose policies that involve higher taxes and a degree of redistribution, as was shown with the adoption of Medicaid and Medicare in 1965. For a major reform to work today, however, two vital conditions would have to be met. First the crisis in the existing system would have to deepen

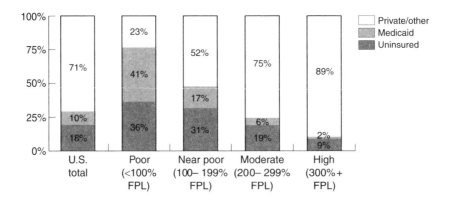

Figure 11.1 Health insurance cover, by poverty level, 1998. The federal poverty level for a family of three was $13,650 in 1998.
Source: Urban Institute estimates of the non-elderly population, based on the March 1999 Current Population Survey

substantially. The most likely scenario for this to happen would be a prolonged recession involving several million lay-offs. As a result a large number of Americans would lose almost all their medical cover. With pervasive job insecurity the national mood might swing in favour of reform. As can be seen from figure 11.1, the uninsured are greatly overrepresented among the poor and the near poor (those whose incomes are below or up to 100 per cent above the federally defined poverty level). These are precisely the people who would be among the first to be laid off during a recession.

Second, it would require formidable political leadership to translate this changed mood into a workable legislative package. Most commentators agree that had the Clinton administration acted with greater speed and resolve in 1993 reform was achievable. As we have seen, however, even by the time the package was unveiled in September 1993 the economic and political conditions had passed their best. Today, even if the economy were to deteriorate, the Bush administration is ideologically disinclined to act. Bush is intent on spending the budget surplus on tax reductions, not on grandiose new programmes. Even if the president was intent on reform, Congress is deeply divided along party lines, and those with an interest in the present system, including the insurance companies and the elderly, are as determined as ever to stand their ground.

This is not to deny that piecemeal reform is possible – indeed, some has already taken place. In 1997 President Clinton signed the Balanced Budget Act, which included the creation of the Children's Health Insurance Program, or CHIP. The programme provides funds for the states to finance medical care for children in families whose incomes are too high for Medicaid eligibility but who cannot afford private health insurance. States can choose whether or not they wish to contribute to the programme, and by 1999 forty-six of the fifty states had elected to join. Although CHIP looks like an improvement on the old system it has a number of disadvantages. Benefit levels vary by state; many families are reluctant to subject themselves to the means tests involved; others simply do not know about it or feel that it is administratively too complicated. Perhaps the greatest disadvantage of this and other means-tested programmes is that many working families feel there is a stigma attached to receiving medical 'welfare'. As a result, they often prefer to pay as they go and hope that their children will not need extended and extremely expensive hospital care.

THE NEW FEDERALISM, GEORGE W. BUSH AND THE FUTURE OF HEALTH CARE REFORM

As is shown in chapter 13, in the social policy area the New Federalism has signalled a significant shift of power away from the federal government and towards the states. In health care this transition is also occurring, as the close state involvement in the CHIP programme shows. In addition the National Governors' Association has proposed radical changes in the administration of the Medicaid programme that would allow the states to extend cover to many more poor people while reducing the cost of benefits to the average recipient. As at present administered Medicaid benefits are means-tested so that citizens qualify either for full coverage or none at all. Under the bipartisan reforms proposed by the governors, poorer working families at present excluded from the system would be eligible for some but not all benefits covered by Medicaid. The proposal is quite radical because it would allow the governors to use some Medicaid funds to pay for employee contributions under employer-sponsored health schemes.

All the indications are the Bush administration will support the plan. The new Secretary of Health and Human Services is Tommy Thompson, who, as Governor of Wisconsin, created a welfare system in his state that was to become the model for the 1996 national welfare reform. While the scheme would increase cover for many poorer working families, it might also reduce the cover of many existing recipients. The reason is simple: state Medicaid costs are rising at almost 10 per cent a year, and more flexibility in the administration of the programme must, if these are to be contained, mean some limit on the universal cover at present enjoyed by most Medicaid recipients. Thus the logic of the New Federalism will be extended. *More*, not less, selectivity in the provision of benefits will ensue. These changes are, therefore, a long way from the comprehensive reforms originally proposed by the Clinton administration.

As far as the Bush administration is concerned, all the changes proposed are in the same piecemeal direction. George W. Bush has proposed the introduction of a health credit of up to $1,000 per individual and $2,000 per family to cover up to 90 per cent of health care costs for poorer families not covered by Medicaid or CHIP. In addition the administration supports the extension of tax breaks for those who save towards the cost of medical care. For the old, help with prescription drug costs and a range of extended benefits for the less well off have been proposed. In sum, these changes will tinker with the system but will do nothing to solve the fundamental problem: a limited and increasingly costly supply of health care services combined with a very rapidly increasing demand for such services. The health care problem encapsulates what is perhaps the most fundamental problem of modern America. How do you satisfy the public's apparently insatiable demand for better public services without at the same time increasing taxes and challenging the prevailing ideology of self-reliance? It is almost certainly the case that the 'health care mess' will persist until some sort of national economic emergency throws up such anomalies and gross inequities that the federal government will be forced to act. Such was the case with the New Deal. In the meantime the United States will continue to find itself in the absurd position of spending more on health care than any other country while failing to satisfy the health care expectations of the mass of its population.

NOTES

1   During the 2000 election campaign, for example, the two candidates vied with each other over who would do most to solve a number of discrete health care problems, including the cost of prescription drugs for seniors.
2   Theodore Marmor, *The Politics of Medicare* (London, Routledge, 1970), chapter 1.
3   Theda Skocpol, *Health Care Reform and the Turn against Government* (New York, Norton, 1987), p. 22.
4   Ibid., p. 25.
5   Paul Starr, 'What happened to health care reform?', *American Prospect*, 6, 1 December 1995, p. 3.
6   Watson Wyatt Worldwide, http://www.watsonwyatt.com/homepage/us/res/hcc20001-tm.htm.

12 Capital Punishment: the Politics of Retribution

- ■ THE DEATH PENALTY IN HISTORICAL PERSPECTIVE
- ■ THE COURTS AND CAPITAL PUNISHMENT
- ■ CAPITAL PUNISHMENT IN THE TWENTY-FIRST CENTURY: THE DEBATE CONTINUES
- ■ THE FUTURE OF CAPITAL PUNISHMENT

Since the *Gregg* v. *Georgia* 1976 Supreme Court decision, which effectively reinstated the use of the death penalty in the American states, more than 700 individuals have been executed. To many foreign observers the practice is both abhorrent and irrational. No other developed democratic country uses the death penalty in this way. Few countries execute with the frequency characteristic of America. And of those that do – for example, China, Afghanistan and Pakistan – all are poor and autocratic.

The issue raises a number of questions. Why is the United States so much the exception? Why do the American public show such a high level of support for capital punishment? Why, in the face of evidence showing no great advantage in continuing with it, does the practice persist? In order to answer these questions it is necessary to trace the history of capital punishment in the United States.

THE DEATH PENALTY IN HISTORICAL PERSPECTIVE

There was nothing unusual or exceptional about the use of the death penalty during America's colonial period. As in England, the death penalty was considered a normal part of the judicial process. Also as in England, the range of crimes subject to the penalty was wide. For example, under the Duke's Laws, enacted in New York colony in 1665, striking one's parents or denying the 'true God' was punishable by death.[1] Perhaps unsurprisingly such draconian penalties were rarely invoked, but for major crimes, and in particular murder, the death penalty was the standard punishment. (For all the American colonies executions rarely exceeded twenty a year.) From the very beginning, therefore, the death penalty was held in reserve and used only as a last resort. As Lifton and Mitchell note:

> The extension of the death penalty to minor crimes came to resemble medieval codes in some states but greatly differed from them *in a reluctance to carry out* the policy. In that way it resembles America's present approach to the death penalty. From the outset in America, capital punishment was more a need than a practice. Americans apparently want to feel that they are in control of evil and have an

answer for it, but that answer becomes less convincing, and certainly less appealing, at the moment of truth.[2]

The first stirrings of opposition to capital punishment came with the publication of Cesare Beccaria's essay *On Crimes and Punishment* in 1767. While this work was notably influential in Europe (the death penalty was subsequently abolished in Tuscany and Austria), it also influenced a number of American intellectuals, including some signatories to the Declaration of Independence.[3] However, it was not until the nineteenth century that serious attempts at abolition were made. Naturally, given the federal structure of the United States, it was left to the states to decide on their own policies. Michigan was the first to abolish the death penalty for all offences but treason in 1846, with Wisconsin and Rhode Island imposing a complete ban soon after. Most states retained the death penalty, however, although most abolished mandatory executions or the requirement for the death penalty to be imposed for capital offences irrespective of the circumstances. As can be seen from figure 12.1, the number of executions did rise rapidly during the late nineteenth century, although this was also a period of very rapid population growth, so *relative* growth in the use of the punishment was modest.

During the twentieth century the use of capital punishment has been through four distinct phases. In the twenty-year period down to America's entry to the First World War in 1917, six more states banned the death penalty while three more confined it to rare crimes such as treason and the murder of uniformed police officers. This was, of course, the Progressive era, which was generally characterized by social reform and the moral improvement of society. Even so, and again in line with population growth, the number of executions continued to rise. By the beginning of the century the geographical pattern that was to persist until the twenty-first century was set. Most executions were carried out in the southern and mountain states. By way of contrast, most opposition to the death penalty came from the upper Mid-western states and the north-east. As far as the south was concerned, capital punishment had acquired a decidedly racial dimension. African Americans were significantly more likely to be put to death than whites. Even the crimes qualifying for capital punishment sometimes carried racial connotations. In many southern states rape and statutory rape were capital offences – an innovation that was specifically designed to deter sexual relations between the races.

From the 1920s through the 1940s the liberalizing trend that had changed policy in the northern states was reversed. A number of states reinstated the penalty and the number of executions rose sharply, especially in the 1930–45 period. (Figure 12.1.) This increase was even greater than the statistics suggest, because this was a period of low population growth. Indeed, the combination of depression and war meant that the population grew less rapidly during these years than at any time before or since. There are a number of reasons why in spite of low population growth executions increased. During and after the First World War a 'red scare' or a conviction that 'alien' and 'un-American' forces – socialism and communism – threatened the United States gripped the public consciousness. These sentiments helped dampen liberal opinion. More important, the Eighteenth

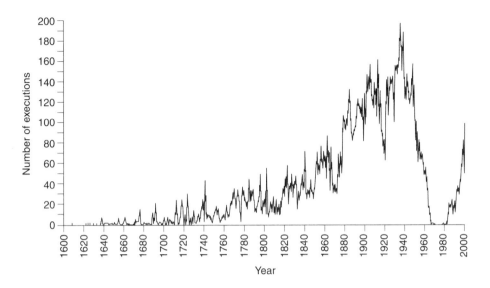

Figure 12.1 Executions, by year, 1608–2000.
Source: http://www.deathpenaltyinfo.org/history1.html, p. 1

Amendment, ratified in 1919, had introduced a blanket prohibition on the production, distribution and sale of all alcoholic liquor. A crime wave based on illegal liquor soon followed, involving high levels of violence and gang warfare. These events radicalized penal policy and led some states to reintroduce the death penalty and, where it was already in place, to impose it more frequently.

What may be called the ideology of crime and punishment also changed during these years. Criminologists believed that the death penalty was a necessary social deterrent. In its absence social order would break down. Many were also influenced by 'eugenics' or the belief that genetically 'inferior' or 'flawed' individuals should be removed from society. Although this movement was to inflict its greatest horrors in Nazi Germany, it was very influential in the United States. Along with such measures as the sterilization of criminals and the insane, capital punishment was seen as a means of 'cleansing' society of its undesirables. Finally, the Great Depression, which lasted for almost all of the 1930s, brought increased crime rates and civil disorder, including violent industrial disputes. As figure 12.1 shows, executions soared, so that by the late 1930s around 200 souls were being put to death every year.

From the 1950s to the mid-1970s the mood changed again. Affluence, full employment and the advance of liberal ideas in criminology and in the broader society led first to a much lower frequency of punishment and second to judicial challenges to the constitutionality of the death penalty. So, while there were 1,289 executions in the 1940s, the total fell to 715 in the 1950s and just 191 between 1960 and 1976. As in the 1930s, changed sentiment resulted from a combination of factors. Intellectual fashions changed. After the horrors of the Second World

War and its aftermath opinion turned against the identification and removal of the weak and unworthy as a solution to society's ills. Eugenics was discredited. Instead the belief that the family and social environment were largely responsible for individuals' behaviour gained currency. As a result, many believed that a combination of education and a change of environment could rehabilitate even the worst offenders.

Such views became particularly influential in Europe, where most countries had abolished capital punishment by the end of the 1960s. At first it looked as though the United States would follow suit. From the early 1970s a succession of Supreme Court decisions cast doubt on the constitutionality of the death penalty and thus led all states to suspend its use until a definitive judgement was provided. This judicial context has dominated the issue ever since. Let us look at it in more detail.

THE COURTS AND CAPITAL PUNISHMENT

Until the 1960s it was assumed that the death penalty was permitted by the Fifth Amendment (which refers specifically to 'capital crime'), the Eighth Amendment (which bans only 'cruel and unusual' punishments) and the Fourteenth Amendment (which bans states from denying 'life' without 'due process of law'). However, reformers were keen to establish that the ways in which capital punishment was being administered did deny condemned persons due process of law. In particular the rules of evidence varied greatly from state to state and judges often had great discretion over who was executed and who was spared. In addition they argued that the gas chamber and electric chair (the main means of execution at the time) did indeed constitute 'cruel and unusual' punishments. During the 1960s the Supreme Court established that capital cases could be 'bifurcated' or divided into a jury judgement on guilt and a second jury judgement on the appropriate punishment. However, it was not until 1972 that the Court concluded that, as at present administered, capital punishment could constitute a 'cruel and unusual' punishment. Hence in *Furman* v. *Georgia*, in a five to four vote, the Court struck down the death penalty as a violation of the Eighth Amendment. The case involved an African American male who had been convicted of murder in Georgia. (The petition also included two capital rape cases in Georgia and Texas.) However, the convicting juries had not been issued with any guidelines or limits on their discretion. As a result, three of the Supreme Court justices, writing the majority opinion, concluded that the resulting arbitrariness of the decision represented a cruel and unusual punishment. (Two other justices found that capital punishment was *per se* unconstitutional and thus favoured a total ban on its use.)

The *Furman* decision was crucial in a number of respects. First, it effectively stopped all executions in the United States (figure 12.1) and was hailed by liberals as a step towards a total ban. More than 600 condemned persons on Death Row therefore won at least a temporary reprieve. In addition some of justices argued that, as then administered, capital punishment discriminated against certain social groups and in particular African Americans. However, the fact that the actual decision of the Court did not find capital punishment as such unconstitutional meant that outright abolition had not occurred. Instead the Court implied that the thirty-nine states with capital offences should draw up strict and consistently applied guidelines governing jury discretion before executions could resume.

It was not until 1976 that the Court clarified its decision. In *Gregg* v. *Georgia*, in a seven-to-two decision, the Court argued that Gregg, who had been convicted of armed robbery and murder, could be executed only if the jury had fully considered both aggravating and mitigating circumstances. In effect this decision re-established the constitutionality of capital punishment by arguing that, as long as juries properly investigated and took into account the circumstances of every individual case, the ultimate penalty could be imposed. The decision also confirmed that mandatory sentences were unacceptable. In every case the particular circumstances would guide jury decisions, and, as an extra guarantee, capital convictions would have an automatic right of appeal to a higher court. Nonetheless *Gregg* was immediately criticized for dodging the central issue. As Lief Carter has noted:

> Basic criticisms of the reasoning in *Gregg* focus on the plurality's [the Court majority] failure to connect persuasively its initial claim that the Eighth Amendment embodies a basic concept of human dignity with its conclusion that sentencers may consider a wide range of information in deciding whether to apply the penalty. If, in other words, human dignity stands as an independent moral criterion for deciding when a punishment is cruel and unusual, the plurality should have read into the amendment the specific moral and factual conditions that aggravate and mitigate the case for capital punishment.[4]

As a result of this failing, executions were resumed, but the basic objections outlined in the *Furman* decisions, namely the arbitrary nature of capital sentences, were not met. Juries could – and indeed do – vary enormously in the ways in which they take into account mitigating and aggravating circumstances. We will return to this point later. A further surprising feature of *Gregg* was that many of the liberals on the Court concurred in the majority decision. It may be that they were influenced by public opinion that was increasingly supportive of the death penalty. By 1975 support for the death penalty was rising rapidly. (Figure 12.2.)

Since *Gregg* all further attempts to abolish capital punishment have failed. Indeed, death sentences increased rapidly after 1976 (Gary Gilmore was the first post-*Gregg* person to be executed – by firing squad – in Utah in 1976) although, because the appeal process can take many years, it was not until the mid-1980s that the actual number of executions increased appreciably. (Figure 12.6.) Further court cases have limited the use of the death penalty in some circumstances. For example, in *Coker* v. *Georgia* (1976) the imposition of the death penalty for rape where the woman is not killed was declared unconstitutional. This decision was considered a victory for civil rights activists, who had long argued that categorizing rape as a capital crime was a cover for discouraging sexual contact between the races. In *Thompson* v. *Oklahoma* (1988) the Supreme Court established that it was unconstitutional to execute persons aged fifteen or under at the

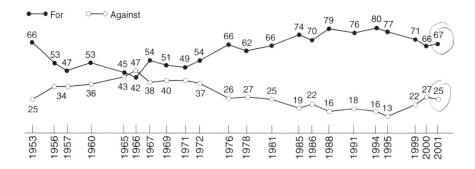

Figure 12.2 Public opinion on the death penalty, 1953–2001. Responses to the question 'Are you in favour of the death penalty for a person convicted of murder?'
Source: http://www.gallup.com/poll/indicators/inddeath_pen.asp, p. 1

time of the crime. Even so, several persons aged seventeen at the time of the crime have been executed, as has one aged sixteen at the time of the offence. Many more teenagers are on Death Row awaiting execution.

Some decisions have reinforced the use of the death penalty. For example, in *McKleskey* v. *Kemp* the Court decided that the fact that African Americans are disproportionately represented on Death Row was not in itself unconstitutional. Defence counsel would have to show evidence of racial discrimination in individual cases before race could be admitted as a mitigating factor. The Court has also failed to address several germane issues, including the suitability of the *means* of execution and the fact that enduring the sometimes very long appeal process (most of those eventually executed linger on Death Row for ten years or more) itself constitutes a cruel and unusual punishment.

CAPITAL PUNISHMENT IN THE TWENTY-FIRST CENTURY: THE DEBATE CONTINUES

Debate on the status of capital punishment became increasingly heated during the 1990s. There are a number of reasons. First, and most important, both the public and informed opinion have become increasingly concerned that the ways in which the penalty is used in the American states raise important questions of equity and justice. In particular, the allegedly arbitrary nature of executions remains firmly on the agenda. This is demonstrated well by examining some simple statistics on executions. For example, the following anomalies demonstrate the importance of the views and determination of prosecuting attorneys and how aggressively they seek the ultimate sanction available to the state:

■ The city of Baltimore averaged 320 murders a year during the 1990s but had only one inmate on Death Row. Suburban Baltimore County, which averaged less than thirty murders a year, had four.

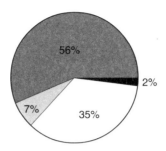

Figure 12.3   Race of defendants executed. The numbers executed are as follows (percentage of the total in parentheses): black 249 (35%), hispanic 49 (7%), white 391 (56%), Asian and Native American 13 (2%).
Source: http://deathpenaltyinfo.org/dpirace.html, pp. 1–2

- Under the direction of aggressive prosecutors, Hamilton County in Ohio has more inmates on Death Row, about fifty, than any other county in the state – even Cuyahoga, which has over half a million more residents. In fact, if you slay someone in Hamilton, you're seven times more likely to face the death penalty than in the state as a whole.
- Tiny Baldwin County Georgia, population 42,000, had five people on Death Row in 1999, one more than Fulton County, which includes the city of Atlanta and has 772,000 people. Baldwin averages two murders a year, Fulton about 200.[5]

This arbitrariness does, of course, extend to interstate variations in the use of executions. Down to March 2001, four states of the thirty-eight with the death penalty accounted for more than half of all executions since 1977 (Texas, Oklahoma, Virginia and Florida). As disturbing is the racial profile of those convicted and actually executed. As can be seen from figures 12.3–5, African Americans are grossly overrepresented both among Death Row inmates and among those subsequently executed. Note also that the vast majority of capital cases involve white victims (83 per cent) but that only 50 per cent of murder victims are white. In other words, taking all capital cases, African Americans have a substantially greater chance of being sentenced to death for the murder of whites than have whites.

  Much debate also surrounds the *methods* of execution employed by the states. As figure 12.6 and table 12.1 show, the vast majority of states now use lethal injection as their sole or main means of execution. However, the electric chair is still used in ten states and the gas chamber, hanging and firing squad remain on the statute book in a number of states, even if they are rarely employed. Death by lethal injection has spread because it generally avoids the technical problems associated with hanging, the gas chamber and the electric chair. In all three instances the number of botched executions has been high. While in almost all cases death ensued, in most some delay involving all manner of unpleasantness

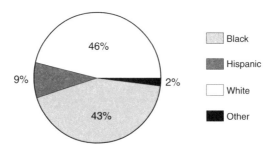

Figure 12.4   Race of Death Row inmates. The numbers are: black 1,595, white 1,719, hispanic 328, other 84.
Source: http://deathpenaltyinfo.org/dpirace.html, pp. 1–2

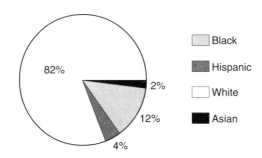

Figure 12.5   Race of victims in capital cases.
Source: http://deathpenaltyinfo.org/dpirace.html, pp. 1–2

occurred. The hardy reader may want to access the details of the thirty-two such unfortunate incidents at http://www.deathpenaltyinfo.org/botched.html. Interestingly, death by lethal injection has also involved a number of technical difficulties – the most common being problems accessing usable veins in convicts with a history of drug abuse.

Publicity about such gruesome incidents has helped to fuel debate on the use of the death penalty, as has the execution of minors (at the time of the offence) and of women. Perhaps the most celebrated case of a female execution was that of Karla Faye Tucker in Texas in 1998. Tucker was executed in spite of her likability, her conversion to Christianity after a long period of rehabilitation and her obvious contrition. Governor (now President) George W. Bush refused to intervene on her behalf. In fact, following her execution, support for the death penalty in Texas declined for the first time since the 1960s. This trend mirrored the national picture, with those in favour of the death penalty falling to a low of 66 per cent in 2000 (although it moved up to 67 per cent in early 2001). (Figure 12.2.) This is

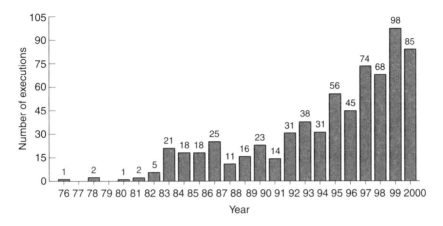

Figure 12.6 Total executions, 1976–2000.
Source: http://deathpenaltyinfo.org/dpiexec.html, p. 1

Table 12.1 Executions, by method, 1976

Method	No. of executions	No. of states authorizing[a]
Lethal injection	537	36
Electrocution	149	10[b]
Gas chamber	11	5[c]
Hanging	3	2[c]
Firing squad	2	2[c]

a   Some states authorize more than one method.
b   The sole method in two states.
c   All have lethal injection as an alternative method.
Source: http://www.deathpenaltyinfo.org/dpicexec.html, p. 1.

quite a turn-round from the peak of 80 per cent in September 1994, although it still represents a substantial increase on the 1960s figures, when the population was divided roughly fifty–fifty on the issue. (Figure 12.2.)

Survey data also reveal the basis of people's support for the death penalty. By far the most often cited reason is the biblical one of an eye for eye. (Typically around 50 per cent of those who support capital punishment will cite this reason.) Of the other reasons offered, saving the cost of imprisonment and the deterrent effect are the most often mentioned. Neither is supported by the facts. The long appeal process and special conditions on Death Row add up to a more expensive burden on taxpayers than life without parole. When all other factors such as income and race are taken into account, states without the death penalty are no more likely to suffer higher crime than those with capital punishment.

In fact a majority of people in many of the abolitionist countries, including the United Kingdom, also support the death penalty, but little in the way of political support for its reinstatement exists. This contrasts sharply with the United States during the 1960s and early 1970s, when *de facto* abolition existed. Many voters were very unhappy that the federal courts were denying the democratic majority their way and, in the context of rising crime rates, their demands were eventually heeded. Of course, in the United States issues of crime and punishment are usually considered matters for state rather than Federal governments, and this has been especially so with regard to the death penalty. The Supreme Court has never challenged the states' prerogative in this area and there is little evidence that it will do so in the foreseeable future. Hence the current debate does not directly involve national politicians. True, the federal government also has the death penalty on the statute book – although it was in effect never used until the 2001 execution of Timothy McVeigh for the Oklahoma City bombing. But no recent presidential candidate has made capital punishment an electoral issue. All recent candidates, Democrat and Republican, have supported the death penalty. Instead the debate rages at the state and local level, where such matters as consistency in the application of the penalty and the possible execution of innocent people dominate discourse. Most recently the more extensive use of DNA evidence has effectively cleared a number of Death Row inmates. Indeed, in Illinois Governor George Ryan declared a moratorium on the death penalty until a commission had reported on its use. Governor Ryan was concerned that as many convicted persons were being exonerated by DNA and other evidence as were being executed. In the circumstances, and although he personally supported the death penalty, he could not endorse the present system.

THE FUTURE OF CAPITAL PUNISHMENT

As earlier suggested, it is extremely unlikely that the Supreme Court will establish a precedent-setting decision in this area. Even liberal Supreme Courts have shied away from the issue in the past. Today the Court is dominated by a conservative majority which has been increasingly deferential to states' rights and increasingly reluctant to establish national standards as far as moral and social issues are concerned. (See chapter 6.) Indeed, the Court's position on the issue is likely to become more rather than less conservative, given that any appointments made by George W. Bush will almost certainly move the Court further to the right. Any meaningful change is therefore likely to come from individual states. Already some larger northern and western states execute very few of those condemned to death. Having reinstated the penalty in 1995, New York has yet to put anyone to death, and California, the most populous state, has executed just eight since 1976. Should there be a change of policy in one of the states that use the penalty extensively it may act as an example for the others. This process may already have begun with the Illinois moratorium, which has so far not provoked great public opposition. On the contrary, it may have resulted in deeper reflection on the obvious inequities inherent in the use of the sanction. As one

Republican Illinois state representative has noted, 'even the most conservative individuals realize that there's a problem'.[6] None the less, we are a long way from a halt to the killings. In the period 17 January to 10 March 2001 Oklahoma alone executed nine people.

Non-Americans will continue to be both horrified and fascinated with the institution of state-mandated homicide in the United States. As in other areas of public policy, the United States seems to pursue its own course and is largely uninterested in the example set by other countries. Europeans may condemn the inefficient and inequitable ways in which the American states administer the death penalty. Their criticisms will fall on deaf ears, however. If there is to be a meaningful move towards abolition it will result from debate within and possibly between the American states. 'Outsiders', including even the institutions of the federal government, are unlikely to play a major role. The most likely outcome of the present debate is that the reluctance to use the death penalty that prevails in the vast majority of states will be extended to the half-dozen or so that use the punishment more extensively. DNA and other evidence showing conclusively that some innocents have been executed may have this effect. Outright abolition is highly unlikely, however, given that most Americans continue to view capital punishment as a form of just and necessary retribution to be visited upon the evil. In this sense support for the death penalty does have religious roots. For those who hold such views, arguments based on deterrence, costs and equity are wholly unconvincing. For them the punishment for the taking of life has to be the forfeit of life. When moral absolutes of this kind are invoked, no amount of evidence on deterrence or efficiency is likely to have any effect.

NOTES

1   Laura E. Randa, *Society's Final Solution: A History and Discussion of the Death Penalty* (Lanham MD, University Press of America, 1997), p. 23.
2   Robert Jay Lifton and Greg Mitchell, *Who owns Death? Capital Punishment, the American Conscience, and the End of Executions* (New York, Morrow, 2000), pp. 23–4.
3   *History of the Death Penalty*, Death Penalty Information Center, http://www.deathpenaltyinfo.org/history2.html, p. 2.
4   Leif H. Carter entry in Kermit L. Hall (ed.), *The Oxford Companion to the Supreme Court* (New York and Oxford, Oxford University Press, 1992), p. 349.
5   Lifton and Mitchell, *Who owns Death?*, p. 124.
6   Cited in ibid., p. 242.

13 Welfare Reform: Providing for the Old but not for the Poor?

- THE EARLY DAYS: 'PROTECTING SOLDIERS AND MOTHERS'
- THREE FAILED REFORM ATTEMPTS
- THE 1990S REFORMS: THE END OF WELFARE AS WE KNOW IT?
- WELFARE REFORM: HAS IT WORKED?
- CONCLUSION: PROTECTING THE OLD BUT NOT THE POOR: THE NEW AMERICAN PHILOSOPHY?

Welfare, or government help for the needy, has inspired one of the longest-running and most abrasive debates in recent American history. While the issue has been a source of controversy in most developed capitalist countries, only in the United States has an influential body of opinion challenged the very idea of welfare. So debate has raged not only round the questions of how much should be provided and who should qualify for aid, but also round the issue of whether welfare aid should be provided at all. In most countries the first government programmes designed to provide for the poor were legislated late in the nineteenth century or early in the twentieth. By the 1960s the principle of *comprehensive* public assistance or the provision of an income 'safety net' for all those with low incomes was enshrined in the laws of most northern European countries. In the United States, however, welfare has never been provided on a comprehensive basis. Throughout, some social groups have been excluded from benefits, and from the very beginning federal and state programmes have emphasized the needs of children in families over other groups.

In marked contrast, social security or income support for the old, widowed and disabled is provided on an extensive basis. Indeed, benefit levels are substantially higher than in many European countries, including the United Kingdom. At first sight, the reasons for the disparity between welfare and social security are obvious. Social security benefits are based on the contributions all American workers and employers make on their payrolls. Welfare benefits are non-contributory and are instead paid for out of general taxation. In other words, social security is directly funded, welfare is not. While this is broadly true – although, as will be shown later, not entirely so – it fails to explain American's apparent antipathy to welfare. To understand this issue it is necessary to trace American attitudes to state provision for the needy and the history of such assistance.

THE EARLY DAYS: 'PROTECTING SOLDIERS AND MOTHERS'[1]

The first move away from charitable provision and towards government aid occurred during the second half of the nineteenth century when a number of states
created 'mothers' pensions' so that widowed women would not have to depend
on charity or send their children into foster care or orphanages. At the same time,
the federal government had introduced quite generous war pensions for Civil
War veterans and their dependants. By 1910 28 per cent of all elderly men and
almost one-third of northern men were in receipt of such pensions.[2] For other
social groups, while limited welfare assistance had been introduced in some states,
charity remained the main means of support for the needy. As in a number of
other countries, the Great Depression of the 1930s and its attendant economic
distress produced calls for the introduction of new federal programmes to fill
what were very substantial gaps in state provision. The resulting 1935 Social
Security Act created two major new programmes. For the old, disabled and widowed a system of contributory social security was established. Although initially
a number of groups were excluded (notably agricultural and domestic workers),
the new law would eventually provide old age and disability pensions for the
mass of American citizens. The programme was to be administered entirely by
the federal government, which would oversee a trust fund created for the specific
purpose of financing future expenditure. It was always assumed that social security would be actuarially sound, or self-financing over the long term.

In stark contrast, the Act also created a non-contributory welfare system that
was highly selective both in terms of its eligibility criteria and in terms of benefit
levels. Hence Aid for Families with Dependent Children (AFDC) provided welfare only for mothers with children. Men and childless woman were not eligible.
In addition the programme would be administered by the states on a matching
basis. Federal grants would provide aid up to a minimum level; states wanting to
spend more could do so. The eventual result was widely varying benefit levels
that were to persist right down to the 1990s, when the programme was replaced
with a new programme, Temporary Assistance for Needy Families (TANF). As
table 13.1 shows, the southern states were the most niggardly in providing assistance. This pattern reflects the very different political cultures prevalent among
the American states. Generally the southern and mountain states are conservative while the northern and Pacific states are liberal. Although the resulting
inequities have long bothered liberals, they have not been a cause of great concern among the public at large. Indeed, the main criticism of AFDC was that
benefits were too generous and that the programme was out of control.

THREE FAILED REFORM ATTEMPTS

Without doubt, much of the antipathy to AFDC stemmed from the notions of
self-reliance that infuse much American thinking on welfare. Why, people ask,
should able-bodied women be in receipt of 'hand-outs' when they could work to

Table 13.1 Average Aid for Dependent Family payments per family in selected regions and AFDC population as % of regional population, 1990

	US	South[a]	ENC[b]	Pacific[c]
Average AFDC monthly payment per family ($US)	396	223	379	606
AFDC recipients as % of total population	6.5	6.6	7.0	8.4

a   Ten southern states.
b   East North Central region: Ohio, Indiana, Illinois, Missouri, and Wisconsin.
c   Washington, Oregon, California, Alaska, and Hawaii.
Source: US Department of Commerce, *Statistical Abstract of the United States* (1996), adapted from tables 599 and 600.

support their families? Such sentiments were reinforced by a gradual easing of the eligibility criteria for AFDC. In 1961, for example, states were given the option also to include unemployed fathers under the programme. Most did so. This and other changes were a result of the much more liberal political environment that prevailed during the Kennedy and Johnson years, when combating poverty became a major policy priority. Indeed, Lyndon Johnson actually declared a 'War on Poverty' in 1964. Some of the resulting programmes, including Food Stamps (tokens that can be exchanged for food and groceries), Medicaid and housing subsidies, greatly complicated the administration of welfare benefits. Depending on where they lived, recipients might find themselves eligible for a range of benefits that in total added up to much more than could be gleaned from gainful employment at minimum wage rates. Thus the incentive to work was reduced. As can be seen from figure 13.1, by the late 1960s the welfare rolls had swelled to around 3 per cent of the population. Although the figure was not high by some international standards, successive administrations vowed to clear up the 'welfare mess' through comprehensive reform.

However, over the ensuing two decades every attempt at wholesale reform failed – in spite of the best efforts of the Nixon, Carter and Reagan administrations. There were two main reasons – one relates to changing beliefs and values about welfare and the other to the specifics of the reform process. A brief description of the three reform attempts illustrates the point.

NIXON AND WELFARE REFORM

On coming to power in 1969 Richard Nixon was unable to dismantle the Great Society programmes. On the contrary, the prevailing ethos was that the federal government had an obligation to provide a minimum income for all American families. A strongly Democratic Congress and many of his own policy advisers believed this.[3] Nixon therefore proposed a Family Assistance Plan (FAP) that was remarkably radical for a Republican administration. FAP offered a guaranteed

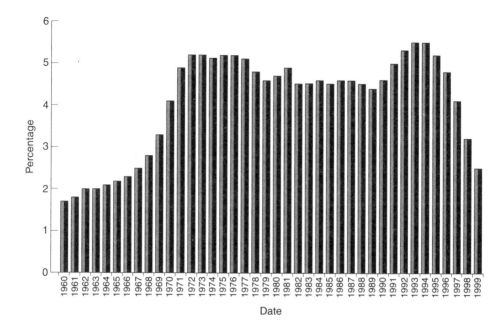

Figure 13.1 Percentage of the US population on welfare since 1960.
Source: US Department of Health and Human Services at http://www.acf.dhhs.gov/news/stats/6090ch2.html, p. 1

income for all parents with young children, tied to a strong work incentive scheme. As parents' income rose so their welfare benefits would fall, hence the 'poverty trap' element in the existing AFDC system would be avoided. There is little doubt that had the president accorded FAP high priority it might have been enacted. However, Nixon was personally averse to the more generous elements in the plan and failed to provide coherent and consistent legislative leadership. Among liberals in Congress the complaint was that FAP recipients might under certain circumstances lose some of their existing benefits, including Medicaid. They therefore opposed it for being insufficiently comprehensive. Although the FAP was eventually abandoned in December 1972, the Nixon administration did change the welfare and social security agenda. Supplementary Security Income, or welfare benefits for elderly people and the disabled with insufficient social security benefits, was introduced and was eventually to become a large programme. In addition Earned Income Tax Credits (EITC) were created to provide some incentive for welfare recipients to work. The principle behind EITC (that the tax system should be used to encourage rather than discourage people from working) was to become central to the major reforms of the 1990s.

Carter and Welfare Reform

By the late 1970s, when Jimmy Carter attempted another reform effort, the political mood had changed substantially. The number of welfare recipients had soared (figure 13.1) and the national fiscal condition had deteriorated. As a result, an FAP-type reform would have proved both expensive and politically unpopular. Carter pressed ahead none the less. What eventually transpired was the Better Jobs and Incomes Plan (BJIP), which combined public service employment, a cash assistance programme to replace AFDC, Supplementary Security Income and Food Stamps and an expended Earned Income Tax Credit. A federal minimum family income level would be established that could be supplemented by state payments. Although the plan appeared to be well thought out, it had one fatal flaw: the working poor, many of whom already received Food Stamps, would, at least in official parlance, be placed in the same category as the non-working poor. As a result around 19 million people would be 'added' to the welfare rolls, i.e. would be transformed into welfare recipients. In addition the plan had the potential to become very expensive, especially if the United States suffered an economic downturn. A further problem was that the Carter administration suffered from numerous interdepartmental conflicts involving Cabinet secretaries defending pet programmes, many of which (housing subsidies, Food Stamps) would have disappeared under the plan.[4] Add to this a president whose policy agenda was crowded with numerous reforms and who was personally less than enthusiastic about the plan, and the seeds of failure were sown. Sure enough, the BJIP died in Congress.

The Reagan revolution, welfare and social security

Throughout the Nixon, Ford and Carter years, the size of the social security programme increased steadily. Although officially funded out of a trust fund, officials in the Reagan administration were particularly concerned that escalating social security costs were adding to federal expenditure and therefore to the budget deficit. Ronald Reagan himself was a long-time opponent of the idea of social security and early on in his presidency proposed major cuts in funding. The political reality, however, was that social security was electorally sacrosanct. Any attempt to cut benefits would provoke the wrath of America's politically powerful senior citizens. While Reagan soon abandoned these plans, he pressed on with reform of the welfare system. In 1981 the administration asked Congress for deep cuts in federal social spending and especially in welfare, housing subsidies and Food Stamps. These were eventually granted in the context of an associated consolidation of eighty-three federal programmes into six block grants made available to the states. The principle of devolving the administration of programmes to the states was strengthened in a more radical 1982 proposal that would have involved 'swapping' the three largest welfare programmes with the states. Thus the states would assume all responsibility for AFDC and Food Stamps while the federal government would assume full control of Medicaid. Reagan also proposed that the states would initially receive federal revenue to pay for these programmes but that it would be gradually phased out so that the federal government's involvement in welfare would end in 1991.

Unfortunately for Reagan, these proposals came at a time when the economy was in deep recession. Officials of the Office of Management and the Budget (OMB) warned that Medicaid was one of the fastest-growing programmes in the budget. At the same time the states were reluctant to take on the full cost of providing welfare, and Congress was loath to endorse what looked like even greater cuts than those imposed in 1981. Reagan was successful in passing the Family Support Act in 1988, however, which gave the states the option of waiving AFDC rules in favour of state-run programmes that increased the incentive to work and reduced truancy among families on welfare. Central to this reform was the idea that federal and state job training programmes could be provided for welfare recipients. As a result they would be able to compete in the job market and escape the 'trap' of lifelong welfare dependence.

What is interesting about these three reform attempts is just how much they reflect a changed policy agenda from the 1960s through to the 1980s. There are only two constants throughout – insistence that any reforms should rationalize the present system and that they should restore the incentive to work among the poor. The changes are much more significant:

1   A switch from federal to state provision. In the late 1960s and early 1970s there was a presumption in favour of the federal role. By the 1980s the presumption was that the states would play the major part in welfare provision.
2   A switch from concern with minimum income standards and equity to concern with lowering costs and actually reducing the number of welfare recipients. By the late 1980s Republicans and Democrats alike agreed that any reform of welfare would have to reduce dependence on government, whether federal or state.
3   A further deepening of the gulf between the political status of social security and that of welfare. It had always been present, but originally the two areas had been the product of the same item of legislation (the 1935 Social Security Act). By the late 1980s the two were worlds apart. Even Supplementary Security Income, which was originally conceived as a programme for the old, changed in shape. By the 1990s it was recast as a programme mainly for the disabled and in particular for long-term sick and disabled children. In other words the welfare debate was increasingly framed in terms of the deserving poor (notably children and the disabled) and the undeserving poor (everybody else).

THE 1990s REFORMS: THE END OF WELFARE AS WE KNOW IT?

While there was no further attempt at reform by the Bush administration (1989–93), an increasing number of states were given permission to waive AFDC rules so as to encourage welfare recipients to return to work. Under Republican Governor Tommy Thompson, Wisconsin was the first state to attempt a complete overhaul of its welfare provision. It was very successful in reducing both the cost of welfare and the number receiving public assistance. Bill Clinton came into office intent on major reform of both the health and the welfare systems; following the failure of health care reform in 1993 and 1994 he turned his attention to the welfare agenda. From the very beginning his administration favoured reforms that encouraged welfare recipients to take up employment. So much had the agenda changed from the 1960s that the underlying assumption of the legislative debate was that, the disabled aside, welfare should be given only as a stopgap until poorer Americans could return to work or receive training in preparation for entering the labour force.

What eventually transpired was the 1996 Personal Responsibility and Work Opportunity Reconciliation Act (PRWORA). Although hailed as a bipartisan effort, it had all the hallmarks of a Republican rather than Democratic piece of legislation. House Speaker Newt Gingrich and the cohort of rightist Republicans elected in November 1994 enthusiastically supported it. Indeed, welfare reform of the sort embodied in the Act had been a key item in Gingrich's *Contract with America*, the Republican 'manifesto' of the 104th Congress. Without a doubt PRWORA was the most radical departure from the basic architecture of welfare created by the 1935 Social Security Act. Its main provisions were:

1   AFDC was replaced with Temporary Assistance for Needy Families (TANF). TANF also incorporates the main federal job training programme, Job Opportunity and Basic Skills Training (JOBS). Thus for the first time welfare payments and job training were to be combined.
2   TANF was to be administered entirely by the states (or by Native American tribes where appropriate). Each state was to receive a block grant from the federal government, which was set at a level that would enable it to maintain historical benefit levels. The grant was set at around $16.8 billion each year through fiscal year 2002.
3   Each state was given enormous flexibility over how it ran its TANF programme so long as it used the federal money in a manner 'reasonably calculated to accomplish the purposes of TANF'. The purposes are: 'to provide assistance to needy families so that children can be cared for in their own homes; to reduce dependency by promoting job preparation, work and marriage; to prevent out-of-wedlock pregnancies; and to encourage the formation and maintenance of two-parent families'.[5]
4   By the end of the 1990s forty-six states had designed TANF programmes, every one of which limited welfare recipients' eligibility to five years maximum and obliged them to undergo training if appropriate. In most cases welfare recipients were required to work after two years of benefits. By fiscal year 2002 at least 50 per cent of recipients must either be involved in work activities or have left the rolls. The rules on child care are also very strict by European standards. In the words of a TANF press release, 'Non-exempt adults [disabled and those with very young children] who are not working

must participate in community service two months after they start receiving benefits. Single parents with a child under six who cannot find child care cannot be penalized for failure to meet the work requirements . . . failure to participate in work can result in either a reduction or termination of benefits to the family'.[6]

Additional incentives and penalties were put in place to discourage abortions and out-of-wedlock births and to encourage states to provide child care. The states were also eligible for 'performance bonuses' for successfully moving people out of welfare and into work.

WELFARE REFORM: HAS IT WORKED?

As table 13.2 shows, the reduction in the welfare rolls since the enactment of PRWORA has been dramatic. It should also be noted, however, that the welfare rolls were falling quite rapidly before TANF was in place, although some states had already introduced work incentive programmes prior to the enactment of the 1996 law. No one disputes that part of the reason for the decline in welfare recipients relates to the booming economy – although nowhere near as many left welfare during previous economic upturns. For example, in the 1984–8 period the reductions were modest. (Figure 13.1.) Another reason for the sharp decline may be that other federal programmes, including the expansion of the Earned Income Tax Credit, encouraged many erstwhile welfare recipients to take up work.

Interestingly, almost the entire welfare debate has revolved around the issue of numbers. Both Republicans and Democrats have pointed to the data in

Table 13.2   Temporary Assistance for Needy Families (TANF), % of total US population, 1990–2000

Year	Recipients	US population	% of population
1990	11,460,382	249,913,000	4.6
1991	12,592,269	252,650,000	5.0
1992	13,625,342	255,419,000	5.3
1993	14,142,710	258,137,000	5.5
1994	14,225,591	260,372,000	5.5
1995	13,652,232	263,034,000	5.2
1996	12,648,859	265,284,000	4.8
1997	10,936,298	267,636,000	4.1
1998	8,770,376	270,029,000	3.2
1999	7,202,639	272,690,813	2.6
June 2000*	5,780,543	275,130,000	2.1

*Most recent available.
Source: HHS Administration for Children and Families.

table 13.2 and claimed credit for 'ending welfare as we know it'. Much less attention has been paid to the deeper consequences of reform. Two major areas are of concern: the effects of reform on America's poor and disadvantaged, and the longer-term fiscal viability of reform in the face of an economic downturn. Preliminary studies suggest that not all former welfare recipients are actually working. About 40 per cent are not and are relying on partners and families for support. Moreover the very poorest families – the bottom fifth of single mothers with children – have actually lost ground since welfare reform. Their incomes have declined as benefits have been cut. One study showed, for example, that in 1997 more than 420,000 children were living in 'extreme poverty' (defined as a family income of less than $6,400 a year for a mother with two children).[7] Most of the reductions in income suffered by this group result from tighter Medicaid and Food Stamps eligibility rules. Rules designed to reduce out-of-wedlock childbirth clearly have not worked. A 1999 study showed that in the two years 1996 and 1997 eleven states showed an improvement in out-of-wedlock births but thirty-nine states showed deterioration. As of 2000 thirty-two in every 100 births in the United States are to unmarried women. Also of significance is the fact that the proportion of white welfare recipients has fallen since reform. In other words the changes have been less effective among the African American and Hispanic communities than among whites. One Brookings study shows that welfare recipients are even more likely than before to be inner-city residents in the older industrial cities of the north-east, south and Mid-west.[8] What appears to be happening is that those areas with the highest levels of poverty and deprivation have benefited least from reform. Hence the lowest levels of reduction in the rolls have been in New York City, Cook County (Chicago), Wayne County (Detroit), Philadelphia and Los Angeles County. In these and comparable cities reductions have typically been around 20–30 per cent rather than the national average of 40–50 per cent.[9] In some areas case loads have actually increased. Some commentators argue that the way in which TANF works actually permits the states too much discretion over programme design. As a result many cities are not receiving as much funding as they need to meet the particular and often very difficult needs of the welfare population.

Of course, all these studies were conducted during the boom years of the 1995–2000 period. In 2001 the economy slipped into recession and many commentators agree that the real test of welfare reform will come during an economic downturn. After 2002 the level of federal funding is likely to fall as block grants of a predetermined size are phased out. In order to maintain benefit levels states will have to dip into their own resources. And if this occurs in the context of continuing recession the resulting distress could be widespread. Moreover an economic downturn would hit the most vulnerable first – those in the lowest-paid jobs and those already dependent on TANF and other programmes.

What all this amounts to is a massive devolution of responsibility for welfare to the states. With a conservative Republican administration now in office the federal role in this area will likely be reduced to pre-New Deal levels. Much therefore depends on the capacity of the states to fill the gaps left by the reduced federal role. This in turn depends on the state of the national economy. All the evidence from the past suggests that when the states find themselves in fiscal distress they turn cap in hand to the federal government for help. But things may be different now. Most state governments accept their new role and many will fight hard to maintain their new-found freedom. Whether they can do so in the face of a prolonged economic crisis remains to be seen.

CONCLUSION: PROTECTING THE OLD BUT NOT THE POOR: THE NEW AMERICAN PHILOSOPHY?

With the coming of the New Deal, and later the Great Society, the United States made significant if sometimes halting steps towards adopting comprehensive pro-grammes designed to assist society's most vulnerable members. By the mid-1970s the old and disabled were well protected against economic hardship and the economic costs of ill health. By the turn of the century protection for these social groups was, if anything, more rather than less extensive. Even conservative Republican administrations, including the Reagan and George W. Bush presidencies, understood that social security and Medicare were politically sacrosanct. Indeed, during the 2000 presidential election campaign Bush and Democratic candidate Al Gore vied with each other over how much they would do to meet the spiralling costs of seniors' prescription drugs. On pensions the Republicans may talk of the need eventually to replace social security with private pension provision, but they are highly unlikely to do anything that fundamentally challenges the existing system. Compare this with the situation in Britain, where supplementing or even replacing state pensions with private schemes is firmly on the political agenda. Even Labour politicians support rationalization of state pensions. Admittedly, birth and immigration rates are lower in the United Kingdom than in the United States and hence the capacity of future generations to fund the pensions of the old will be limited. But American pensions are substantially more generous, and few experts believe that the existing system can continue indefinitely in the absence of reform and/or increased taxes.

While the old and disabled remain protected by the federal government, the status of assistance for the poor has changed out of all recognition. For a short period from the 1950s to the 1970s an influential body of American opinion believed that those who found themselves in poverty and were unable to work should be provided with benefits under federal programmes. Such programmes gradually increased in size and scope until they reached a peak in the late 1970s. But many Americans remained unhappy with this situation. There was, they thought, something unwholesome about able-bodied adults receiving federal hand-outs, and reform of what were always selective benefits was always on the political agenda. At first, during the Nixon years, there was talk of a guaranteed income for all. Later the emphasis shifted to 'Workfare' and to reducing the number of welfare recipients. By the 1990s the aim was even more ambitious: the virtual elimination of welfare except for the sick, disabled and very young children in poor families.

Disquiet with the 'burgeoning' welfare rolls was more ideological than economic in nature. The two largest welfare programmes, AFDC and Food Stamps, never amounted to more than about 3 per cent of the federal budget, compared with 32 per cent for Medicare and Social Security. Admittedly Medicaid has been more expensive (around 6 per cent of the budget) but no one has seriously suggested that children in poor families (the main recipients of the programme) should be denied medical care. So influential was the ideological aversion to welfare that it converted even a Democratic president to the idea that the federal role in this area could come virtually to an end. By 2002 this will almost have happened. It is now the states who are in the front line – albeit with the help of federal aid in the form of block grants. What this means in practice is that how the poor are treated by government will vary, even more than in the past, from state to state and even from county to county. The pressure to work is already intense, and this now applies to mothers with young children. Whether these reforms will actually achieve their aim – the inculcation of the work ethic so as to eliminate a culture of dependence among an excluded underclass – seems doubtful. Already evidence suggests that the very poorest living in the most deprived areas are those who have responded least well to the TANF programme. Charities in these areas report substantial increases in the demand for food and shelter. But the most telling statistic is that most families that leave welfare remain in poverty. The reforms may have reduced the rolls and saved some money but they have done little to reduce poverty.

NOTES

1   This phrase is from Theda Skocpol's *Protecting Soldiers and Mothers: The Political Origins of Social Policy in the United States* (Cambridge MA, Harvard University Press, 1992).
2   Theda Skocpol, 'From beginning to end: has twentieth-century social policy come full circle?', in Morton Keller and R. Shep Melnick, *Taking Stock: American Government in the Twentieth Century* (New York and Cambridge, Cambridge University Press, 1999), p. 255.
3   For a discussion see David McKay, *Domestic Policy and Ideology: Presidents and the American State, 1964–1987* (Cambridge, Cambridge University Press, 1989), chapter 4.
4   McKay, *Domestic Policy and Ideology*, chapter 5.
5   Cited in Administration for Children and Families, press release, US Department of Health and Human Services, http://www.acf/dhhs.gov/programs/opa/facts/tanf/htm, p. 1.
6   Administration for Children and Families, pp. 1–2.
7   Data from the Children's Defense Fund.
8   Brookings Institution, Center on Urban and Metropolitan Policy, *The State of Welfare Caseloads in America's Cities, 1999* (Washington DC, February 1999).
9   As above, appendix B.

14 Abortion: the Right to Life Debate

- A Brief History of Abortion and the Abortion Issue
- Roe v. Wade
- The Constitutional Argument
- Philosophy and Science
- The Difficult Cases: Rape, Incest and the Death of the Mother
- Conclusion

For every 100 children born in the United States, thirty are aborted.[1] Every year about 1.3 million American women have abortions, and since 1973 – the year the Supreme Court handed down its (in)famous *Roe* v. *Wade* decision – over 30 million have undergone the procedure.[2] Such numbers sicken many Americans. Indeed, a tiny hard core of pro-lifers are so sickened by what they regard as the 'murder of the unborn child' that they are prepared to impose on others the ultimate sanction. In several high-profile cases in the 1990s pro-life activists took the lives of three doctors, two nurses, one clinic escort and one security guard involved in abortion procedures.[3]

Undoubtedly, the abortion debate is one of America's most emotive and vituperative. At the same time, however, opinion polls show that abortion is not an issue that most Americans are deeply concerned about. Moreover, while roughly equal proportions describe themselves as pro-life and pro-choice (47 per cent versus 45 per cent respectively), most are not committed to a hard-line position. A majority (51 per cent) thinks that abortion should be neither wholly legal nor illegal, believing instead that it should depend upon the circumstances. Other evidence also supports the contention that Americans are more comfortable with a moderate position. Thirty-four per cent think abortion laws should be stricter and just 17 per cent less strict, while 46 per cent said they should remain as they are. Moreover, 67 per cent oppose a constitutional amendment to overrule *Roe* v. *Wade*, the Supreme Court decision that established a constitutional right to an abortion, while just 30 per cent favour it.[4] While each of these questions taps slightly different sentiments and passions, overall the responses do not give the impression of a citizenry that is passionately divided on the abortion issue.

Yet the murders mentioned above, plus the many other death threats, bombings, assaults and acts of arson and vandalism, demonstrate that the abortion debate today is highly charged. This is because, as on so many issues, the debate is not between moderate Americans seeking a compromise solution to a difficult policy issue. It is instead between two fairly extreme and unrepresentative groups for whom compromise is anathema and total victory the only solution. Before we examine the content of the debate between the pro-life and pro-choice groups, it is useful to summarize the history of the abortion issue and to set out the law as it applies today. This knowledge, while important for its own sake, will help us understand the medical, philosophical, emotional and political arguments that dominate debate.

A Brief History of Abortion and the Abortion Issue

In the early 1800s federal and state laws restricting abortion were practically non-existent. From the 1820s through to the 1950s, however, anti-abortion statutes were introduced in all the states. The reasons for restricting the availability of abortions were several. Some anti-abortion campaigners were genuinely concerned about the threat abortion posed to the mother's health: hygiene was poor, medical techniques were primitive and thus death rates were high. Other campaigners and in particular qualified physicians and their nascent pressure group, the American Medical Association (AMA), sought to exclude non-qualified, unofficial deliverers of medical services (herbalists, homeopaths, midwives, faith healers and so on) from practising medicine, including performing abortions. In part this was due to genuine concern with women's health, but it was also designed to exclude competition and professionalize medical practice. Others campaigned against abortion because they thought it a moral crime, along with prostitution, pornography and other vices. Still others, who today would probably be labelled anti-feminists, worried about increasingly assertive women who sought to control their fertility and perhaps challenge the subordination of women in the home and in public life. Finally, at a time of high immigration of Catholics and eastern Europeans, others worried about the low birth rate of native-born white Protestant women; they feared that the Anglo-Saxon stock that built America was threatened by this 'invasion' of sexualized, fertile 'foreigners'. The sanctity of the life of the unborn child was, then, hardly the primary message of the anti-abortion campaigners. Instead, they were driven by a myriad of concerns, including women's health, private economic gain, a fear of changing gender relations, and nativist or racist sentiments.[5]

Given the scope and depth of such interests, it is not surprising that they succeeded, mainly through state legislatures, in curtailing women's ability to abort their pregnancy. Several loopholes for women remained, however. Some states permitted abortion in cases of rape or incest, or if the foetus was deformed. More significantly, most states also permitted abortion if childbirth 'threatened' the life of the mother. The ambiguity entailed in such a diagnosis meant that women with a sympathetic doctor could in certain states use legal (and relatively safe) abortion as a method of birth control. This abortion avenue was increasingly threatened, however, as improvements in medical technology made childbirth much less dangerous and thus abortion much more difficult to justify. By the 1950s medicine had become so advanced and death in childbirth so rare that doctors conducting abortions were liable to prosecution. Partly in response, some doctors sought to clarify their legal position.

While doctors were mainly concerned about the legal aspects of the abortion procedure, others, most notably women themselves, increasingly sought to challenge both the ban on abortion and other restrictions placed on women in the home and the workplace. In the 1950s, and especially the 1960s, the status of women changed as the second-wave feminist movement politicized gender relations and drew attention to the 'patriarchal' nature of modern society. In this more liberal and sexually permissive society, women, rallying to the cry of 'The personal is political' and reacting against male control over their bodies, sought control of their own fertility. One way they did so was to challenge existing and restrictive anti-abortion laws in many of the states. In some they were successful, but in most they were not. The failure to liberalize the law led to a change in strategy. Just as the civil rights movement increasingly looked to the federal government for policy solutions in the 1950s and 1960s, so too did pro-choice campaigners – as they came to be known. However, as the executive and legislative branches failed to champion abortion reform, the pro-choicers' attention turned to the US Supreme Court. As the campaigners quickly realized, a Court decision constitutionally protecting a woman's right to terminate her pregnancy would force all the states to make abortion legal. To the surprise of many, this it did in the landmark 1973 *Roe* v. *Wade* decision.

ROE v. *WADE*

The majority opinion in *Roe* ruled that a woman has the right to an abortion, but also that this right is not absolute. The opinion divided a woman's pregnancy into three equal parts, or trimesters, as they are called. During the first three months, or trimester, a woman can choose whether to terminate the pregnancy, and during the second and third trimesters a state can regulate or outlaw abortion.

Dividing up a woman's pregnancy into trimesters was certainly one of the more peculiar Supreme Court decisions. It was based not on a strict interpretation of the constitution but on previous Court decisions that had established a right to personal privacy, and on scientific evidence and medical testimony. *Roe* essentially performed a balancing act between a woman's privacy and a state's interest in the health of the mother and in the 'potentiality of human life'.

A state, the Court said, has no 'interest' in the foetus or the life of the mother during the first trimester because a woman at that stage enjoys a right to privacy; she can thus choose what to do with own body. Like the abortion 'right', however, the right to privacy does not explicitly appear in the constitution. Rather, based on a particular reading of the Bill of Rights, the Court in a series of cases – most notably in *Griswold* v. *Connecticut* (1965) – established that certain zones of privacy were protected by the due process or 'liberty' clause of the Fourteenth Amendment. A woman's right to privacy, however, is not absolute. It has to be balanced against a state's interest in the health of the mother and in the foetus. The Court said that during the second trimester a state's interest in the health of the mother becomes more compelling than a woman's right to privacy. Therefore a state can if it wishes regulate abortion during this stage when the procedure threatens the mother's health.[6] Finally, the Court stated that during the third and last trimester the state's interest in the foetus becomes compelling because at that point, it was believed, the foetus is 'viable' – in other words, it can survive outside the womb. Thus abortion is outlawed unless the life or health of the mother is threatened.

Predictably, the Supreme Court's decision outraged pro-lifers. Indeed, the delicate balancing act performed by Harry Blackmun, the Supreme Court justice who wrote the opinion, ignited one of the most controversial and ill-tempered disputes in US history, which runs to this day.

The Constitutional Argument

Unsurprisingly, one of the most frequently heard and most powerful arguments used by opponents of *Roe* is that the Supreme Court's decision is unconstitutional. Nowhere in the constitution is abortion (or privacy or individual choice) mentioned. Thus it is not within the Court's remit to make decisions and force them upon the states. Rather, as the Tenth Amendment of the constitution says, 'The powers not delegated to the United States by the Constitution, nor prohibited by it to the States, are reserved to the States respectively, or to the people.' Abortion should, in short, be an issue for each of the fifty states, not for the federal government. Indeed, even some Supreme Court observers politically sympathetic to *Roe* recognized that it 'derived more from medical and social policy than from constitutional law . . . As a practical matter it was not a bad solution. As a constitutional matter, it was absurd.'[7] Indeed, the changing medical 'facts' led the Court to abandon the rigid trimester solution in the case of *Planned Parenthood* v. *Casey* (1992). The Court instead said a state has an interest in the 'potential life' of the foetus throughout the pregnancy. A state cannot, however, place an 'undue burden' on a woman seeking an abortion before viability. The Court did not, however, overturn the core of its earlier *Roe* decision, stating that a woman has a constitutional right to an abortion.

The ambiguous nature of *Roe*, derived from the delicate balancing of various interests, has provided ample opportunity for Congress, the office of the presidency, the state governments and even later Courts to restrict access to abortions. For example, 86 per cent of American counties have no abortion provider.[8] Half the states limit public funding of abortion to cases of rape, incest or when the life of the mother is in danger. Most hospitals do not perform abortions. Some states require minors to notify and receive the consent of their parents to have a termination, while others have implemented a 'cooling off' period between the decision to abort and the procedure, which is intended to encourage women to change their minds.

By the early 1990s, after twelve years of Republican presidential appointments to the Supreme Court, it looked as though the increasingly conservative Court would soon overturn its landmark *Roe* decision. The four solidly anti-abortion justices – Chief Justice William Rehnquist and Associate Justices Byron White,

Antonin Scalia and Clarence Thomas – needed just one more to join their coterie. However, the defeat of President Bush in 1992 by Democrat Bill Clinton gave the pro-choice side some breathing room. The solid anti-*Roe* four became three when Clinton appointed the pro-choice Ruth Bader Ginsburg to replace White on his retirement in 1993. His appointment of pro-choice Stephen Breyer in 1994 to replace pro-choice Harry Blackmun reconfirmed the pro-*Roe* majority of six, with Breyer joining Ginsburg, Sandra Day O'Connor, David Souter, Anthony Kennedy and John Paul Stevens. Ford appointee Stevens and Reagan appointee Kennedy sometimes join the anti-*Roe* three in restricting access to abortion, but not when *Roe*'s constitutional protection of abortion is threatened.

However, the 2000 presidential election defeat of pro-choice Al Gore by pro-life George Bush junior does not bode well for those seeking to protect women's right to choose.[9] The replacement of just two pro-choice justices with pro-life ones could spell the end of *Roe*. Unfortunately for the pro-choice forces, two of the pro-life justices – O'Connor and Stevens – may be close to retirement, and any Bush junior replacements would almost certainly be pro-life. The pro-choice hope rests on the possibility that O'Connor and Stevens will postpone retirement until the election of another pro-choice and probably Democrat president. The re-election of Bush in 2004 would almost certainly kill *Roe*. Immediately after his inauguration as President Bush told a group of pro-lifers:

> We share a great goal: to work toward a day when every child is welcomed in life and protected in law. We know this will not come easily, or all at once. But the goal leads us onward: to build a culture of life, affirming that every person, at every stage and season of life, is created equal in God's image.
>
> The promises of our Declaration of Independence are not just for the strong, the independent, or the healthy. They are for everyone – including *unborn children*. We are a society with enough compassion and wealth and love to care for both mothers and their children, to seek the promise and potential in every human life. I believe that we are making progress toward that goal.[10]

Putting some flesh on his rhetorical bones, Bush junior signed an executive order restoring his Republican predecessors' 'Mexico City policy', which rules that US organizations operating overseas must not perform abortions[11] or promote abortion as a method of family planning if they are to receive any federal monies. He also appointed the hard-line anti-abortionist John Ashcroft to the position of US Attorney General, and has indicated his opposition to the controversial 'abortion pill' RU486.

The new political landscape in Washington DC certainly looks favourable to the pro-life forces. However, pro-choice groups will never give up the fight. The debate today is as passionate and vituperative as it has ever been. It is, though, not a debate in which a majority of Americans participate, or even are that interested. As we saw earlier, most Americans support the *status quo* and do not consider the issue one of their most pressing concerns. The debate reported below, then, is actually more of a war between two very passionate enemies who will not give an inch. Most pro-life groups – such as National Right to Life (NRL) and the American Life League (ALL) – will not tolerate the spectre of abortion even when pregnancy is a result of rape or incest. Conversely, pro-choice groups will not tolerate restricting women's right to choose, even when that choice is clearly a lifestyle decision or effectively *ex post facto* contraception. The absolutist nature of each position may at first glance seem insensitive, extremist, vulgar even. As we shall see, however, they are perfectly logical positions derived from very different, but passionately held, premises.

PHILOSOPHY AND SCIENCE

At the core of the pro-life position is one fundamental premise: human life begins at the fertilization of an egg by a sperm. This premise, pro-lifers claim, is not a philosophical or religious opinion but a scientific fact. Thus, quite simply and undeniably, abortion is murder because it takes the life of an 'unborn child'. At fertilization a new and unique 'person' is created or 'born', with 'his' or 'her' own genetic code. This is the first step on the continuum of life, which progresses from zygote through foetus, birth, childhood, adolescence, adulthood and finally death. For the pro-choice advocate, however, a foetus is only a 'potential life'; only at birth does it become an actual or real life. Undoubtedly there is something physical inside the mother, and it will become a child, but life can exist only after birth. For pro-choice groups the only life to be considered is that of the woman. Her right to choose to abort or not is absolute. It cannot be weighed against any rights a potential life may or may not have; they are simply incomparable. Even when the foetus is viable – that is, it could survive outside the womb – pro-choicers maintain their potential-life position. Not doing so would be to admit that the right to choose is not absolute, and that the rights of the mother do not always trump those of the foetus. Not doing so would be to concede a central philosophical point, and would result in the crumbling of the edifice upon which the pro-choice argument is built. Their position needs to be absolutist because they are fighting an enemy with an absolutist position. Pro-lifers, too, are apt to reject the concept of viability, which suggests that the unborn baby's right to life is contingent upon its development in the womb. The consequence of this would be a weakening of their argument that that right is absolute and that abortion is always wrong.

It should be noted that talk of killing unborn children and murdering unborn babies is not the language only of the most radical pro-lifers. Such phrases are widely used, including by President George W. Bush. In the same vein, places where abortions are performed are never clinics or hospitals but 'abortion mills'. And those people performing terminations are not doctors or physicians but abortionists or murderers – who perhaps themselves deserve to die for their actions. While, to an outside observer, the language of some pro-lifers can be shocking in its venom, the clinical language of pro-choicers can appear cold and insensitively shocking, too. For example, one pro-choice advocate describes a first trimester abortion procedure (suction curettage) thus:

> The embryo is very small and composed of watery, jelly-like tissue that is easily shredded and removed by the suction of the pump. . . . In fact, the total amount of

tissue, including the entire pregnancy – embryo, placenta, and other tissues – removed is one tablespoon.

D&E and D&X,[12] two later-term abortion procedures, are described respectively thus:

> When her cervix is dilated enough, to about the size of a nickel, the physician can then insert forceps into her uterus to crush or cut her foetus into parts, which are then removed . . . In the D&X method, a woman's foetus is extracted whole, up to the head, which is the biggest part of the foetus . . . The skull is collapsed by suctioning out the brain, and the head then fits through the small opening cervix.[13]

Compare these with a pro-life description of a 'salt poisoning', or saline injection, abortion procedure:

> The abortionist sticks a long needle into the mother's womb. The needle contains salt which is then injected into the amniotic fluid surrounding the baby. The baby breathes in, swallows the salt and dies from salt poisoning, dehydration, brain haemorrhage and convulsions. Taking nearly an hour to die, the baby's skin is completely burned, turns red and deteriorates. The baby is in pain the entire time. The mother goes into labor 24–28 hours later and delivers a dead baby.[14]

Whether the unborn suffers pain or not is a matter of debate. Pro-lifers point to 'scientific' evidence suggesting that the pre-born and soon-to-be-dead baby suffers 'organic' pain. The evidence is technical, complex and mixed, and this is certainly not the place to resolve the dispute, even if it were possible. What is clear, however, is that the pro-life pain argument is part of a wider attempt to give the unborn human characteristics. The aim is to elicit empathy for a fellow human being. To this end, as well as ascribing the sensation of pain to the pre-born baby, pro-lifers describe in detail its development in the womb. They claim that it has vital organs and measurable brain waves at six weeks; that it can respond to stimuli and 'grasp' objects at eight; that it 'sucks' its thumb and has fingerprints at ten; that it 'inhales and exhales' amniotic fluid at eleven, and that it has fingernails and eyelashes and can kick at sixteen. These and later developments can be found with accompanying pictures of the 'innocent pre-born' babies on most pro-life websites.

Unsurprisingly, most pro-choice advocates reject the pro-life claim that abortion causes pain, if pain is defined both physically and psychologically. On the whole, though, pro-choicers are not comfortable with the pain argument, especially when the discussion is about foetal pain during later stages of pregnancy. For pro-choicers, pain is usually discussed in relative terms. Whatever pain a foetus may or may not suffer, it cannot, pro-choicers argue, compare with the psychological pain a woman would have to endure having an unwanted baby.

> Calling for laws that define an embryo as a 'person', with equal rights to or greater than those of women, is arrogant and absurd. Subjugating women – living, breathing, thinking, feeling, hoping, suffering human beings – to the needs of a tablespoon

of insentient, unaware tissue is perverse. Equating a human being with a hollow
ball of cells trivializes everything we value about humanity.[15]

The mental health of the woman, then, trumps the physical pain of the foetus.
Equally, so does the woman's physical health. A major tenet in the pro-choicers'
armoury is that legal abortion is necessary to prevent the unnecessary suffering
of women. They argue that women are always going to have abortions, whether
they are legally available or not. Abortions will always be used as a final resort to
prevent the birth of an unwanted child. Thus, because illegal abortions are more
dangerous than legal ones, it is only right that abortion is made legal; illegal
abortion penalizes, persecutes and threatens women's health unnecessarily. Some
pro-lifers respond that abortion, even if legal, is not a safe procedure. They point
to research showing that women who have had terminations are more likely than
non-aborting women to suffer breast cancer, to miscarry future pregnancies, to
have ectopic pregnancies, to be infertile, to have uterine infections, perforations
and haemorrhaging, and to have babies with abnormalities. Other pro-lifers respond, in an argument perhaps not compatible with the previous one, that rarely
is the physical health of the mother at serious risk in childbirth. They contend
that the vast majority of abortions are carried out for lifestyle reasons – perhaps
because the woman does not want a baby, does not want one yet, or does not
want one by the potential father, for example – not health considerations. Pro-
choice advocates respond in turn that no woman should ever be forced to have a
child she does not want, because it would compromise her mental health. And
the argument begins again. On each side, to every argument, there is a response.
And to that response there is a further response. The debate never moves on.

Pro-choicers argue that it is not just the health of the mother that is protected
by the constitutional right to abortion but children's health too. Their argument
has several strands. One is that abortion results in healthier babies because the
combination of advanced scanning technology, blood tests and abortion ensures
that foetuses with severe abnormalities can be aborted. Another is that pregnant
women in ill health give birth to poorly babies; thus abortion for health reasons
helps ensure the birth of healthy babies. Another is that women who abort one
pregnancy are more likely to have a healthy baby next time. Yet another is that
forcing a woman to have an unwanted pregnancy could result in severe mental
health problems for the (unwanted) child as well as for the mother. To all these
points pro-lifers respond that a less than perfectly healthy baby is better than a
dead baby; the 'solution' of murder is hardly commensurate with the problem of
ill health. They also point out that we should not play God with others' lives;
who are we to make a decision about whether someone's life would be worth
living or not? Linked with this is worry that the selection of foetuses on health
grounds may lead to selection on, say, gender grounds (as it has done in one-
child China), or eye colour, or skin colour, or whatever. Taken one stage further,
they say, the selection logic could lead to the extermination of unwanted people.
All life, including that of the unborn, disabled or not, is sacred and must be
protected.

THE DIFFICULT CASES: RAPE, INCEST AND THE DEATH OF THE MOTHER

Pro-choicers often become frustrated arguing with pro-lifers because they will not be shifted from their absolutist position that life begins at fertilization and therefore that abortion is murder. In an attempt to get pro-lifers to admit that abortion is not always wrong they often raise three difficult cases: those of rape, incest and when the life (rather than just the health) of the mother is at stake. Surely, they say, abortion cannot be wrong when the woman is pregnant because of rape or incest, or when she could die if forced to endure childbirth. At this point some pro-lifers back down. While they continue to argue that abortion is still wrong, they acknowledge that banning it under such circumstances would be politically impossible and morally unacceptable to a majority of Americans. More hard-line pro-lifers, however, maintain that abortion is always murder and murder is always wrong, even in cases of rape, incest or the death of the mother.

They argue that abortion in cases of rape and incest punishes only the innocent victim: the child. The child should not be made a scapegoat for another's crime. Aborting the innocent child because of another's crime creates two victims and two crimes, and two wrongs do not make a right. What's more, they say, the circumstances of the conception are not relevant: the pre-born child has a right to life, and that right is inviolate even if the mother does not consent to impregnation or if the father is a blood relative of the mother. A logistic objection is also raised. If abortion is permitted only in cases of rape, how would society and/or the law distinguish between a rape victim and someone falsely claiming to be a rape victim in order to acquire an abortion? Pro-lifers point to one high-profile example of such a case. Norma McCorvey, better known as Jane Roe of *Roe* v. *Wade*, claimed to the Supreme Court that she had been gang-raped. Many years later she admitted she had lied. Making women try to prove they had been raped would, pro-lifers argue, be disastrous.

Pro-lifers also point out that only in extremely rare circumstances is a mother's life genuinely threatened by childbirth – for example, if the woman has an ectopic pregnancy or cancer of the uterus. In such cases every effort should be made to save both the mother's and the baby's life. However, when it is absolutely apparent that the mother will die during childbirth, then whatever operation is required to save her life must be performed. Have pro-choicers finally got even hard-line pro-lifers to admit that abortion is not always wrong? The answer is no:

> In some conditions . . . a treatment may be required which indirectly kills the preborn. But in such cases, the treatment does not legally or morally qualify as an abortion. When removing a cancerous uterus, the intent is to save the mother; every effort to save the child should still be made. Thus even if the child dies, the treatment is still fully justified. The death of the child was never *intended*. In contrast, for an abortion the intent is always the same: to kill the preborn child.[16]

CONCLUSION

On his retirement in 1994 Supreme Court Justice Harry Blackmun, *Roe*'s author, said of his most famous decision, 'I think it was right in 1973, and I think it is right today. I think it's a step that had to be taken as we go down the road toward the full emancipation of women.'[17] Randal Terry of Operation Rescue, a radical anti-abortion group committed to picketing abortion clinics, made clear his opposition to Blackmun's sentiments: 'I despise [feminism because it is] out to destroy . . . the Christian heritage of motherhood and what it means to be alive.'[18] Many in the pro-life camp think along similar lines. They believe in 'traditional' or conservative family values, such as monogamy, marriage and motherhood, and they are God-fearing fundamentalist or evangelical folk. In opposition are the ungodly radical feminists who, according to conservatives, promote promiscuity, polygamy, and homosexuality even. The pro-choicers in turn regard traditional values with suspicion. In their discourse such values were and are used to oppress women, subjugating their individuality, freedom and sexuality while privileging male power. One way to fight this patriarchal system is to take control of their bodies and minds, to resist oppression at every point, including male control of their fertility.

Part of the conflict between pro-lifers and pro-choicers, then, is not about abortion at all. Part of it is actually about ideology and, linked with it, existential being. For both sides the abortion issue is a convenient and high-profile battlefield on which the war for the hearts and minds of the American people is fought. The culture war that began in the 1960s is not a traditional war. It is a civil war between left and right, between conservatives and liberals; it is about what sort of country America should be, and about how Americans should live. It is being fought today, and abortion is one of the battlefields.

NOTES

1   Because the abortion debate is highly charged, and because words are so important in framing the terms of the debate and the scope of the conflict, there is no such thing as neutral language on this issue. In an attempt to remain neutral, I have where possible used the language of the pro-life side when discussing its position and arguments and used the language of the pro-choice side when discussing its. When discussing abortion outside these contexts I have attempted to alternate between pro-life and pro-choice language, or have tried to say nothing either would find offensive. The first line of the chapter is indicative. I have not said whether the thirty aborted are pre-born babies or foetuses. That is for the reader to decide.

2   National Right to Life Committee at http://www.nrlc.org; Harold W. Stanley and Richard G. Niemi, *Vital Statistics on American Politics, 1999–2000* (Washington DC, CQ Press, 2000). Some pro-life groups claim that the real number of abortions is far higher. The American Life League, for example, estimates that since 1967, the year some states legalized abortion, there have been over 500 million. This staggering figure is arrived at by summing the 30 million or so surgical abortions to a

claimed 486 million chemical abortions resulting from ingestion of 'abortifacients' such as the 'morning after' pill.

3   While mainstream pro-life groups such as National Right to Life condemn violence, others, while not explicitly condoning it, often speak about understanding the reasons why some individuals are driven to violence. Pro-choice groups claim the failure to condemn violence positively creates an atmosphere conducive to it. More radical pro-life groups, such as the Pro-life Action League and Lambs of Christ, have advocated physical conflict and violence. They defend, even encourage, the murder (or 'death', as they see it) of 'murderers' (or abortionists) on the grounds that it is 'justifiable homicide'.

4   Gallup polls, 30 March–2 April, 6–9, 25–8 October 2000; 10–14 January 2001. See http://www.gallup.com/poll/releases/pr010122.asp.

5   See Leslie J. Reagan, *When Abortion was a Crime: Women, Medicine, and Law in the United States, 1867–1973* (Berkeley CA, University of California Press, 1996). Surprisingly, the Catholic Church did not play a major role in the nineteenth-century debates. While it took an anti-abortion position, this did not crystallize into an important tenet of the faith until the twentieth century.

6   A state cannot regulate abortion for health reasons during the first trimester because during this stage childbirth is more hazardous than abortion; regulation thus makes no sense.

7   Robert Woodward and Scott Armstrong, *The Brethren* (New York, Simon & Schuster, 1979), p. 237. However, many highly respected law professors do believe that the constitution protects a woman's right to choose. This position is eloquently and convincingly articulated in Laurence H. Tribe's *Abortion: The Clash of Absolutes* (New York, Norton, 1992).

8   National Abortion and Reproductive Rights Action League at http://naral.org/mediaresources/fact/terrorism.html.

9   In his early political days as US Senator for Tennessee, Al Gore was pro-life. His flip to a pro-choice position coincided with the elevation of his political ambition to nation-wide office.

10 22 January 2001, message to March for Life participants.

11 Unless the abortion is to save the life of the mother, or where the pregnancy is due to rape or incest.

12 D&X is the controversial abortion procedure also known as the 'partial birth' abortion.

13 Margaret Sykes at http://prochoice.about.com/newissues/prochoice/library/bllatetermconf2.htm.

14 American Life League, http://www.all.org/issues/abmethod.htm.

15 Margaret Sykes at http://prochoice.about.com/newissues/prochoice/library/weekly/aa051799c.htm.

16 American Life League, http://www.all.org/issues/argue14htm (emphasis in original).

17 Quoted in Karen O'Connor, *No Neutral Ground: Abortion Politics in an Age of Absolutes* (Boulder CO, Westview Press, 1996), p. 3.

18 Quoted in James Risen and Judy L. Thomas, *Wrath of Angels: The American Abortion War* (New York, Basic Books, 1998), p. 297.

15 Manifest Destiny and Realpolitik: Realism versus Idealism in Foreign Policy

- ■ THE REALIST–IDEALIST DEBATE
- ■ THE CASE FOR REALISM
- ■ THE CASE FOR IDEALISM
- ■ CONCLUSION

THE REALIST–IDEALIST DEBATE

The debate between realists and idealists is far from being unique to the study of American politics and foreign policy; it is ingrained in the very notion of what states should do in the international arena and how they ought to conduct themselves. Nevertheless, the realist/idealist divide has often been most visible and apparent in the conduct of American foreign policy. Some policy makers – Woodrow Wilson, Jimmy Carter and Ronald Reagan are often cited as especially striking examples – have taken the idealist route, seeing America's role in terms of a moral crusade in favour of classically 'American' ideals such as democracy, free markets or human rights. Others – Theodore Roosevelt, Richard Nixon and Henry Kissinger are usually mentioned here – have seen foreign policy primarily as an exercise in the pursuit of power and interests. In other words, they adopt a classically realist concern with the self-interest of the American state and with what can practically be achieved in an international system that is often hostile to American objectives.[1]

What issues separate the idealists from the realists? What is the realist/idealist debate about? Realism in its purest form argues that statesmen ought to absolutely disregard considerations like human rights in favour of a focus on the 'national interest'. Classic *Realpolitik* arguments suggest that one ought to pursue that policy which maximizes the national interest, quite regardless of whether the policy seems 'moral' or not. Niccolo Machiavelli made this case in *The Prince*, where he argued that leaders must deal with the world as it is, not as they would wish it to be. On the other hand, in its purest form idealism argues that one ought to take the moral route in all circumstances, regardless of whether doing what's right is in the national interest or not.

The assumptions of realism contrast markedly with those of idealism, as James McCormick notes. The key assumptions of realism are that:

1   States are the primary actors in the international system.
2   States are motivated, and ought to be motivated, by their own interests and the search for power.
3   The distribution or balance of power is the key to international stability.
4   Relations between states should be geared to achieving such an international balance of power, not to changing one another's domestic economic or political systems.

Idealism, on the other hand, is motivated by the ideas that:

1   The state is only one of the most important actors in the international system.
2   Values and not interests should and do shape a state's behaviour.
3   Social and economic issues are as important to maintaining order as the military distribution of power.
4   General international conditions dominate the considerations of states, rather than narrow self-interest.

Global security and well-being, in other words, are as important as national security. While realists are more likely to have a pessimistic view of human nature, idealists often take a more positive view.[2]

Applied to American foreign policy, Henry Kissinger captures the essential distinction between the two approaches well when he talks about the reasons why America chose to abandon its long-held 'isolationist' foreign policy in the early twentieth century. He discusses the reasoning of the realist president Theodore Roosevelt and the idealist president Woodrow Wilson in choosing to project America into a world role:

> Roosevelt was a sophisticated analyst of the balance of power. He insisted on an international role for America because its national interest demanded it, and because a global balance of power was inconceivable to him without American participation. For Wilson, the justification of America's international role was messianic. America had an obligation, not to the balance of power, but to spread its principles throughout the world.[3]

The idealist/realist debate was present at the founding of the republic. The essentially idealistic Thomas Jefferson disagreed markedly with the realist Alexander Hamilton on many foreign policy issues.[4] Arguably, though, idealism as an approach is more 'natural' to the American belief system, in the sense that it draws upon instincts and ideas to which most US citizens subscribe. Realist scholars like Hans Morgenthau were always intensely aware of this, and Morgenthau wrote books which were at least in part intended to dissuade US policy makers from adopting a 'naive' idealist approach to world affairs. And yet realism has always had a place in American thinking. During the Second World War President Franklin Roosevelt believed that – regardless of whether he approved of Stalin's regime at home – balance of power considerations and the dictates of *Realpolitik* required the United States to ally itself with whomever was prepared to join it in the fight against Hitler. In the 1940s, when the United States was providing assistance to the dictator Rafael Trujillo in the Dominican Republic, F.D.R. came under fire from critics who pointed out that Trujillo was no friend of democracy. Roosevelt, though, gave a famous reply that has often been quoted since. 'Trujillo may be a son of a bitch,' he said, 'but he's our son of a bitch.' Immigration from realist-minded Europe during the twentieth century appears to have reinforced this strain in American thinking, Henry Kissinger, Hans Morgenthau and Zbigniew Brzezinksi (Carter's National Security Adviser) all being prominent European-born realists who came to America and affected US foreign policy in important ways.

Idealism, it is worth noting, has both right- and left-wing variations, both of which were in evidence during the Cold War. Conservative idealists like Ronald Reagan saw themselves as engaged in a war against an 'Evil Empire', a conflict of wrong versus right and good versus evil; they sought not simply to 'balance' the international order but to eradicate what they saw as a morally bankrupt political system. Liberal idealists like Jimmy Carter, on the other hand, saw international politics as a moral crusade, but their morality was different. Carter thought that too much attention had been paid to the conflict with the Soviets, and that the United States ought to practise abroad what it preached at home. He believed that, if America's commitment to human rights was to mean anything, the country should cease supporting right-wing regimes in Latin America that violated this principle (for instance). America's commitment to human rights, he insisted in his 1977 inaugural address, had to be 'absolute'.

During the Cold War these differences of perspective were somewhat muffled by the larger conflict in question. At least before Vietnam, American idealists and American realists shared a common enemy (the Soviet Union) and a common objective (the defeat of global communism). From the days of Harry Truman to the mid-point of George Bush senior's spell in the White House – a span of over forty years – virtually all US presidents pursued a similar overall objective: contain communism and the expansion of Soviet influence in the world. Though there were important differences in the strategies that different presidents adopted to try to achieve this objective,[5] all were basically after the same thing. The beauty of 'containment' as a policy was that both conservative idealists and realists could support it. Idealists such as John Foster Dulles could support the policy because it meshed well with his moral crusade to destroy 'godless communism'. Realists like Kissinger sought more dispassionately to counter what they saw as the challenge of a major rival to American power and a source of instability in the international system. Soviet communism, then, was both a challenge to American ideas and a challenge to American power,[6] and each school could focus on the aspect that especially concerned it.

Realists and idealists could also agree to support the new grand design on which US post-war foreign economic policy was founded. From the mid-1940s onwards, America sought to build a new international economic system along free trading lines. Realists could support free trade as being in America's own interests, something that bolstered American hegemony. Idealists could take pride in the seemingly generous way in which America sought to rebuild Europe after the Second World War (through the Marshall Plan, for instance) and in the notion that free trade was in everyone's interests, not just those of the United States.

The end of the Cold War, however, thrust the age-old realist/idealist debate on to the centre stage once more. With the old Soviet enemy gone – and the long-established policy of containment of Soviet ambitions no longer relevant – the question naturally arose as to what shape US foreign policy ought to take in the post-Cold War world. Some saw a sea change in the nature of international politics itself, ushering in a world in which idealist objectives such as the pursuit of democracy and individual freedoms could now be given priority. Others of a more realist bent saw new threats to overcome, a more complex but perhaps even less safe environment in which the United States must continue to limit its objectives to the direct preservation of national interests. The United States could no longer afford to play the role of 'globocop', as one observer put it, and should concentrate on preserving its own power and interests.

The 2000 presidential debates between the Republican candidate George W. Bush and the Democrat Al Gore again threw this ever-present debate into sharp relief. The divisions were especially clear on the use of military force. Bush maintained that he would use military force only in situations where US interests were directly under threat, arguing for 'realism in the service of American ideals'. Asked during the presidential debate of 11 October 2000 to say what the guiding principle of a Bush foreign policy would be, the Republican candidate took a classic realist line:

> The first question is what's in the best interest of the United States? What's in the best interest of our people? When it comes to foreign policy, that will be my guiding question. Is it in our nation's interests?

Bush said that he would support the use of American military force only under limited conditions:

> If it's in our vital national interests – our territory is threatened, our people could be harmed, our defence alliances are threatened, our friends in the Middle East are threatened. Also, if the mission is clear, if we were prepared and trained to win, if forces were of high morale and well equipped. And finally, whether or not there was an exit strategy.

This prohibition on the wider use of force extended to the use of humanitarian intervention in cases of ethnic cleansing or genocide. The United States, Bush made clear, would not intervene in such situations except where doing so directly aided its strategic interests. He rejected what he called the 'overextension' of American power and the use of intervention for 'nation-building' purposes.

Al Gore, on the other hand, defined the scope of his foreign policy objectives more broadly, adopting a clearly idealist approach:

> I see our greatest . . . national strength coming from what we stand for in the world. I see it as a question of values. It is a great tribute to our Founders that 224 years later, this nation is now looked to by the peoples on every other continent, and the peoples from every part of this earth as a kind of model for what their future could be.

Cases of genocide, he noted, did not always directly affect the US mainland, but it was nevertheless morally incumbent upon America, as the leader of the free world, to act in such a situation. It would be wrong for the United States to simply stand aside and let genocidal acts occur. It ought to exercise its moral duty to act in such a circumstance, he argued. While Bush favours the withdrawal of US peace-keeping forces from the Balkans as soon as possible, Gore argued that the United States should stay in the region until it is fully stabilized. Gore also emphasized the importance of working with multilateral institutions such as NATO and the United Nations, while Bush favoured a more unilateral approach. America would go it alone if need be and would seek to avoid participation in UN peace-keeping missions.

Bush's narrow victory at the 2000 presidential election presumably means that the United States will again adopt the kind of cautious, interest-based foreign policy strategy usually favoured by his father between 1989 and 1993, in contrast to the idealist-infused approach of the Carter administration and the early Clinton administration. If historical experience is anything to go by, the foreign policy positions of President Bush, and the differences between Gore and Bush, are likely to be smoothed out somewhat by the imperatives of the American political system. The belligerent foreign policy rhetoric of Eisenhower towards the Soviets during the 1952 presidential campaign gave way to a policy of containment similar to that of Harry Truman, just as candidate Clinton's pro-human rights stance on China metamorphosed into an accommodative, pro-trade stance once he became President Clinton. Even if it turns out to be so, however, ideas do matter in setting the tone and objectives of foreign policy. Moreover, the debate between idealists and realists is not likely to go away. The following sections examine the arguments of both schools of thought in relation to contemporary American foreign policy.

THE CASE FOR REALISM

Realists generally oppose giving 'moral' concerns priority in foreign policy, whether this involves aggressive pro-human rights policies or humanitarian intervention to prevent internal 'wrongdoing'. There are a number of reasons for this.

The first relates to the practical and political difficulty of intervening in the domestic affairs of another state. This is partly a matter of international norms and diplomatic practice and partly a matter of practical politics. Interference in the internal affairs of another state – even if we do not happen to like its domestic policies – is a violation of its sovereignty, realists note. States have a right to determine the nature of their own domestic policies, however distasteful we may find them. George Bush expressed this view well in the presidential debates when he opined, 'I'm not so sure the role of the United States is to go around the world and say, this is the way it's got to be.' Realists point out that when the United States does interfere with the domestic affairs of other states, however, it invites (or at least leaves itself open to) the charge of 'imperialism', confirming the arguments of its worst critics. Making the United States unpopular in the world does not serve American interests; indeed, it hinders its ability to pursue them. Aside from other undesirable effects, realists note that Jimmy Carter's human rights policy unwittingly heightened tension between the two superpowers. Not unnaturally, Soviet leaders took offence at Carter's condemnation of their record on the issue – without any concomitant improvement in the Soviet Union's human rights record to compensate for the heightening of tension. Conceivably, Carter's warnings to the Shah of Iran on human rights may also have weakened a pro-American regime and helped to usher in the decidedly anti-American Ayatollah Khomeini. Similarly, George W. Bush has condemned Bill Clinton's intervention in Haiti in 1994 as a misguided exercise in 'nation building' that did more harm than good. Though he was noticeably careful during the presidential debates to avoid giving other specific examples where Bill Clinton committed US troops abroad, he made his opposition to the general concept of moralistic intervention clear.

Second, realists see humanitarianism or moralism as a luxury the country cannot often afford, at least where American ideals and interests push policy in different directions. When this occurs, say realists, we ought to put our own interests first. During the Cold War, for instance, it was often necessary for the United States to 'look the other way' when the Shah of Iran's police violently suppressed internal dissent, or the regime of Augusto Pinochet tortured and killed Chileans who opposed his government. Stalin's repressive measures at home had to be ignored during the war. Even though such practices sat uneasily with American belief in democracy and a limited state, the alternatives – in one case the risk of communism establishing a toehold in Latin America, in the other the danger of allowing Hitler to gain control of the entire European continent – were even worse. It would have been nice if the United States could have chosen to reject such allies, but befriending them served a higher (and ultimately moral) goal. It would also be nice, realists say, if we could only align ourselves with states whose leaders share our moral and political beliefs, but the practice of power politics often does not allow us that luxury.

The end of the Cold War has not altered the need to put American interests first, according to this view, for there are new and different threats on the horizon which demand the attention of policy makers. Realists insist that the United States will on occasion have to violate its own best instincts and ideals in order to protect American interests, however regrettable this may be. One cannot try to remake the world; one must take it as it is, be faithful to moral principles where we can but always be willing to bend them with the purpose of preserving the interests of the state.

A further reason why contemporary US realists favour an interest-based approach to foreign policy relates to recent history. They point to the experience of American administrations which *have* tried to place morality and human rights at the centre of foreign policy, noting that these examples illustrate the difficulties, if not the impossibility, of doing so. The administration of Jimmy Carter is an oft cited example. In previous years – notably under Kennedy, Eisenhower and Nixon – foreign policy had come to be dominated by realist prescriptions and ideas. US policy in Latin America, for instance, had been based on the realist argument that you ought to suspend moral qualms in world politics when those qualms conflict with the national interest. So the United States had been quite willing to support extreme right-wing regimes – regimes which often violated human rights by denying freedom of speech, denying freedom of assembly, using torture, holding political prisoners and so on – as long as the regime was pro-United States, or at least anti-communist. US policy had been based upon the realist 'lesser of two evils' strategy: that you support one evil regime because the alternative is even worse. Again, realists say, this is ultimately a moral strategy in the longer term, because the alternative – communism – would have been *more* immoral, and would lead to even greater violations of human rights.

Carter's ideas were simple enough in principle and enjoyed broad political appeal: liberals liked the policy because it condemned the past behaviour of the CIA and overzealous Cold Warriors, and conservatives liked it because it appeared to condemn the Soviet Union and China for their human rights records. Nevertheless, Carter's experience in office provides an object lesson for those who would set out to base their policies on moral precepts. First of all, Carter had difficulty in defining what human rights meant: different members of the administration had different ideas of what rights they were meant to be protecting. Some thought that it was primarily civil and political rights; others thought they ought to protect economic and social rights as well. The second difficulty lay in deciding how far violations of human rights would be penalized in recalcitrant nations. One strategy was to cut off military aid, and this was done in a whole host of cases, such as Chile, Argentina, Uruguay, Uganda and Mozambique. But the main sanction was public and private condemnation, or 'jawboning': trying to bring human rights violations to the world's attention and to turn world opinion against them.

Ultimately Carter's experiment failed. His officials realized that – for reasons of *Realpolitik* – they would simply have to maintain links with certain states in vital regions of the world, even though they violated the rights of their own citizens. So, like previous presidents, Carter maintained friendly relations with the Shah of Iran. And this in spite of the Shah's very poor human rights record, because Carter worried that if the Shah fell a regime sympathetic to the Soviet Union might replace him, giving communism a toehold in a vital and strategically important region of the world. The experience of the Clinton administration – particularly the humiliation in Somalia in October 1993, when eighteen American soldiers were killed and seventy-five wounded in an attempt to capture the Somali 'war lord' Mohammed Farah Aideed – are also often cited by realists as an object lesson in the dangers of seeking to remake the world in America's image. Contemporary US realism tends to reject the kind of multilateralism favoured by the Clinton administration as a general rule, though it is unclear whether this distaste will persist in the long term or whether it reflects the personal preference of George W. Bush for more unilateral ways of doing things.

THE CASE FOR IDEALISM

American idealists are generally in favour of giving moral considerations priority in foreign policy. The realists claim that doing so is a luxury they often counter with the argument that realists have created a false dichotomy. Doing what is morally right is often also in the national interest as well, so that one often *does not have to choose* between one or the other. This argument was very often present in President Clinton's rhetoric, and Al Gore similarly emphasized the notion during the 2000 presidential debates, when he argued that 'If our national security is at stake, if we have allies, if we've tried every other course, if we're sure military action will succeed, if the costs are proportionate to the benefits, we should get involved.'

This sounds like a realist speaking, but Gore's words undoubtedly reflected his conviction that intervention in Bosnia and Kosovo – to cite two prominent examples – served both American moral ideals about what is right *and* its strategic interest in a stable Europe and a strong NATO. In short, American idealists maintain that political reality can be moral reality and that human nature is capable of being moulded and shaped by social institutions; but they also contend that creating such a reality need not involve any diminution of America's interests and power.

A second argument in favour of idealism is simply that it is what the American people want. Opinion polls show that most ordinary Americans favour a foreign policy based on values and ideals rather than interests.[7] This leads American presidents to present their policies to the public in idealist terms, even where their true motivation is basically realist. As Terry Deibel notes:

> ordinary Americans mainly seem uncomfortable with the idea that their nation might throw its weight around in the world simply to protect their own security. They want their country to use its power for good, too . . . no president ever told the American people that he was leading them to war to preserve the balance of power; Americans rather have fought 'in the cause of humanity' (1898), to make the world 'safe for democracy' (1917), to revenge 'an unprovoked and dastardly attack' (1941), 'to prevent a third world war' (1950), to defend 'the value of an American commitment' (1965), or 'to forge . . . a new world order' (1991).

American citizens, as Deibel notes, want a policy which 'globalizes American values'.[8] Most Americans support the idea that the United States should not maintain friendly relations with states that consistently violate the rights of their citizens, and that recalcitrant states should change their behaviour if they want to do business with America. As previously noted, then, idealism is probably more instinctively appealing as a set of ideas than realism, because it lends itself to an external pursuit of the things that Americans favour domestically. Jimmy Carter's concern with human rights represents a classic reflection of where most Americans stand on foreign policy. His conception of morality was simple and direct. Carter believed that America's foreign policy had to be dictated by a desire to promote human rights around the world, and that America's behaviour abroad ought to reflect its values, principles and beliefs at home. Carter was a neo-Wilsonian, in the sense that he very much wanted to remake the world in America's image and wanted the United States to set the moral standard which others would follow. As he put it in his inaugural address in 1977, 'Our commitment to human rights must be absolute . . . Because we are free, we can never be indifferent to the fate of freedom everywhere. Our moral sense dictates a clearcut preference for those societies which share with us an abiding respect for individual human rights'. Advances in modern telecommunications have also heightened concern with human rights. With the spread of satellite television it has now become possible to view what is happening around the world at a moment's notice. Events such as those in Tiananmen Square in China, for example, or the treatment of Bosnian Muslims in the Balkan conflict, are now seen live around the world as they are happening. This has inevitably provoked heightened concern with human rights violations because it has brought about a heightened *awareness* of those violations.

A third argument relates to America's place in the world and its status as the world's foremost economic and political power. 'Manifest Destiny', or a conviction that the United States has a historic obligation to improve the moral condition of humankind, has always been an influence on its foreign policy. At first this applied to colonizing the North American continent. Later it was applied more broadly to the Western hemisphere and finally to support for the spread of democracy and human rights throughout the world. Hence a powerful movement among American elites has held that America has a special duty to act. Mark Stoler calls this 'the mission concept', or the belief by Americans in a divinely inspired duty to 'spread their superior concepts and institutions to the rest of the world, and thereby to improve and transform that world'.[9] This messianic belief was certainly evident in the thinking of Wilson, Carter and Reagan in particular, and a less strident version was advocated by Al Gore in the 2000 presidential debates. Idealists continue to view America's role as an indispensable one, as a matter of values and not just self-interest. Even if the United States no longer has the capacity to lead alone, through playing the dominant role in multilateral institutions it can continue to exercise its power for good. Thus contemporary idealism exhibits a preference for multilateralism. Again, however, it is not clear how persistent this current taste will be, given that there is nothing intrinsic to idealism that would lead to the use of multilateral (as opposed to unilateral) techniques.

A final contemporary argument in favour of idealism is that it reflects a trend towards a more 'sane' and rational world. The world has reached the point where the behaviour of most Western states reflects the impact of both concern about the national interest and moral concern about things like human rights. The horrors of the Second World War convinced a lot of academics and practitioners alike that treaties and institutions needed to be put in place in the post-war world which would not only preserve the peace but preserve the rights of individuals as human beings. Signatories to the UN Charter, created in 1945, for instance, pledged to promote human rights and to use violence only where it was necessary to repel aggression by others. In 1946 the UN Commission on Human Rights was created. In 1948 came the Universal Declaration of Human Rights, which was passed by the UN General Assembly. In 1953 came the European Convention on Human Rights, in 1966 the International Covenant on Civil and Political Rights and in 1975 the Helsinki agreements, which included provisions relating to human rights. While the creation of all these treaties and agreements has not rid the world of human rights infringements, their existence shows a clear commitment to the aim of eradicating human rights violations. The institutionalization of the human rights agenda through international treaties is an important step on the road towards this final goal. The United States should continue to foster the process, say idealists.

CONCLUSION

The portraits of two schools of foreign policy which we have painted in this chapter are to some extent caricatures or 'ideal types', because in the real world no one ever states arguments about morality and the national interest in such an explicit way. In practice, no American policy maker ever argues that government ought to completely disregard moral values, or that it ought to pay no heed to what seems to be in the national interest. In practice, then, the debate is not one of absolutes, but one of emphasis; analysts disagree with one another as to which should be given priority, but very few argue solely for one or the other. The realist Hans Morgenthau, for instance, proposed in *Politics among Nations* that realism is actually a set of *moral* precepts based on the realities of diplomacy and the world as it actually works, while idealism is a set of moral principles based on wishful thinking about how we would like the world to work. 'There can be no political morality without prudence,' he argues, 'that is, without consideration of the political consequences of seemingly moral action.'[10] Hence realists do not ignore moral considerations in foreign policy, but they do often subordinate them to interests and power. Idealists, on the other hand, tend to reverse this priority.

The 2000 presidential debates illustrate this point. Bush was careful to note the importance of 'idealism without illusions', while Gore spoke often of the importance of America's strategic interests. The differences between the two men were matters of degree and emphasis. Most contemporary realists and idealists are also united by a commitment to internationalism, the notion that America must remain actively committed in the world rather than returning to its isolationist past. National Security Adviser Condoleeza Rice has said that America cannot operate a '911 service' (the equivalent of dialling 999 in Britain) for the rest of the world, and this reflects the Bush administration's antipathy to sending American troops into hostile situations on ethical grounds. Contemporary US realists should not be viewed as anti-interventionist or neo-isolationist, however; they are isolationist when it meshes with American interests as they perceive them, and interventionist when that seems to serve those same interests better. We can expect the Bush administration to play as active a role in the world as the Clinton administration did; we should not expect it to play that role for quite the same reasons, however.

NOTES

1   Henry Kissinger, *Diplomacy* (New York, Simon & Schuster, 1994).
2   James McCormick, *American Foreign Policy and Process* (Itasca IL, Peacock, 1992), pp. 118–19.
3   Kissinger, *Diplomacy*, pp. 29–30.
4   Charles Kegley and Eugene Wittkopf, *American Foreign Policy: Pattern and Process*, fifth edition (New York, St Martin's Press, 1996), pp. 34–5; Kissinger, *Diplomacy*, pp. 30–4; Michael Hunt, *Ideology and US Foreign Policy* (New Haven CT, Yale University Press, 1987).
5   See especially John Lewis Gaddis, *Strategies of Containment* (New York, Oxford University Press, 1982).
6   Kegley and Wittkopf, *American Foreign Policy*, pp. 50–3.
7   Dick Morris, *Behind the Oval Office: Winning the Presidency in the Nineties* (New York, Random House, 1997), p. 6.
8   Terry Deibel, 'Strategies before containment: patterns for the future', *International Security*, 16 (1992), pp. 79–108, at p. 94.
9   Mark Stoler, 'The mission concept and the role of ideology in American foreign policy: a historical assessment', *Jerusalem Journal of International Relations*, 9 (1987), 45–67, at pp. 45–6.
10 Hans Morgenthau, *Politics among Nations: The Struggle for Power and Peace*, fourth edition (New York, Knopf, 1967), p. 10.

16 America as a Global Economic Player: Free Trade versus Protectionism

- ■ THE BATTLE OVER NAFTA
- ■ THE WTO AND THE 'BATTLE OF SEATTLE'
- ■ THE CONTEMPORARY CASE FOR FREE TRADE AND GLOBALIZATION
- ■ THE CASE AGAINST FREE TRADE AND GLOBALIZATION
- ■ A CASE OF 'DOUBLETHINK'?

The debate between free-traders and protectionists has a long pedigree in the United States, as elsewhere. At one level, this issue can be considered purely as an abstract academic debate. Neoclassical economists, for instance, have long insisted that all nations would be better off if they practised free trade and specialized in those products in which they possess a 'comparative advantage'. At another level, however, it is an active political debate with real-world consequences. As Robert Gilpin notes, 'the issues are concerned with the effects of international trade on domestic welfare and industrial development, the economic and political effects of increasing interdependence, and the role of government policies and corporate power in the distribution of benefits'.[1] Ever since the founding of the republic these controversial topics have fostered a debate between those who believe that America's national interest and well-being lie in wholehearted immersion and participation in the international economy, on the one hand, and those who believe that these goals are best fostered through protecting the economy from the vicissitudes and instabilities of the outside world, on the other. While free-traders argue that all will be better off if markets are open and barriers to trade dismantled, protectionists argue for the use of restrictions (such as tariffs and quotas) to reduce the flow of imports. In America these restrictions most often take the form of guarantees by government that key industries and agricultural sectors will be shielded from competition that might otherwise be harmful to their economic viability.

As an abstract belief, the commitment to free trade and free markets is well documented in the United States; the notions that economic growth and prosperity are maximized when the entrepreneurial spirit and capitalism in general are given free rein is part of the political culture. As Isaiah Frank notes, the United States has long been a major advocate of free trade. Yet it also 'has a long record of protection of particular industries which in recent years has often taken the form of restrictive measures to counter trade practices abroad deemed unilaterally to be unfair'.[2] Both as a practice and as a set of ideas, US protectionism has deep roots, and there has always been a protectionist school in American foreign economic policy thinking. Alexander Hamilton advocated a strong form of 'economic nationalism' as far back as 1791, when he presented his *Report on the Subject of Manufactures* to the House of Representatives.[3] Hamilton emphasized the idea of government-led economic development as a prerequisite for the development of a modern industrial base, and in so doing provided an intellectual justification for protectionism.

From the early 1800s to the mid-1930s the United States made extensive use of protectionism in its economic dealings with the rest of the world. In the heyday of British economic power the United States was effectively compelled to industrialize behind a protective tariff wall in order to protect its nascent economic base, and in the 1930s – as the Great Depression took hold across the developed world – Congress passed the Smoot–Hawley Tariff Act. The Act imposed trading restrictions on a variety of industrial and agricultural imports, and was passed over the advice of many economists (who accurately predicted that it would lead to retaliation from other states). As Frank notes:

> the enactment of that tariff entailed the most intense 'log-rolling' in which congressmen traded votes with one another, seeking higher tariffs for producers in their own states and districts which competed with imports. The process was driven by the realisation that more votes were at stake in the concentrated import-competing industries where jobs and incomes were threatened than among the more diffused and less organised consumer and export interests which stood to gain from free trade.[4]

Understandably, Smoot–Hawley and the retaliation by other states which followed it precipitated a rapid decline in international trade at a time when the global economy was already in recession, and this memory has undoubtedly helped to bolster America's post-war commitment to free trade. After the passage of the Reciprocal Trade Agreements Act of 1934 the United States gradually moved towards the goal of freer trade. Under American leadership, a new liberal economic order was erected at the Bretton Woods conference of 1944. The International Monetary Fund (IMF), the World Bank and the General Agreement on Tariffs and Trade (GATT) were the institutional symbols of this new order – what Gilpin calls the 'Pax Americana' – and its core principle was free trade. Since the 1970s, however, a number of forces have combined to create a resurgence of protectionist ideas and practice. With the widespread perception of an America in decline, the rise of the East Asian newly industrializing countries (NICs), an unstable international climate evidenced by the oil shocks of 1973 and 1979 and increased economic interdependence and globalization, protectionist sentiments have come increasingly to the fore. As America's economic position in the world has come to seem more fragile and precarious than it was, so the demands for protection of American industry have increased.

Protectionist pressures also gained considerable impetus during the 1980s as a result of America's huge trading deficits. Interestingly, the early years of the Reagan administration – which espoused free markets and free trade as articles of faith – were a period of especially high protectionism in America. Largely as a response to the huge trade deficits of the time, a whole host of measures were adopted to try to redress America's trading imbalances and protect its industries from outside competition. Trade with Japan and the European Union, for instance, was and continues to be managed rather than 'free'.

Complete freedom of trade in the international arena, of course, has always been an aspiration rather than a reality, for all nations erect barriers to trade of some sort. Protection of particular sectors of American industry continued even in the supposed heyday of free trade. The steel industry, for example, has long been protected through an informal system of cartelization and price fixing. According to Harry Schutt, this 'is an inevitable choice for any US industry threatened by foreign imports, given the traditional American repugnance for directly subsidizing the costs of the private sector'. Japanese steel imports have been effectively kept to a minimum by informal agreements in which Japanese companies are compelled to limit their exports to the United States.[5]

The post-Second World War system has to a large extent been founded on the external application of America's internally held free-market ideals. At the same time, however, another well established feature of American politics and society pulls policy making in another direction. Protectionist sentiments tend to be dominant in societies in which powerful sectional interests have a say in the making of policy, and this is obviously a condition closely met by the characteristics of the American political system. While many textbooks emphasize the point that protectionist measures are nowadays most popular among Third World states, the nature of American society and the 'open' structure of its political system – designed to create various access points at which policies can be initiated or frustrated – mean that protectionism has always been a force to reckon with. We shall return to this point in the concluding section of this chapter. The simultaneous popularity of free trade and protectionism is puzzling to outside observers, and it merits further discussion.

Two related international trade issues provoked intense controversy in the United States during the 1990s and continue to divide observers today: the debate over the ratification of the North American Free Trade Agreement (NAFTA) in 1994, and the creation of the World Trade Organization (WTO) associated with the ongoing GATT talks, which occurred the following year. Both issues involve the ever-present debate between the ideas of free trade and protectionism. We will now turn to the controversies over these issues as an illustration of the nature of the contemporary debate.

THE BATTLE OVER NAFTA

On 17 November 1993 Congress ratified the North American Free Trade Agreement. Briefly, NAFTA abolished tariff and other barriers to trade between the United States, Mexico and Canada, effectively creating a free market for goods and services between the three nations. NAFTA passed in the House of Representatives by a majority of 234 to 200 and in the Senate by a majority of sixty-one to thirty-eight.

The domestic political forces arrayed against it had been formidable, however, and NAFTA had initially looked like a political non-starter. Indeed, the battle over NAFTA pitted President Bill Clinton against his own congressional party. The Democratic leadership in the House of Representatives was firmly set against ratification of the deal, with both House majority leader Richard Gephardt and majority whip David Bonior voicing their opposition. President Clinton himself had failed to voice support for NAFTA during the 1992 presidential election campaign. This was undoubtedly a reflection of the fact that, as Martin Walker notes, 'free trade was political dynamite, an issue that sent deep cleavages through both parties'.[6] Clinton had to walk a delicate tightrope between his own free-trading instincts and the protectionist impulses of his core constituents, and this required him initially to fudge the issue of whether he was for or against it. Once in office, however, Clinton became an advocate of the treaty, inheriting a policy and an agreement whose details had mostly been hammered out by his predecessor. His own views became somewhat clearer and he felt able to support NAFTA openly. According to Bob Woodward, Bill Clinton 'believed in free trade'; moreover, there were other (more political) reasons for supporting NAFTA as well. Since his Republican predecessor had negotiated the agreement, supporting NAFTA would politically neutralize the issue of trade and take it off the table.[7] NAFTA would establish Clinton's credentials as a new kind of Democrat, providing the substantiation of a claim that many of his advisers thought had helped him win the 1992 presidential election.

Given the strong coalition of forces opposing NAFTA, Clinton needed a large number of Republican votes in order to carry the day. As Martin Walker notes, 'the boldest actions of Clinton's presidency were to defy and split his own Democratic party in Congress to force through the North American Free Trade Agreement and the GATT world trade pact'.[8] Even so, a majority of congressional Democrats voted against NAFTA, and the split between the White House and the House leaders Gephardt and Bonior was especially obvious.

The Democratic Party's hostility to the agreement can be traced in large part to protectionist concerns, primarily the suspicion by many of its core or heartland groups that NAFTA would fundamentally damage their economic livelihoods and interests. Companies and their workers were concerned that jobs would be lost as US consumers gained access to cheaper goods and services from Mexico and Canada. The labour unions, for example, were especially determined to defeat the agreement, and put particularly heavy pressure on Democratic members of Congress to vote against it;[9] the heavyweight unions, such as the AFL-CIO, were vociferous in their opposition. The congressional black caucus and former Democratic Party candidate Jesse Jackson had similar misgivings.

Robert Reich, in his memoir of his years as Labor Secretary under Bill Clinton, paints a vivid picture of just how vehement his own party's resistance to NAFTA was. In September 1993 Reich visited Bill Ford, then Chairman of the House Education and Labour Committee, with close links to the AFL-CIO, in an attempt to persuade the latter to vote for the agreement. He quotes Ford thus:

NAFTA's a piece of crap. It'll cost this nation hundreds of thousands of good jobs. And you want me to *legitimize* it, to put my blessing on it, to make it look respectable . . . ? Delude people into thinking they can *get* a good job when the good jobs are vanishing? What *planet* are you on?[10]

The opposition of organized labour has not diminished in the years since NAFTA was passed. According to AFL-CIO figures, by 1997 the agreement had cost 420,000 jobs. The organization 'Public Citizen', which also opposes NAFTA, puts the figure more conservatively at 200,000 jobs by 1998. Even though it concedes that the aggregate number of persons in employment in the United States has gone up since 1994, it maintains that the number would have been higher had NAFTA been rejected. NAFTA was also opposed by a variety of individuals outside the Democratic Party, which added to the chorus of criticism: the conservative journalist and Reform Party candidate Pat Buchanan, the consumer advocate and Green Party candidate Ralph Nader and the Reform Party presidential candidate and Texan billionaire Ross Perot all weighed in against NAFTA. Echoing the concern of the labour unions, Perot memorably predicted that Americans would hear 'a giant sucking sound' as jobs left the United States bound for Mexico.

Free trade has been America's declared foreign economic policy objective since the end of the Second World War. And yet the odd nature of the anti-NAFTA coalition reflects a deep ambivalence about free trade in America today. Pat Buchanan and Jesse Jackson, for instance, can rarely have found themselves on the same side of an issue before NAFTA. Perot and Nader also made something of an 'odd couple', resembling the pairing of Walter Matthau and Jack Lemmon in the film of the same name. Although the outlines of NAFTA were developed by the Bush administration, some conservatives were just as uneasy about the danger to jobs as US liberals were. The threat (real or imagined) posed to US businesses by Mexican and Canadian competition also placed rank-and-file workers and corporation directors in the same boat.

In a sense the 'amended' version of NAFTA that Congress approved was as much a protectionist agreement as a free-trade one. For in order to gain a sufficient number of votes to pass the agreement, guarantees had to be given to a whole host of interests that their livelihoods would not be jeopardized by increased trade with Mexico and Canada. As Elizabeth Drew notes, 'the deals were so numerous that it seemed as if a "For Sale" sign had been hung over the White House'.[11] Orange growers in Florida, for instance, had to be given guarantees that the Clinton administration would provide them with financial assistance should competition with Mexico prove too damaging. Similar guarantees had to be provided to sugar growers in Louisiana, Minnesota and North Dakota, to peanut growers in Georgia and to most of the vegetable and citrus-growing communities in America. As Joe Califano notes, each interest had to be massaged and assuaged in order to get the agreement passed at all.[12] It should also be noted that, since NAFTA is a regional trading agreement that excludes other states, it is protectionist in an external sense as well. Nevertheless, its proponents defended it as an example of free trade in action, and most of its opponents continue to attack it as such.

THE WTO AND THE 'BATTLE OF SEATTLE'

In 1995 the Uruguay Round of the GATT negotiations was finally completed, almost a decade after it had begun. The same negotiations also resulted in the creation of the World Trade Organization, a body that has been given new powers to extend the global provision of free trade. The major new power enjoyed by the WTO is the authority to settle trade disputes between its 135 member states. It was also given new rule-making powers that (among other things) extend the number of products and services covered by the GATT. This was a significant extension of the powers and authority of the GATT, and it was heralded by supporters of global free trade as a major step forward. In Kegley and Wittkopf's words, the creation of WTO 'struck a blow for liberalism'.[13] It was also in accord with the Clinton administration's stated objective of 'enlarging' the growth of free markets around the globe.

Not everyone in the United States was pleased with this development, however. In November 1999 the members of the WTO met in Seattle to begin what they hoped would be the opening shot in the millennium round of talks about freer trade. The good mood of the liberal marketeers was to receive a severe jolt, however, as between 50,000 and 100,000 anti-free trade and anti-globalization protesters descended in droves on the city. The streets were full of banners proclaiming general opposition to capitalism and in particular contempt for the WTO. In all likelihood, the malcontents were not all out-and-out protectionists. Some were environmentalists complaining that business interests were being placed before the interests of the planet, some were concerned about the effects of increased globalization on American jobs, while others were concerned about the effects of the WTO on human rights and women's issues. But the common thread within this diverse coalition appears to have been opposition to unbridled free trade and to the expanded enforcement powers that the WTO now enjoys. While the concern of the organized opponents of NAFTA was largely (though not exclusively) with the economic costs it might have, the Seattle demonstration was an indication of wider discontent with the political and moral results of globalization as well.

The contemporary American arguments about free trade and increased globalization are relatively straightforward and easy to understand. They are summarized below.

THE CONTEMPORARY CASE FOR FREE TRADE AND GLOBALIZATION

All the following are propositions to which George W. Bush, Bill Clinton and Al Gore as advocates of freer trade would subscribe:

1   Free trade is a 'job creator'. Supporters of NAFTA and the WTO argue that the United States will be economically 'better off' if the expansion of free trade continues. They note that the immediate post-war years were the high

point of America's economic power, and that they were also the high point of free trade internationally. It was no accident that the post-war economic boom of the 1950s and 1960s was paired with a free-trade system, for the latter is said to have caused the former. Economists also argue that all countries will be better off if they concentrate their production and export efforts upon those goods and services in which they have a 'comparative advantage'.

2   All sections of society will benefit from free trade, since it creates employment and growth for everyone. There is thus no contradiction between a more globalized world and a fairer one, for the poor will benefit from gains from free trade just as the rich do.

3   Protectionist policies invite harmful retaliation. A return to the policies of the 1930s would harm all states, particularly the less developed countries (LDCs). The Smoot–Hawley Act, and the beggar-my-neighbour trade policies which many states resorted to in retaliation, greatly reduced economic growth across the Western world.

4   Protectionist policies harm consumers in the domestic economy. They do so by compelling consumers to purchase domestically produced goods that may be of inferior quality to imported versions, more highly priced, or both. This distorts the market process and introduces a great deal of inefficiency into the economic process. It also hurts the foreign producers of goods and may cost jobs abroad.

THE CASE AGAINST FREE TRADE AND GLOBALIZATION

1   According to its opponents, free trade reinforces existing economic relations, causing the poor to become poorer and the rich to become richer. Trade liberalization reinforces the position of those who already enjoy economic benefits, while undermining that of the disadvantaged.

2   Free trade is a 'job destroyer'. It has cost American jobs, closed factories and ruined livelihoods. The US trade deficit with Mexico and Canada more than quadrupled between 1993 and 1997, from $9 billion to $39 billion. Labour unions argue that NAFTA and the WTO have led to a major loss of employment and growth opportunities. Unskilled workers and the disadvantaged in general are particularly hard hit by sudden shifts in the economy, since they find it difficult to adapt to 'new realities'. The long-time consumer rights advocate and Green Party candidate Ralph Nader estimated in an interview with the *San Francisco Chronicle* in October 1996 that by that year the United States had already 'exported' 350,000 to 400,000 jobs. Conservative columnist and activist Pat Buchanan shares this position.

3   Free trade reinforces exploitation in poorer states, encouraging human rights violations: most notably lower wages, the use of sweatshop, often child and female labour, the denial of union rights and the weakening of worker safety regulations. According to AFL-CIO figures, Mexican wages fell by 36 per cent between 1993 and 1997. In order to undercut US prices and maximize profits, Mexican companies (for instance) appear to be increasingly

exploiting their work forces. NAFTA does supposedly contain safeguards to ensure that workers' rights are protected, but critics say that they have not worked.

4   Free trade is a misnomer and in its current form infringes the rights of consumers. Ralph Nader argues that NAFTA and the WTO seek to manage trade between states to the advantage of big corporate interests, not to make it 'freer'. 'We've progressed by subordinating the commercial to the human rights, labour rights and environmental rights imperatives,' Nader argued in July 2000. 'The WTO reverses that.' Much of NAFTA and the WTO agreement are actually attempts to manage trade. 'True free trade would take only one page for a trade agreement. How come there are hundreds of pages, and thousands of regulations?' Nader asks in one of his 2000 campaign leaflets. 'It's corporate-managed trade.'

5   Free trade damages the environment. There is an inherent tension, many argue, between 'Green' concern about the planet and the profit-maximizing dictates of big business. Concern about the environment and quality of life takes second place to economic imperatives.

A Case of 'Doublethink'?

As noted earlier in this chapter, the simultaneous popularity of both protectionism and free trade in the United States is a genuine puzzle to many students of its politics. There is perhaps a kind of Orwellian 'doublethink' being practised here, as Harry Schutt suggests. Even though Western politicians and economists have consistently sung the praises of free trade since the 1940s, the international economy has never actually reached the point where it could be described as genuinely 'free'.[14] And yet, in America's case at least, the contradictory practices in this area of policy making probably derive in large part from the ways in which the separate branches of its political system are compelled to 'think differently'.

Presidents and members of Congress confront different patterns of electoral incentives. Isaiah Frank argues that protectionist pressures in the United States 'are a reaction to pressures from special domestic groups acting rationally in their own interests . . . traditionally, Congress has responded to the concentrated and well-organized pressures of special groups whose jobs and incomes are threatened by imports'.[15] Members of Congress have a local constituency-oriented focus and are hence more likely to advocate protectionism, especially where well organized interests exist which seek to limit external competition. Presidents, on the other hand, can afford to take a national focus, and may be more likely to favour free trade (if, that is, one accepts the liberal argument that free trade is in the interests of the nation as a whole, which all post-war US presidents have done). There was nothing especially unusual, then, in the fact that President Clinton saw a different side of the issue from many in Congress when confronting the issue of NAFTA.

In his book *The Deadlock of Democracy* James McGregor Burns argued that there are actually four major political parties in the United States: presidential Democrats, congressional Democrats, presidential Republicans and congressional Republicans.[16] This way of looking at the parties is arguably quite useful for understanding debates about international trade, for the current dispute essentially pits the presidential parties (plus the congressional Republicans) against the congressional Democrats. The 2000 presidential debates illustrated how close together the two main *presidential* parties are on free trade. Although they differed slightly on the degree to which they would link trade with environmental and workers' rights issues, both George W. Bush and Al Gore made it clear that they were enthusiastic advocates of NAFTA and the WTO. (Though for understandable political reasons Gore largely avoided mentioning this on the campaign trail in order to avoid offending labour unions and often used the term 'free and fair trade'.) In a speech delivered at the APEC business summit on 16 November 1998 Gore made it clear that he was no friend of protectionism. 'In the end,' he insisted, 'in this global economy, protectionism will only protect us from prosperity itself.' He argued also that freer trade would create jobs. Bush was even more vocal in his praise of the doctrine of free trade during the presidential campaign, insisting that the case for free trade was 'not just monetary but moral'. On a visit to Mexico in April 2000 Bush pledged to tear down trade barriers from Alaska 'to the tip of Cape Horn'.

Some international relations theorists – especially a group known as the hegemonic stability theorists – worry that a series of protectionist 'trade wars' similar to those which followed the enactment of Smoot–Hawley are just around the corner.[17] They argue that the existence of a free-trading international order is dependent upon the existence of a 'hegemonic' power both willing and able to police such an order. But with the decline of the current hegemon from its pre-eminent position, this means that we can soon expect the international collapse of free trade and a return to the practices of the 1930s (when the absence of a hegemon was also paired with a collapse in trade). Critics of this position counter that the free-trade regime will probably continue to exist long after American hegemony has waned.[18] Both positions, however, focus largely on America's continued *capacity* to police a free-trading economic order, as opposed to its *willingness* to continue to play such a role. But the latter may well be as crucial as the former. We cannot overlook the importance of the debate going on in America today as to whether free trade is actually in America's interests. For this internal debate – who wins, who loses – will be crucial to determining the foreign-policy behaviour of a nation which continues to dominate the international political and economic system.

NOTES

1   Robert Gilpin, *The Political Economy of International Relations* (Princeton NJ, Princeton University Press, 1987), p. 183.
2   Isaiah Frank, 'Towards freer trade among nations: a US perspective', in John Nieuwenhuysen (ed.), *Towards Freer Trade between Nations* (Oxford, Oxford University Press, 1989), p. 44.

3 Gilpin, *Political Economy of International Relations*, pp. 180–1.
4 Frank, 'Towards freer trade', p. 45.
5 Harry Schutt, *The Myth of Free Trade: Patterns of Protectionism since 1945* (Oxford, Blackwell, 1985), p. 155.
6 Martin Walker, *Clinton: The President they Deserve* (London, Vintage, 1997), p. 287.
7 Bob Woodward, *The Agenda: Inside the Clinton White House* (New York, Simon & Schuster, 1994), p. 55.
8 Walker, *Clinton*, pp. 285–6.
9 Elizabeth Drew, *On the Edge: The Clinton Presidency* (New York, Simon & Schuster, 1994), p. 343.
10 Robert Reich, *Locked in the Cabinet* (New York, Knopf, 1997), p. 124.
11 Drew, *On the Edge*, pp. 341–2.
12 Joe Califano, 'The imperial Congress', *New York Times* magazine, 23 January 1994.
13 Charles Kegley and Eugene Wittkopf, *World Poltics: Trend and Transformation*, eighth edition (New York, Bedford/St Martin's Press, 2001), p. 262.
14 Schutt, *The Myth of Free Trade*, p. 1.
15 Frank, 'Towards freer trade', p. 55.
16 James McGregor Burns, *The Deadlock of Democracy: Four-party Politics in America* (Englewood Cliffs NJ, Prentice-Hall, 1963).
17 See, for instance, Robert Gilpin, *War and Change in World Politics* (London, Cambridge University Press, 1981).
18 Robert Keohane, *After Hegemony: Cooperation and Discord in the World Political Economy* (Princeton NJ, Princeton University Press, 1984).

Further Reading

PART I INSTITUTIONS AND PROCESSES

1 DIVIDED GOVERNMENT: DOES IT MATTER?

The best summary of the divided government debate is by Morris Fiorina, *Divided Government* (second edition, New York and London, Macmillan, 1995). For a discussion of the origins of divided government see Gary C. Jacobson, *The Electoral Origins of Divided Government: Competition in the US House Elections, 1946–1988* (Boulder CO, Westview Press, 1990). For a discussion of the role of the presidency in divided government see Byron Shafer, *Bifurcated Politics* (Cambridge MA, Harvard University Press, 1988). On the consequences of divided control see David R. Mayhew, *Divided we Govern: Party Control, Lawmaking and Investigations* (New Haven CT, Yale University Press, 1991). For a critical perspective on divided government see James L. Sundquist, 'Needed: a political theory for the new era of coalition government in the United States', *Political Science Quarterly*, 103 (1988), pp. 613–35; also his *Constitutional Reform and Effective Government* (Washington DC, Brookings Institution, 1987). Quantitative studies of the phenomenon are provided by Gary W. Cox and Samuel Kernell (eds), *The Politics of Divided Government* (Boulder CO, Westview Press, 1991).

2 TRUST IN GOVERNMENT: A CRISIS OF DEMOCRACY?

The most accessible text on American's distrust of government is Gavin Esler, *The United States of Anger: The People and the American Dream* (London, Penguin, 1997). Other good introductory texts include Joseph S. Nye junior, Philip D. Zelikow and David C. King (eds), *Why People don't Trust Government* (Cambridge MA, Harvard University Press, 1997), and Susan J. Tolchin, *The Angry American: How Voter Rage is Changing the Nation* (Boulder CO, Westview Press, 1996). Two detailed and sophisticated volumes are Pippa Norris (ed.), *Critical Citizens: Global Support for Democratic Governance* (Oxford, Oxford University Press, 1999) and Susan J. Pharr and Robert D. Putnam (eds), *Disaffected Democracies: What's Troubling the Trilateral Countries?* (Princeton NJ,

Princeton University Press, 2000). Data on Americans' attitudes to their government can be found at the National Election Studies' and the Pew Research Center's websites at http://www.umich.edu/~nes/nesguide/gd-index.htm#5 and http://www.people-press.org/trustrpt.htm.

3 VOTING AND NON-VOTING: AMERICA'S FLAWED DEMOCRACY?

The classic discussion of the party identification approach is Angus Campbell, Phillip E. Converse, Warren E. Miller and Donald E. Stokes, *The American Voter* (New York, Wiley, 1960). Norman Nie, Sydney Verba and John R. Petrocik's *The Changing American Voter* (Cambridge MA, Harvard University Press, 1976) is a direct response to the earlier work from an issue voting perspective. A good deal more up to date is Warren Miller and Merrill Shanks, *The New American Voter* (London, Harvard University Press, 1996), although undergraduates may find it quite demanding. On political participation in the United States generally the classic discussion is Sidney Verba and Norman Nie's *Participation in America: Political Democracy and Social Equality* (London, Harper & Row, 1972), although the statistics they provide are now out of date. A more contemporary analysis is Robert Putnam's highly readable *Bowling Alone: The Collapse and Revival of American Community* (New York, Simon & Schuster, 2000). The most important empirical analysis of the question of non-voting is Ruy Teixeira's *Why Americans don't Vote: Turnout Decline in the United States, 1960–1984* (London, Greenwood Press, 1987). Also especially worth looking at is Walter Dean Burnham's *The Current Crisis in American Politics* (Oxford, Oxford University Press, 1982). Up-to-date figures on US and comparative voter turnout can be found on the Internet; the Federal Election Commission's site, www.fec.gov, is particularly useful, as is the Center for Voting and Democracy at www.igc.org.

4 CAMPAIGN FINANCE REFORM: CREATING A LEVEL PLAYING FIELD

For a stinging critique of the campaign finance system see Elizabeth Drew, *The Corruption of American Politics: What went Wrong and Why* (New York, Overlook Press, 2000). Slightly dated now but also very useful is her earlier work *Politics and Money: The New Road to Corruption* (New York, Macmillan, 1983). Brooks Jackson's *Honest Graft* (New York, Knopf, 1988) is a journalistic work in similar vein. For a critique of the system from a political scientist's perspective see Lance Bennett, *The Governing Crisis: Media, Money and Marketing in American Elections* (New York, St Martin's Press, 1992). There are numerous up-to-date sources of information on campaign finance issues available on the worldwide web, but among the most useful sites are the Brookings Institution coverage at www.brookings.org and the politics sections of the *Washington Post* at www.washingtonpost.com and the *New York Times* at www.nytimes.com.

5 CONTAINING PRESIDENTIAL POWER

An excellent textbook on all aspects of the American presidency is Norman Thomas and Joseph Pika, *The Politics of the Presidency* (fourth edition, Washington DC, CQ Press, 1997). Every student of the subject should consult Richard Neustadt's classic book *Presidential Power and the Modern Presidents: The Politics of Leadership from Roosevelt to Reagan* (New York, Free Press, 1990). The most widely cited critique of presidential power is Arthur Schlesinger's *The Imperial Presidency* (Boston MA, Houghton Mifflin, 1973). The epilogue to the 1989 edition updates his analysis to the Reagan era. A representative example of the opposing argument is Gordon Jones and John Marini (eds), *Imperial Congress: Crisis in the Separation of Powers* (New York: Pharos Books, 1988). Balanced accounts of the powers of Congress and the president in relation to foreign policy are provided in James Lindsay, *Congress and the Politics of US Foreign Policy* (London, Johns Hopkins University Press, 1994), and Louis Fisher, *Presidential War Power* (Lawrence KS, University of Kansas Press, 1995).

6 THE SUPREME COURT: THE POLITICS OF JUDICIAL ACTIVISM

On the Burger Court see Vincent Blasi (ed.), *The Burger Court: The Counter-revolution that Wasn't* (New Haven CT, Yale University Press). For an up-to-date summary of the leading Court decisions see Kermit L. Hall (ed.), *The Oxford Guide to United States Supreme Court Decisions* (New York and Oxford, Oxford University Press, 1999). Kermit Hall has also edited an excellent guide to the Court, *The Oxford Companion to the Supreme Court* (Oxford and New York, Oxford University Press, 1992). An insider's view of the Court by an ex-clerk to Harry Blackmun is by Edward Lazarus, *Closed Chambers: The Rise, Fall and Future of the Modern Supreme Court* (New York and Harmondsworth, Penguin, 1999). David Savage, *Turning Right: The Making of the Rehnquist Supreme Court* (New York, Wiley, 1992) provides a graphic account of the move to the right in the early Rehnquist Court. Jethro K. Lieberman, *A Practical Companion to the Constitution* (Berkeley CA, Los Angeles and London, University of California Press, 1999) provides good background information on major Court decisions.

7 DIRECT DEMOCRACY: POWER TO THE PEOPLE?

The Initiative and Referendum Institute maintains the best on-line direct democracy resource at http://www.iandrinstitute.org. One of the classic direct democracy texts is David Magleby, *Direct Legislation: Voting on Ballot Propositions in the United States* (Baltimore MD, Johns Hopkins University Press, 1984). A more recent and more specialist book is Shaun Bowler, Todd Donovan and Caroline J. Tolbert (eds), *Citizens as Legislators: Direct Democracy in the United States*

(Columbus OH, Ohio State University Press, 1998). Two very accessible books by journalists unhappy with the direct democracy process are David S. Broder, *Democracy Derailed: Initiative Campaigns and the Power of Money* (New York, Harcourt, 2000), and Peter Schrag, *Paradise Lost: California's Experience, America's Future* (New York, New Press, 1998). Two very good books that examine single initiatives rather than direct democracy as a whole are Lydia Chavez, *The Color Bind: California's Battle to End Affirmative Action* (Berkeley CA and Los Angeles, University of California Press, 1998), and David O. Sears and Jack Citrin, *Tax Revolt: Something for Nothing in California* (Cambridge MA, Harvard University Press, 1985). If you want to widen the scope of your reading to include countries other than the United States consider David Butler and Austin Ranney's edited volume *Referendums around the World: The Growing Use of Direct Democracy* (Washington DC, AEI Press, 1994).

Part II Policies

8 Gun Control: The Right to Bear Arms

Pro-gun information and arguments can be found on the National Rifle Association's website at http://www.nra.org. Counter-arguments can be found on the websites of Handgun Control and the Coalition to Stop Gun Violence at http://www.handguncontrol.org and http://www.csgv.org. For details of Americans' opinions on guns and gun control go to Gallup's site at http://www.gallup.com/poll/indicators/indGuns.asp. An excellent text, which includes a wide range of articles on the history, use and abuse of guns, is Jan E. Dizard, Robert Merrill Muth and Stephen P. Andrews (eds), *Guns in America: A Reader* (London, New York University Press, 1999). The most comprehensive review of why Congress has failed to pass meaningful gun-control legislation is Robert Spitzer, *The Politics of Gun Control* (Chatham NJ, Chatham House, 1995).

9 Immigration: a Nation State or a State of Nations?

A good introductory text on immigration policy is Louis DeSipio and Rodolfo O. de la Garza, *Making Americans, Remaking America: Immigration and Immigration Policy* (Boulder CO, Westview Press, 1998). An excellent exposition of the arguments used by those seeking to restrict immigration can be found in David M. Reimers, *Unwelcome Strangers: American Identity and the Turn against Immigration* (New York, Columbia University Press, 1998). Many interesting articles on contemporary anti-immigrant sentiment are included in Juan F. Perea (ed.), *Immigrants Out! The New Nativism and the Anti-immigrant Impulse in the United States* (New York, New York University Press, 1997). For an insight into the lives of Mexican immigrants see Augusta Dwyer, *On the Line: Life on the US–Mexico Border* (London, Latin America Bureau, 1994) and (for a fictional account) T. Coraghessan Boyle, *The Tortilla Curtain* (London, Bloomsbury,

1996). General information can be found on the Census Bureau's and Immigration and Naturalization Service's websites at http://www.census.gov and http://www.ins.gov.

10 AFFIRMATIVE ACTION: THE CONTINUING DILEMMA

Two excellent edited volumes on affirmative action are Stephen Steinberg (ed.), *Race and Ethnicity in the United States: Issues and Debates* (Oxford, Blackwell, 2000), and Robert Post and Michael Rogin (eds), *Race and Representation: Affirmative Action* (New York, Zone Books, 1998). The history of Proposition 209, California's anti-affirmative action initiative, is eloquently and accessibly told in Lydia Chavez, *The Color Bind: California's Battle to End Affirmative Action* (Berkeley CA and Los Angeles, University of California Press, 1998).

11 THE POLITICS OF HEALTH CARE: ANXIETY AMID PLENTY

For an account of how Medicare was enacted see Theodore Marmor, *The Politics of Medicare* (London, Routledge, 1970). Numerous accounts of the failure of the Clinton reforms exist; see in particular Theda Skocpol, *Boomerang: Health Care Reform and the Turn against Government* (New York, Norton, 1997); Thomas E. Mann and Norman J. Ornstein, *Intensive Care* (Washington DC, Brookings Institution/American Enterprise Institute, 1995); Paul Starr, 'What happened to health care reform?', *American Prospect*, 6 (1995). For a review of alternative ways of reforming health care see Erik Eckholm (ed.), *Solving America's Health Care Crisis* (New York, *Times* Books/Random House, 1993). A general introduction to the politics of health care policy is Carol S. Weissert and William G. Weissert, *Governing Health: The Politics of Health Policy* (Baltimore MD, Johns Hopkins University Press, 1996). On the same theme see Mark E. Rushevsky and Kant Patel, *Politics, Power and Policy-making: A Case of Health Care Reform in the 1990s* (Armonk NY, Sharpe, 1998).

12 CAPITAL PUNISHMENT: THE POLITICS OF RETRIBUTION

A good history of the death penalty is Laura E. Randa, *Society's Final Solution: A History and Discussion of the Death Penalty* (Lanham MD, University Press of America, 1997). For a recent critique of the death penalty see Robert Jay Lifton and Greg Mitchell, *Who owns Death? Capital Punishment, the American Conscience, and the End of Executions* (New York, Morrow, 2000). For a more comprehensive review of the controversy in this area see Mary E. Williams (ed.), *Capital Punishment: Current Controversies* (San Diego CA, Greenhaven Press, 2000). For a graphic account of the counselling and support provided by Sister Prejean to a condemned man see Helen Prejean, *Dead Man Walking: An Eye Witness Account of the Death Penalty in the United States* (New York, Vintage

Books, 1996). This account was made into a film of the same name starring Susan Sarandon and Sean Penn. Numerous websites are devoted to the capital punishment question; for a sample of good links see, for example, http://www.deathpenaltyinfo.org/history2.html.

13 WELFARE REFORM: PROVIDING FOR THE OLD BUT NOT FOR THE POOR

The best single introduction to the subject is Theda Skocpol's *Protecting Soldiers and Mothers: The Political Origins of Social Policy in the United States* (Cambridge MA, Harvard University Press, 1992). For an account of welfare reform attempts in the Johnson, Nixon, Carter and Reagan presidencies see David McKay, *Domestic Policy and Ideology: Presidents and the American State, 1964–1987* (Cambridge, Cambridge University Press, 1989). A critique of the welfare system is provided by Charles Noble, *Welfare as we Knew it* (Oxford and New York, Oxford University Press, 1997). For a perspective on the 1996 reforms see Theda Skocpol, 'From beginning to end: has twentieth-century social policy come full circle?' in Morton Keller and R. Shep Melnick, *Taking Stock: American Government in the Twentieth Century* (New York and Cambridge, Cambridge University Press, 1999). For up-to-date data on welfare recipients see the Administration for Children and Families, US Department of Health and Human Services, http://www.acf/dhhs.gov/programs/opa/facts/tanf/htm. For a comparative (Anglo-American) perspective see Desmond King, *Actively Seeking Work* (Chicago, University of Chicago Press, 1995).

14 ABORTION: THE RIGHT TO LIFE DEBATE

Mainstream pro-life arguments can be found on websites of the National Right to Life Committee and the American Life League at http://www.nrlc.org and http://www.all.org. More radical arguments can be found on many of the sites of the more extreme groups, such as Operation Rescue's. (These sites include extremely graphic photos of aborted foetuses or 'murdered pre-born children'.) Counter-arguments can be found at the website of America's largest pro-choice pressure group, the National Abortion and Reproductive Rights Action League, at http://www.naral.org. And Americans' opinions on abortion are reported in detail on Gallup's website at http://www.gallup.com/poll/releases/pr010122.asp. An excellent history of abortion in pre-Roe America is Leslie J. Reagan, *When Abortion was a Crime: Women, Medicine, and Law in the United States, 1867–1973* (Berkeley CA and Los Angeles, University of California Press, 1996). Laurence H. Tribe's *Abortion: The Clash of Absolutes* (New York, Norton, 1992) and Karen O'Connor's *No Neutral Ground: Abortion Politics in an Age of Absolutes* (Boulder CO, Westview Press, 1996) are both accessible and relatively balanced books on this emotive topic. Finally, a very detailed but fascinating picture of contemporary pro-life radicals is presented in James Risen and Judy L. Thomas, *Wrath of Angels: The American Abortion War* (New York, Basic Books, 1998).

15 Manifest Destiny and Realpolitik: Realism versus Idealism in Foreign Policy

For a classically realist perspective on American foreign policy see Henry Kissinger, *Diplomacy* (New York, Simon & Schuster, 1994). The best textbooks to consult in this area are James McCormick, *American Foreign Policy and Process* (Itasca IL, Peacock, 1992), and Charles Kegley and Eugene Wittkopf, *American Foreign Policy: Pattern and Process* (fifth edition, New York, St Martin's Press, 1996), both of which attempt a rather more balanced approach than Kissinger. John Lewis Gaddis's classic *Strategies of Containment* (New York, Oxford University Press, 1982) provides a detailed but partial account of most of the strategies adopted by US presidents during the Cold War. Richard Melanson, *American Foreign Policy since the Vietnam War: The Search for Consensus, from Nixon to Clinton* (Armonk NY, Sharpe, 1996), and Stephen Ambrose, *Rise to Globalism: American Foreign Policy since 1938* (London, Penguin, 1993), include discussions of recent administrations. For up-to-date statements by contemporary American realists and idealists see the latest editions of the journals *Foreign Affairs* and *Foreign Policy*.

16 America as a Global Economic Player: Free Trade versus Protectionism

A classic albeit slightly dated discussion of the theoretical arguments on both sides of this issue can be found in Robert Gilpin, *The Political Economy of International Relations* (Princeton NJ, Princeton University Press, 1987). The battle over NAFTA viewed from the Clinton administration perspective is particularly well treated in Elizabeth Drew, *On the Edge: The Clinton Presidency* (New York, Simon & Schuster, 1994). A defence of free trade can be found in most elementary economics textbooks, and examples of the modern protectionist argument can be found on the AFL-CIO's website at www.aflcio.org. For Ralph Nader's position see his *The Case against 'Free Trade': GATT, NAFTA and the Globalization of Corporate Power* (San Francisco, Earth Island Books, 1993). Up-to-date analyses of free trade versus protectionist issues can also be found in Graham Dunkley, *The Free Trade Adventure: The WTO, the Uruguay Round and Globalism* (London, Zed Books, 2000), and William Orme, *Understanding NAFTA: Mexico, Free Trade and the New North America* (Austin TX, University of Texas Press, 1996).

Index

abortion 161–2, 170
    constitutional argument 164–6
    philosophy and science 166–8
    rape, incest and death of the mother 169
    Roe v. *Wade* 68, 72, 76, 161, 163–5,
        169, 170
    Supreme Court 68, 72, 74, 76, 161,
        163–5, 169, 170
Adarand Constructors v. *Pena* 73
advertisements, political
    campaign finance reform 46–7, 49
    trust in government 26
affirmative action 118, 126–7
    case against 123–5
    case for 122–3
    class-based 125–6
    history 118–22
    Supreme Court 70, 71–2, 73–4
AFL-CIO
    campaign finance reform 53
    free trade v. protectionism 186, 187,
        189
    health care 130
Aideed, Mohammed Farah 178
Aid for Families with Dependent Children
        (AFDC) 151–2, 153, 154, 155–6, 160
American Life League (ALL) 165
American Medical Association (AMA)
        129, 133
    abortion 162
Americans for Gun Safety (AGS) 103
apportionment 70
Arab Muslim immigrants 113
Ashcroft, John 165
Audubon Society 109
Austria 33
Authoritarian Reflex 27

Baker, James Jay 99
Balanced Budget Act (1997) 136
Beccaria, Cesare 140
Beck, Roy 110
Bennett, Lance 50–1, 52–3
Better Jobs and Income Plan (BJIP) 154
bilingual education 115–16
Blackmun, Harry 72
    abortion 164, 165, 170
Blue Cross 129
Blue Shield 129
Bok, Derek 22–3
Boland, Edward 62
Boland amendments 62
Bonior, David 186
Borjas, George 110
Bork, Robert 72–3
Bowler, Shaun 83, 85–6, 88
Bradley, Bill 35
Brady, James 95, 103
Brady, Sarah 95, 103
Brady Bill (1993) 73, 95, 96, 100–1, 102
Brandeis, Louis 69
Brennan, Justice 72, 75
Brest, Paul 71
Breyer, Stephen 165
Briggs, Vernon, Jr 110, 111
Brimelow, Peter 110, 113, 114
Broder, David 88–9
Brody, Richard 40
Brown v. *Board of Education* 68, 71, 119
Bryer, Stephen 72
Brzezinski, Zbigniew 174
Buchanan, Pat 187, 189
Buckley v. *Valeo* 45, 46, 47, 49, 50, 53
budget
    direct democracy 89

divided government   14, 16
health care   132
Bureau of Alcohol, Tobacco and Firearms
   (BATF)   101
Burger, Warren   69, 70, 72
   gun control   101–2
Burger Court   69–72, 75
   gun control   101–2
Burnham, Walter Dean   40, 41
Burns, James McGregor   56, 190–1
Bush, George H. (Sr)
   abortion   165
   divided government   11, 12
   foreign policy   174
   free trade v. protectionism   187
   presidential power   60, 64
   trust in government   24, 26
   welfare   155
Bush, George W. (Jr)
   abortion   165, 166
   capital punishment   146, 148
   foreign policy   175–6, 177, 178, 181
   free trade v. protectionism   188, 191
   gun control   97, 98, 104
   health care   136, 137
   presidential elections (2000)   31, 33,
      35
   Supreme Court   68, 74, 75, 76
   welfare reform   159
Bush v. Gore   68, 74, 75, 76
Byrd, Robert   133

Califano, Joe   59, 64, 187
California Teachers' Association   115
campaign finance
   direct democracy   85, 87
   gun control   102
   reform   44–7, 52–3: case against   47–8;
      case for   48–50; money and politics
      50–1
   see also fund raising
Campbell, Angus   34, 35, 36
Canada
   health care   132
   NAFTA   185–7, 189
capitalism   29
capital punishment   139
   current debate   144–8
   future   148–9
   historical perspective   139–42

Supreme Court   72, 139, 142–4, 148
Carrying Concealed Weapons (CCW)
   laws   103
Carter, Jimmy
   divided government   11
   foreign policy   172, 174, 176, 177, 178,
      179–80
   health care   130
   presidential power   60, 63
   Supreme Court   69
   trust in government   25
   welfare reform   16, 154
Casey, William   62
children
   health care   136–7
   welfare   151–2, 153, 154, 155–7,
      159–60
Children's Health Insurance Program
   (CHIP)   136–7
Chile   177
China   52
Cisneros, Henry   59
Citadel Military Academy   74
civic republicanism, decline of   28, 29
civil liberties   70
civil rights
   direct democracy   83
   Supreme Court   70, 71
Civil Rights Act (1964)   15, 119, 121
Civil Rights Act (1965)   15
Civil War   75, 76, 119
class-based affirmative action   125–6
Cleveland, Grover   31
Clinton, Bill
   abortion   165
   affirmative action   121
   campaign finance reform   52
   divided and unified government   12, 15,
      17
   elections (1996)   13
   foreign policy   176, 177, 178, 179, 181
   free trade v. protectionism   186, 187,
      188, 190
   gun control   95, 104
   health care   132–4, 136, 137, 156
   imperial Congress   58, 59, 65
   Supreme Court   72
   trust in government   26
   welfare reform   16, 156–7
Clinton, Hillary Rodham   132, 133

Coalition to Stop Gun Violence
    (CSGV)   102
Coker v. *Georgia*   143
Cold War
    foreign policy   174–5, 177
    trust in government   24, 29
Committee on Political Education (COPE)
    53
communitarianism   28
confrontational politics   17
Congress
    affirmative action   119–20
    campaign finance reform   47
    composition by party, 1961–2001   10
    free trade v. protectionism   184, 186,
        190
    gun control   101
    health care   133, 134, 136
    immigration   106–7, 108
    and president, power distribution *see*
        divided government
    presidential power   55, 57–9, 60–2, 63,
        64–5
    welfare reform   152, 153
    see also House of Representatives; Senate
constitution
    abortion   164–6
    divided government   17–18
    gun control   97, 101–2
    presidential power   57, 59–60
    Supreme Court   67, 68–9
Consumer Product Safety Commission   103
Contract with America   12, 15, 64, 156
Conyers, John   59
Corrado, Anthony   47
corruption
    campaign finance reform   49, 50
    direct democracy   78–9, 84–5
Cox, Archibald   57, 59
Crater, Lief   143
Cronin, Thomas   57, 83, 87
Crovitz, Gordon   58, 63
cultural arguments, immigration debate
    112–16

death penalty *see* capital punishment
Deibel, Terry   179
DeIulio, John   38
Dellinger, Walter   75
democracy

direct *see* direct democracy
    representative   78, 82, 84, 90
Democratic Party
    affirmative action   120, 125
    campaign finance reform   47
    capital punishment   148
    divided government   9–13, 14, 15, 16
    free trade v. protectionism   186, 191
    health care   130
    immigration   108
    imperial Congress   58, 59, 62, 63, 65
    Supreme Court   74
    trust in government   25
    voting behaviour   34–5
    welfare reform   152, 155, 156, 157–8
Department of Labor   120
direct democracy   78–81, 90
    affirmative action   121
    contemporary debate: minority rights
        82–4; special interests and big money
        84–8
    immigration   107, 115
    responsive v. responsible laws   88–9
    theoretical and historical debate   82
disabled people   151, 155, 159
divided government   9–11
    causes   11–13
    consequences   14–17
    presidential power   65
    voters' views   17–18
Dole, Bob   12, 13, 134
Dole, Elizabeth   122
Dominican Republic   174
Donovan, Todd   83, 85–6, 88
Draper, Theodore   63
Dred Scott v. *Sandford*   75, 76, 119
Drew, Elizabeth   45, 49, 50, 187
Duke's Laws   139
Dulles, John Foster   174

Earned Income Tax Credits (EITC)   153,
    154, 157
economic arguments, immigration debate
    109–12
economic performance
    trust in government   23–4, 29
    voting behaviour   36
education levels and voting behaviour   39
Eisenhower, Dwight D.
    budget negotiations   16

foreign policy   176, 177
    presidential power   56
    Supreme Court   70
elderly people
    health care   129–30, 132, 134–5, 137
    pensions   151, 159
    welfare   155, 159
elections and divided government   10–11,
    13
English language and immigration   114–16
environmental arguments
    free trade v. protectionism   190
    immigration   108–9
Esler, Gavin   24
Espy, Mike   59
Ethics in Government Act (1978)   58
eugenics   141, 142
European Convention on Human Rights
    181
exclusionary rule   70

Family Assistance Plan (FAP)   152–3
Family Support Act (1988)   155
Federal Election Campaign Act (FECA)
    1971   44
    1974   44–5, 50, 53
Federal Election Commission   44, 47
Federation for American Immigration
    Reform (FAIR)   108
Feingold, Russ   47
Fernandez, Ken   85–6
focus groups, trust in government   25
Foley, Tom   96
Food Stamps   152, 154, 158, 160
Forbes, Steve   35
Ford, Bill   186–7
Ford, Gerald
    abortion   165
    presidential power   63
    Supreme Court   69, 70
    trust in government   25
    welfare reform   154
foreign policy
    divided government   9, 12, 14, 18
    presidential power   56–7, 58, 59–64
    realist–idealist debate   172–6, 181:
        idealism   179–81; realism   176–8
Foster, Vince   59
Frank, Isaiah   183–4, 190
free speech, and campaign finance

reform   47–8, 50
free trade   183–5, 190–1
    case against   189–90
    case for   188–90
    NAFTA   185–7
    trust in government   23
    WTO   188
Friends of the Earth   109
Fukuyama, Francis   114
fund raising   25
    see also campaign finance
Furman v. Georgia   72, 142–3

Gamble, Barbara   83
Garcia v. San Antonio Metropolitan Transit
    Authority   72
gay rights   74, 83
General Agreement on Tariffs and Trade
    (GATT)   184, 185, 186, 188
generational factors, voting behaviour
    40–1
George III   20
Gephardt, Richard   186
Germany   25
Gideon v. Wainwright   70
Gilmore, Gary   143
Gilpin, Robert   183, 184
Gingrich, Newt
    divided government   12, 15
    imperial Congress   58, 64
    welfare reform   156
Ginsberg, Benjamin   72, 73
Ginsburg, Ruth Bader   72, 165
globalization   183–5, 190–1
    case against   189–90
    case for   188–90
    NAFTA   185–7
    trust in government   23, 29
    WTO   188
Golden, Andrew   100
Goldwater, Barry   35
Gore, Al
    abortion   165
    foreign policy   175–6, 179, 180, 181
    free trade v. protectionism   188, 191
    gun control   98
    presidential elections   11, 31, 33, 35
    Supreme Court   68, 74, 75, 76
    welfare   159
Gore v. Bush   68, 74, 75, 76

Great Britain *see* United Kingdom
Great Compromise   119
Great Depression
    capital punishment   141
    presidential power   55
    protectionism   184
    trust in government   24–5
    welfare   151
Great Society
    divided government   9, 15
    Medicare Bill   130
    welfare reform   152, 159
Green Party   187
Greenstein, Fred   57
Gregg v. *Georgia*   72, 139, 143
Grenzke, Janet   50
gridlock, political   11
Griswold v. *Connecticut*   163
Gulf War   12, 60
gun control   95–6, 104
    arguments against   96–9
    arguments for   99–104
    Supreme Court   73, 100–2
Gun-free School Zones Act   73

Haiti   177
Hall, Richard   51
Hamilton, Alexander   173, 184
Handgun Control   103
hard money, campaign finance reform   45,
    48
Harris, Eric   100
Harrison, Benjamin   31
Hart, Gary   26
Hart, Melissa   46–7
health care   128
    Bush, George W.   137
    Clinton plan   132–4, 156
    controversy   134–7
    future   138
    New Federalism   137
    self-reliance and public
        expectations   128–32
Health Insurance Association of America
    (HIAA)   133
Health Maintenance Organizations (HMOs)
    131, 134, 135
Health Security Act (HSA)   133
hegemonic stability theorists   191
Helms, Jesse   13

Helsinki agreements   181
heroic presidency period   56, 64
Heston, Charlton   96–7
Hill, Anita   73
Hinckley, John   95
Hitler, Adolf   173, 177
Hodgson, Geoffrey   57
Holmes, Oliver Wendell   69
Hopwood v. *Texas*   121
House of Representatives
    composition by party, 1961–2001   10
    divided government   10–11, 12–13
    free trade v. protectionism   186
    presidential power   60, 62, 64
housing subsidies   152
Hughes Court   69, 75, 76
human rights   174, 177, 178, 179–81
Humphrey, Hubert   120
hunting   99
Huntington, Samuel   2, 38

illegal immigration   107, 111
immigration   106–8, 116
    affirmative action   124
    cultural arguments   112–16
    economic arguments   109–12
    environmental arguments   108–9
    foreign policy   174
Immigration and Naturalization Service
    (INS)   107
Immigration Reform and Control Act
    (IRCA, 1986)   107
imperial Congress   55, 57–9, 63, 64–5
imperial presidency   55, 56–7, 63, 64,
    65
incumbency advantage   11–12, 51
inevitable discovery rule   70
information technology (IT)   24
Inglehart, Ronald   27
initiatives   79–81, 85–8, 89
    affirmative action   121
    immigration   107, 115
inner cities, immigration   111
institutional explanations, non-voting
    behaviour   38–9, 41
International Covenant on Civil and
    Political Rights   181
International Monetary Fund (IMF)   184
interpretivists   68–9, 75
Iran   177, 178

Iran-Contra scandal   55, 59, 61–4
Shah   177, 178
issue advertisements   46–7, 49
issue voting model   35–7

Jackson, Andrew   56
Jackson, Jesse   186, 187
Japan   25, 185
Jefferson, Thomas   56, 173
Jim Crow laws   119
Job Opportunities and Basic Skills Training
    (JOBS)   156
jobs
   free trade v. protectionism   187, 188–9
   immigration   109, 110–11
Johnson, Lyndon B.
   affirmative action   120
   presidential power   57, 59, 60, 64
   Supreme Court   69
   trust in government   25
   welfare reform   16, 152
Johnson, Mitchell   100
Jones, Gordon   58, 65
Jones, Paula   59
journalism   26, 29
jurisprudence   68

Kegley, Charles   188
Kemp, Jack   34
Kennedy, Anthony   72, 74, 165
Kennedy, John F.
   assassination   95, 100
   foreign policy   177
   health care   130
   presidential power   56
   Supreme Court   69
   trust in government   26
   welfare reform   152
Kennedy, Robert   100
Key, V. O.   36, 96
Khomeini, Ayatollah   177
King, David   25
King, Martin Luther, Jr   100, 123, 125
Kissinger, Henry   172, 173, 174
Klebold, Dylan   100
Kleck, Gary   98
Klink, Ron   46

Labor, Department of   120
labour unions

campaign finance reform   44, 45, 53
free trade v. protectionism   186–7
language, official   114–16
LaPierre, Wayne   97–8
Lascher, Edward   88
lethal injection, death by   145, 146
liberalism, procedural   28
Lifton, Robert Jay   139–40
Lincoln, Abraham   56
Lindsay, James   61, 65
Line item Veto Act (1996)   64–5

McCain, John
   campaign finance reform   47, 49–50,
      53
   presidential nomination   35
McCain–Feingold Bill   47, 48, 50, 52, 53
McConnell, Mitch   48
McCormick, James   172
McCorvey, Norma   169
McCuan, David   85–6
McFarlane, Robert   62
Machiavelli, Niccolo   172
McKay, David   39
McKleskey v. *Kemp*   144
McVeigh, Timothy   20, 102, 148
Madison, James   56, 82
Magaziner, Ira   132
Mahan v. *Howell*   70
Malbin, Michael   63
Malcolm X   100
Mann, Thomas   49, 50
Mapp v. *Ohio*   70
Marbury v. *Madison*   67, 75
Marini, John   58, 65
Marshall, John   72, 75
Mayhew, David   15
media   26, 29
Medicaid   130, 131, 132, 135, 136
   Clinton health care plan   133
   divided government   15
   New Federalism   137
   welfare reforms   152, 153, 154–5, 158,
      160
Medicare   130, 135, 159, 160
   Clinton health care plan   133
   divided government   15
   trust in government   22
Mexican American Legal Defense
      Fund   115

Mexico
  immigrants from   107, 113–14
  NAFTA   185–7, 189–90
Miller, Warren   40–1
Milliken v. *Bradley*   71
minority rights   82–4
Miranda v. *Arizona*   70, 76
Missouri Compromise   67, 119
Mitchell, George   134
Mitchell, Greg   139–40
Morgenthau, Hans   173, 174, 181
mothers' pensions   151
Muslim immigrants   113

Nader, Ralph   187, 189, 190
NAFTA *see* North American Free Trade
  Agreement
National Council of Senior Citizens   130
National Farmers' Union   130
National Governors' Association   137
National Instant Check System (NICS)
  101
National Rifle Association (NRA)   95–6,
  98, 99, 100, 101–2, 103, 104
National Right to Life (NRL)   165
National Voter Registration Act   33
NATO   176, 179
Neustadt, Richard   55–6
New Deal
  divided government   9
  health care   138
  Supreme Court   67, 69, 75, 76
  welfare   159
New Federalism   137
'New Frontier' programme   130
New World Order   24
Nicaragua, Iran-Contra scandal   59, 61–4
Nichols, Terry   102
Nicholson, Jack   131
Nie, Norman   35, 37, 42
Nix v. *Williams*   70
Nixon, Richard
  affirmative action   120–1
  budget negotiations   16
  campaign finance reform   44
  divided government   11
  foreign policy   172, 177
  health care   130
  presidential power   57, 58, 60, 63, 64
  Supreme Court   68, 69, 73

trust in government   25
Watergate *see* Watergate
welfare reform   16, 152–3, 154, 159
Nixon v. *Shrink Missouri Government PAC*
  52
non-interpretivists   68–9
non-voting   31–3, 41–2
  divided government   13
  theories   37–8: institutional explanations
    38–9; socio-political explanations
    39–41
North, Oliver   62
North American Free Trade Agreement
  (NAFTA)
  effect on health care reforms   133
  free trade v. protectionism   185–7, 188,
    189–90, 191
  trust in government   23

O'Connor, Sandra Day   72, 73, 74
  abortion   165
Office of Management and the Budget
  (OMB)   155
old age pensions   151, 159
Operation Rescue   170
opinion polls, trust in government   25
opportunity, spirit of   2
optimism   2

party identification model, voting behaviour
  34–5, 37
Pasadena Board of Education v. *Spangler*
  71
performance of government
  trust in government   21–4
  voter behaviour   36
Perot, Ross   187
Personal Responsibility and Work
  Opportunity Reconciliation Act
  (PRWORA, 1996)   156–7
pessimism   24
Philadelphia Plan   120
Philip Morris   87
Pika, Joseph   56
Pinochet, Augusto   177
Pioneer Fund   108
Planned Parenthood v. *Casey*   164
Plessy v. *Ferguson*   119
Poindexter, John   62
Political Action Committees (PACs)   44,

45, 50, 51, 53
political explanations, trust in government
    24–6
pornography   74
positivists   68–9, 75
post-imperial presidency   57–9
post-materialism   27
poverty
    affirmative action   125
    health care   130, 131, 136–7
    see also welfare reform
Powell, Colin   34
Powell, Justice   121
preferred provider organizations (PPOs)
    131
president
    and Congress, power distribution see
        divided government
    power   55–6, 64–5: imperial presidency
        thesis   56–7; Iran-Contra scandal
        61–4; post-imperial presidency and the
        imperial Congress   57–9; War Powers
        Resolution   59–61
    veto   16, 17
Printz v. United States   73
procedural liberalism   28
Progressive era
    capital punishment   140
    direct democracy   78–9, 80, 84–5
    divided government   9
prospective issue voting   36
protectionism   183–5, 190–1
    case against   188–9
    case for   189–90
    NAFTA   185–7
    WTO   188
Public Citizen   187
public debates   1–2
Purdy, Patrick Edward   100
purposeful voter model   12, 15
Putnam, Robert
    social capital   28, 29, 41, 42
    voting behaviour   39, 41

Quayle, Dan   34
Quota Acts (1920s)   114

race issues
    affirmative action see affirmative action
    capital punishment   140, 144, 145, 146

immigration   106–7, 108, 110, 113–14,
    115
    welfare reform   158
racial segregation
    affirmative action, history   119
    bilingual education   115
    Supreme Court   71
Ranney, Austin   14
rational choice theory   37, 38
Reagan, Ronald
    abortion   165
    assassination attempt   95
    budget negotiations   16
    divided government   11, 12, 13, 14, 15
    foreign policy   172, 174, 180
    free trade v. protectionism   185
    gun control   95
    presidential power   60, 61–3, 64
    Supreme Court   69, 72
    trust in government   22, 26
    welfare reform   16, 154–5, 159
recalls   79
Reciprocal Trade Agreements Act (1934)
    184
referendums   79
Reform Party   187
Regents of the University of California v.
    Bakke   71, 121, 124
registering to vote   33, 38, 39, 40
Rehnquist, William   72, 74, 75, 76
    abortion   164
Rehnquist Court   72–6
Reich, Robert   186–7
reporting   26, 29
representative democracy   78, 82, 84, 90
Republican Party
    affirmative action   120, 125
    campaign finance reform   47
    capital punishment   148
    divided government   9–13, 15
    free trade v. protectionism   191
    health care   134
    immigration   108
    imperial Congress   58–9, 64–5
    Supreme Court   74
    trust in government   25
    voting behaviour   34–5
    welfare reform   152, 155, 156, 157–8,
        159
resilience of American system   2

retrospective issue voting   36
rhetorical presidency   55
Rice, Condoleeza   181
Roe v. *Wade*   68, 72, 76, 161, 163–5, 169, 170
Roosevelt, Franklin D.
  foreign policy   173–4
  presidential power   55, 56
  Supreme Court   67, 75
  trust in government   26
Roosevelt, Theodore
  campaign finance reform   44
  foreign policy   172, 173
  gun control   99
  presidential power   55, 56
Rose, Richard   57
Ross, Edward   106
Rossiter, Clinton   56
Ryan, George   148

Sandel, Michael   28, 29
Sandinista government   62
Santer, David   72
Santorum, Rick   46
Scalia, Antonin   72, 73, 74, 75, 76
  abortion   165
Schlesinger, Arthur
  affirmative action   126
  imperial presidency   55, 56–7, 58, 61, 63, 64, 65
Schrag, Peter   88, 89
Schutt, Harry   185, 190
Second World War *see* World War II
segregation, racial *see* racial segregation
Senate
  composition by party, 1961–2001   10
  divided government   10–11, 12–13, 15
  free trade v. protectionism   186
  health care   134
  presidential power   60
Shanks, Merrill   40–1
Sierra Club   109
single-issue politics   2
slavery   67, 118–19
Smoot–Hawley Tariff Act   184, 189, 191
Snyder, Jeffrey   98
social capital   28, 29, 41
social security   151, 160
  elderly people   134–5
  trust in government   22

and welfare   150, 155, 159
Social Security Act (1935)   128, 151, 155
  health care   130
  welfare reform   156
sociological school of jurisprudence   68
socio-cultural explanations, trust in government   27–8
socio-political explanations, non-voting behaviour   39–41
soft money, campaign finance reform   45–7, 48, 50
Somalia   178
Souter, David   165
Soviet Union   174–5, 177
Spencer, Glenn   114
split ticket voting   13, 18
Stalin, Joseph   173, 177
Starr, Kenneth   58, 59
Starr, Paul   134
steel industry   185
Stein, Dan   108
Sternberg v. *Carhart*   74
Stevens, John Paul   70, 72, 74, 75
  abortion   165
  campaign finance reform   52
Stoler, Mark   180
Stone Court   69
strict constructionists   69
Sundquist, James L.   14, 15
Supplementary Security Income   153, 154, 155
Supreme Court   67–8, 75–6
  abortion   68, 72, 76, 161, 163–5, 169, 170
  activism, passivism and interpreting the constitution   68–9
  affirmative action   70, 71–2, 73–4, 119, 121, 124
  Burger Court   69–72, 75
  campaign finance reform   44–5, 49, 50, 52, 53
  capital punishment   72, 139, 142–4, 148
  gun control   73, 100–2
  Hughes Court   69, 75, 76
  presidential power   58
  Rehnquist Court   72–6
  Stone Court   69
  Taney Court   75
  Vinson Court   69
  Warren Court   69, 70, 71, 72, 75

Swann v. *Charlotte Mecklenberg*   71
Sweden   33
Switzerland   33

Taft–Hartley Act (1947)   44
Taney Court   75
taxation
  health care   132, 133
  immigration   109, 111
Teixeira, Ruy   40
Temporary Assistance for Needy Families
    (TANF)   151, 156–8, 160
Terry, Randal   170
textbook presidency period   56
Thomas, Clarence   72, 73, 74, 76
  abortion   165
Thomas, Norman   56
Thompson, Tommy   137, 156
Thompson v. *Oklahoma*   143–4
Thurmond, Strom   13
Tillman Act (1907)   44, 52
Tolbert, Caroline   88
Tonkin Gulf Resolution   60
Trujillo, Rafael   174
Truman, Harry
  divided government   17
  foreign policy   174, 176
  presidential power   56
trust in government   20–1, 29
  campaign finance reform   49
  divided government   17
  performance   21–4
  political explanations   24–6
  socio-cultural explanations   27–8
Tucker, Karla Faye   146

'ungovernability'   11
United Kingdom
  first-past-the-post system   31
  pensions   159
  voting behaviour   33, 38, 39
United Nations   176, 180–1
United States v. *Lopez*   73
United States v. *Miller*   101
Universal Declaration of Human
    Rights   180–1
Unz, Ron   115

Van Horne, Terry   46–7
Verba, Sidney   42

veto, presidential   16, 17
Vietnam War
  presidential power   57, 60
  trust in government   25, 29
Vinson Court   69
Violent Crime Control and Law
    Enforcement Act (1994)   95
Virginia Military Academy   74
Voices of Citizens Together   114
voting patterns   31–3, 41–2
  divided government   13, 17–18
  non-voting *see* non-voting
  theories   34: issue voting model   35–7;
    party identification model   34–5
Voting Rights Act (1965)   119

wages and immigration   109, 110–11
Wagner, Robert   128
Walker, Martin   186
Wall Street Journal   112
Walsh, Lawrence   58, 62
War on Poverty   152
war pensions   151
War Powers Resolution (WPR)   55, 59–61
Warren, Earl   69
Warren Court   69, 70, 71, 72, 75
Washington, George   56
Watergate
  campaign finance reform   44
  presidential power   57, 58, 63
  Supreme Court   68
  trust in government   29
Watson, Richard   56
Wayman, Frank   51
welfare reform   150, 159–60
  1990s   155–9
  divided government   15–16
  early days   151
  failed attempts   151–2, 155: Carter
    154; Nixon   152–3; Reagan   154–5
Wertheimer, Fred   49
White, Byron   72
  abortion   164, 166
Whitewater affair   58, 133
Wilson, James   38
Wilson, Pete   121
Wilson, Woodrow
  foreign policy   172, 173, 180
  presidential power   55, 56
Wittkopf, Eugene   188

Woodward, Bob   186
World Bank   184
World Trade Center bombing   113
World Trade Organization (WTO)
    free trade v. protectionism   185, 188,
        189, 190, 191

trust in government   23
World War II
    foreign policy   173, 180
    presidential power   55, 57
    trust in government   24–5